TALKING UNION

Talking
UNION

Judith Stepan-Norris and
Maurice Zeitlin

University of Illinois Press

URBANA AND CHICAGO

Illini Books edition, 1996
© 1996 by the Board of Trustees of the University of Illinois
Manufactured in the United States of America
1   2   3   4   5   C   P   5   4   3   2

This book is printed on acid-free paper.

Library of Congress Cataloging-in-Publication Data

Stepan-Norris, Judith, 1957-
    Talking union / Judith Stepan-Norris and Maurice Zeitlin.
      p.   cm.
    Includes bibliographical references and index.
    ISBN 0-252-02192-4 (cloth : acid-free paper). — ISBN
0-252-06489-5 (pbk. : acid-free paper)
     1. International Union, United Automobile, Aircraft, and
Agricultural Implement Workers of America. Ford Local 600—History.
2. Trade-unions—Michigan—Detroit—History. 3. Labor movement—
Michigan—Detroit—History. I. Zeitlin, Maurice, 1935- .
II. Title.
HD6475.A21787   1996
331.88'1292'0977434—dc20   95-9876
                                         CIP

For the men and women of
Ford Local 600, UAW-CIO,
and others like them everywhere

Talking Union

Words by the Almanac Singers

If you want higher wages let me tell you what to do,
You got to talk to the workers in the shop with you,
You got to build you a union, got to make it strong,
But if you all stick together, boys, t'won't be long,
You get shorter hours—better working conditions—
Vacations with pay—Take the kids to the seashore.

It ain't quite this simple, so I better explain
Just why you got to ride on the union train;
Cause if you wait for the boss to raise your pay,
We'll all be waiting till judgment day;
We'll all be buried—gone to Heaven—
Saint Peter'll be the straw boss then, boys.

Now, you know you're underpaid, but the boss says you ain't;
He speeds up the work till you're about to faint.
You may be down and out, but you ain't beaten,
You can pass out a leaflet and call a meetin'—
Talk it over—speak your mind—
Decide to do something about it.

Course, the boss may persuade some poor damn fool
To go to your meeting and act like a stool;
But you can always tell a stool, though, that's a fact,
He's got a yellow streak a-running down his back;
He doesn't have to stool—he'll always get along—
On what he takes out of blind men's cups.

You got a union, now, and you're sitting pretty;
Put some of the boys on the steering committee.
The boss won't listen when one guy squawks,
But he's got to listen when the union talks—
He better—be mighty lonely—
Everybody decided to walk out on him.

Suppose they're working you so hard it's just outrageous,
And they're paying you all starvation wages,
You go to the boss, and the boss will yell,
"Before I raise your pay I'd see you all in hell."
Well, he's puffing a big cigar and feeling mighty slick,
Cause he thinks he's got your union licked.
He looks out the window, and what does he see
But a thousand pickets, and they all agree
He's a bastard—unfair—slave driver—
Bet he beats his wife.

Now, boys, you've come to the hardest time;
The boss will try to bust your picket line;
He'll call out the police and the national guard,
They'll tell you it's a crime to have a union card.
They'll raid your meeting, and hit you on the head,
They'll call every one of you a goddam red—
Unpatriotic—Moscow agents—trying to steal the atom bomb.

But out in Detroit here's what they found,
And out in Frisco here's what they found,
And out in Pittsburgh here's what they found,
And down at Bethlehem here's what they found,
That if you don't let redbaiting break you up,
And if you don't let stool pigeons break you up,
And if you don't let vigilantes break you up,
And if you don't let race hatred break you up—
You'll win—what I mean, take it easy—but take it.

Contents

Preface

Quotive mark

The men and women who talk with us in these pages made their own history, although not just as they pleased, nor under circumstances they chose, but under "circumstances directly found, given and transmitted from the past."[1] They were active participants in an unprecedented epoch of working-class insurgency and organization, and of radical assaults on the bastions of capital's power, that reshaped class relations and expanded the freedom of the "common people" in America.

So history is seen here not as it is glimpsed and reconstituted by historians on the basis of written documents, but through the participants' eyes, retold in their voices, as they remember living and making it.[2] But understanding that their activities and the battles they fought—in common with countless others—mattered in changing our society emphatically does not imply a "voluntaristic theory" of politics or history. The historical opening for these working-class activists and organizers was provided by an extraordinary crisis of American capitalism; the ensuing "spontaneous" struggles in the factories, mines, and mills; and the consequent political upheavals at all levels of government—local, state, and federal, legislative, executive, and judicial—that "ripped the cloak of civilized decorum from society, leaving exposed naked class conflict."[3] These were indeed rare times and "certainly not of anyone's deliberate making."[4]

But no matter how rare and propitious these times were for "self-organization," the working class did not simply organize itself. No class does. Rather, classes are organized and led in a particular way and by particular activists, organizers, and leaders aligned with particular factions or parties and having particular theories, objectives, and strategies. The process of self-organization of a class involves concrete political struggles within it—and within its organizations—over what its "real" class interests are (and over whether it is a class) and who should organize and lead it. These political struggles are never mere effects of "structures" or "objective conditions"; nor are their consequences pregiven. Rather, the question is, Given certain "circumstances," how *do* men and women make their own history?

This is the question that faced the union men and women whom we meet in these pages. Individually and collectively, within the realm of possibilities open to them, they had to assess their options, make choices, decide, and *act*. Only in acting could they find out how their choices mattered—for themselves and their "circumstances." In short, they had to *engage* history in order to *make* it.

Surely, the rich, often eloquent, wonderfully expressive, and informative excerpts from their interviews provide a reconnaissance of the character and views of these particular individuals. The excerpts also illuminate the character and views of others like them across the nation, who—left, right, and center, black and white, native and foreign born, Jew and Gentile—became self-conscious agitators, organizers, and leaders of industrial workers in America during that ephemeral but decisive historical moment from the 1930s through the 1950s. Of course, these excerpts deepen our knowledge of the inner political life of a specific, unique industrial union. Perhaps more important, what these union men and women say and how they say it provides rare, if retrospective, insight into the consciousness of working-class activists as they experienced the world in crisis and sought not merely to understand it but also to change it.[5]

Acknowledgments

This is a joint work in the fullest sense, so our names appear in alphabetical order. Support for the research program of which this book is a product was provided more than a decade ago by a John Simon Guggenheim Memorial Foundation Fellowship awarded to Zeitlin. Since then, this research program has been generously funded by both the Academic Senate and the Institute of Industrial Relations (IIR) at the University of California, Los Angeles. Daniel J. B. Mitchell and Archie Kleingartner (respectively the IIR's former director and associate director) and David Lewin and Sanford Jacoby (the IIR's current director and associate director) have provided helpful counsel. In preparing the final manuscript of this volume for publication we also benefited from the astute comments and constructive advice of Rick Fantasia and several anonymous reviewers. We also thank Michael Hamilburg, our agent, for his sustaining confidence in the book.

The tape recorded interviews were transcribed—during the halcyon years at the University of California—by staff typists at UCLA's Central Word Processing office under the supervision of Jane Bitar. Jennifer Suet Fong Lim and Jeannie Gruenewald, then undergraduates at UCLA and Zeitlin's administrative assistants, patiently (and carefully) typed and retyped the final manuscript.

TALKING UNION

Introduction

The men and women who talk with us here were among the organizers of a unique local union during the heroic years of industrial unionism in America. The men were also active in the local's leadership—sometimes in fierce opposition to each other—through the late 1950s.[1] "Some of the people that you're now probably interviewing," Henry McCusker chides, "sit down in their building behind a lot of boxes on Joe Stalin's birthday, and sing 'Happy Birthday' to Joe Stalin."

Ford Local 600 of the United Automobile Workers, Congress of Industrial Organizations (UAW-CIO)—whose members worked in the vast factories sprawled on the banks of the Rouge river in Dearborn, Michigan—was (as its newspaper *Ford Facts* used to proclaim) the "biggest local union in the world." But it was also one of the most militant, radical, and democratic unions in America.

"The Rouge," as the workers called it, was "the biggest single industrial unit on earth" and "a completely integrated production system producing finished automobiles and motor vehicles from basic raw products."[2] This singular industrial complex, intended by Henry Ford to be a model of bureaucratic management and technological efficiency, provided a naturally hostile soil for the growth of democracy.[3] Indeed, Local 600 itself was bigger than most *international* unions in the CIO.[4] Yet the local had a vibrant democratic political life: organized parties—mainly the "progressive" versus "right-wing" caucuses—fought for its leadership in hotly contested elections. Progressives (mainly Communists and their radical allies) held most of the local's offices most of the time, but defeat and turnover in office for incumbents in both major caucuses was frequent.

Local 600's uniqueness was rooted in the uniqueness of the Rouge plant itself. Here, the new cars that rolled off its massive assembly line were produced from the ground up. The plant, at which production began in 1920, combined and integrated every basic operation involved in the production of an automobile. Trains hauled raw materials and equipment over the plant's twenty-four miles of railroad tracks, and ships laden with ore and fuel directly discharged their cargoes into two-million-ton concrete storage bins to be processed and transformed into finished products. Its foundry and five-hundred-thousand-horsepower electric powerhouse were the biggest in existence. The major stages of the production process involved in the manufacture of an automobile, from blast furnace to assembly line, were carried out by workers in some twenty different "building units" and subunits: axle, foundry machine shop, frame and cold heading, parts (two buildings), motor (and, in later years, an engine plant), press steel (or stamping), spring and upset, assembly, and even a miscellaneous unit. The Rouge complex also had three plantwide units: tool-and-die, maintenance and construction, and transportation. During World War II, it also had an aircraft unit.

The workers in the steel unit, including the production foundry, jobbing foundry, open hearth furnace, and rolling mill, made the steel that was then stamped into automobile bodies in the press steel unit. In the rubber unit, the workers made the tires; in the plastic unit, the steering wheels; in the glass unit, the windshield and windows, and so on for the other major components that were then fit together to become the latest Ford models.

In a sense, then, the workers at Rouge were employed not in the automobile industry but in many highly diverse industries combined into one megaplant. Their occupation was less auto worker than blast furnace operator, tinsmith, steel worker, carpenter, assembly-line worker, tool-and-die maker, machinist, electrician, glassworker, warehouseman, trucker, pattern maker, or rubber worker—or one of the other *"et ceteras* and so forths who did the work" at River Rouge.[5]

They came, too, from all over the country and all over the world, in all sorts of colors, creeds, and religions. Some fifty-three nationalities—Poles, Bulgarians, and Chinese, Syrians, Jews, Italians, Greeks, and Maltese—were represented at Rouge. The plant consisted, as John Mando told us, of "just a little bit of this and a little bit of that; and it was just one big 'melting pot.' . . . You name them, the nationalities, they were in there."

Contending for the leadership of this veritable microcosm of America's working class was a rich and restive mix of "left-wingers" (Wobblies, anarchists, Socialists, Communists, and Trotskyists), who often were more divided among themselves than united against the right; "plain-and-simple unionists"; and assorted "right-wingers" (the followers of Father Charles Coughlin, the pro-Nazi "radio priest,"[6] adherents of the anti-Semitic "Christian" agitator Gerald L. K. Smith, and the "Actists," members of the Association of Catholic Trade Unionists, who formed the "Catholic vanguard in the conflict with the radicals").[7]

Spies and "stoolies" also abounded in the plant. On the company payroll and posing as production workers, their real job was to aid and abet Ford's "service men" (security guards) to keep out the radicals, agitators, trouble-makers, and—above all—the union. Ford's informers were everywhere, in the plant, in the community, and in the union, directed by "one Harry Bennett, who was," in Victor Reuther's words, "a hired gangster of the Ford Motor Company." In 1937, four years before the local was recognized, Bennett, formally the head of the company's "Labor Relations Department," boasted that half of his "service staff," working undercover in the guise of bona-fide production workers, had taken out cards in the union. Ford's thugs, under Bennett's direct command, intimidated, beat, and sometimes crippled, blinded, or killed, suspected union men or their sympathizers. The company's "private underworld terrorize[d] the workers. . . . The fear in the plant," as reporter Benjamin Stolberg wrote in 1938, was "indescribable."

As Archie Acciacca puts it, "It's almost unbelievable the way Ford was run. It was a real gestapo set-up." Dave Moore, an "inside organizer" in the Rouge plant, was "caught with UAW literature inside [his] shirt. . . . I got the hell beat out of me. . . . They said, 'Nigger, if you ever be caught around the Ford Motor Company again, we'll kill you.' And they got me to the gate." "Risking everything they had," in the words of Stanley Nowak, plenty of workers got caught trying to smuggle union leaflets into the plant. Others managed to bring stacks of them past the guards. Then they would put the stacks of leaflets "on the conveyor belt," Margaret Nowak explains, "and they'd go down the line." "Those leaflets," she adds, "would go out through the whole plant."

These sorts of organizing activities inside Rouge, especially when they led to collective actions by the workers in defiance of the terror, had already begun to make a difference in the atmosphere inside the plant, as John Orr says, even before the local was recognized officially. "I was negotiating wages and working conditions before the union was recognized. At a given signal one day, we all lit cigarettes; that was something new at the Ford Motor Company. Different things we used to do to demonstrate, you know. Always under threat." As the union movement grew, the "bosses. . . tolerated more and more all the time."

But the emergence of a mass union movement at Rouge was a long time coming. Shortly after Rouge went into production, a handful of radicals, most of them Communists, began trying to penetrate and organize it. Not only was Rouge itself a fortress, guarded inside and out, but the city of Dearborn, where the plant was located (and where about one in six of Rouge's workers and their families lived), was also, as Walter Dorosh calls it, "Ford city." Ford's rule over Dearborn was unfettered. The "chief cogs" in his machine of domination over Dearborn's civic life for well over a decade were a leading municipal judge, who was Ford's close friend, and two former Ford security operatives, one of whom was the city's chief of police throughout the late 1920s and 1930s. "Mr. Ford owned the city, lock, stock and barrel," Dorosh says. "He owned the police force, the city council, the mayor, . . . and they passed any ordinance that Ford wanted. . . . You couldn't distribute any leaflets. . . . The police would come out and arrest you, take you to jail and harass you."

Ford also had programs aimed at winning the loyalty of his working men and their family members, especially the immigrants among them, many of whom had been drawn there by his announcement of the "8-hour, $5, profit-sharing day" in January 1914. Some of the foreign-born workers came directly from Ellis Island; others arrived in Detroit only after a hard stint in eastern coal mines and steel mills.

Until Ford opened Rouge in 1920, his Highland Park plant had been his biggest. The workforce was mainly foreign-born, and Ford sought assiduously to "Americanize" them. If they wanted to keep enjoying the benefits of the $5 day, they had to attend "Americanization" and English classes and were pressured to take out citizenship papers. They were also expected to march in Americanization Day celebrations. "Henry Ford really had built up a relationship with the various ethnic groups," Horace Sheffield told us. "The old man gave the churches coal and that sort of thing. . . . [He] built up initially . . . a core leadership group that supported Ford's. . . . The thing that had the greatest impact, really, was Ford shelling out the hard dollars."

Ford encouraged all of his workers to start savings accounts, and the company's "Sociology Department," consisting of thirty social workers and investigators, provided "elementary lessons" in budgeting, as well as instruction on hygiene, home management, and how to shop, including how to select the right cuts of meat. If men wanted to earn that $5 a day (women earned only $2.07 and weren't included in the $5 day—Ford thought they should get married and mind the home), they had to hew to Ford's "code of conduct." This included never spitting on the floor at home and bathing regularly (with "plenty of soap and water"). The company's inspectors would drop in any time to check that beds were made and the house tidy. Its legal department assisted workers in buying homes and warned them not

to buy anything on the installment plan.[8] Such paternalism won Ford
the loyalty of many workers. In Orr's opinion, this loyalty "kept the
Ford workers from organizing until four years after GM and Chrysler
were organized. 'If only the old man knew, he would do something
about it.'" The guys believed that "it was the lesser bosses . . . that imposed all these indignities and all this mess."

Ford also went out of his way to hire blacks, many of whom, like
Moore, who started work at Rouge in 1935, had also come there to
take up Ford's offer for "five bucks a day." Moore dropped out of school
in Ohio and "went up there to get some of that big money." Ford had
"blacks that hired blacks," as William Johnson explains. "They had
blacks in the employment set-up, and these people had extensive contacts to the black churches and black civic organizations." Moore says
that "Ford . . . was more liberal toward the blacks. I shouldn't use the
word 'liberal.' There was nothing liberal in the bastard. He had a strategy that was different than General Motors and Chrysler. . . . They
didn't have blacks on any machine. The best you could do was work
cleaning up the floors, mopping in the restrooms, . . . and things like
that. But Ford had a sprinkling of blacks here and there," although, as
Orr points out, they were mainly "relegated to foundry work, shoveling sand, pouring steel, cleanup jobs in the other production buildings,
dangerous things."

Ford also built homes for blacks out at Inkster. "I say 'homes,'"
Moore remarks, "they were shacks. He would give them land. They
could go out and farm a garden. You could go to his stores and buy
food. . . . After he gave you all this, he said, 'Now you got to pay.'"
Ford's "rehabilitation" of the community in Inkster was repaid by his
black employees through deductions from their pay checks. His "company paternalism," in Johnson's phrase, "fostered [black] allegiance to
the company, and they had a great deal of mistrust for unions."

Orr recalls that "a bunch of us" once had to rescue Shelton Tappes,
an organizer who later became the local's recording secretary, from
irate antiunion fellow blacks in the foundry. "Some guys had a rope
out and were going to hang [him] from the nearest rafter for working
against Mr. Ford. . . . His back was right against the wall, boy, and he
was taking them all on." When the final drive to organize Rouge was
in motion, Detroit's senior NAACP leaders "opposed the organization
of Ford," according to Sheffield. But the NAACP Youth Council, of
which he was president at the time, "favored it." Neither carried much
weight with Ford's black workers. Loyal to Ford and hostile to unions
(which in the AFL had never given them a "fair shake"), a lot of the
black workers "stayed in" during the April 1941 strike. "I got a sound

truck," Sheffield remembers, "and went up and down the Miller Road urging . . . these scabs to come out."

The Rouge regime's unique combination of terrorism and paternalism could delay but it could not prevent the plant's ultimate unionization. In the spring of 1941, the same wave of industrial unionism that four years earlier, in one sit-down strike after another, had compelled the other auto makers to recognize the union, now flowed into Rouge, making even Ford give way.[9]

A little after midnight on April 2, 1941, in the wake of a spate of quick and effective sit-downs inside Rouge, fifty thousand workers walked off of their jobs and into history. The strike that finally broke Ford's resistance had begun. Walking four abreast in a formation that stretched over a mile, the workers marched and sang "Solidarity Forever" and "Old Hank Ford he ain't what he used to be." On April 11, Ford agreed to hold an NLRB election.[10] On May 21, fifty-eight thousand Ford workers voted to join the UAW-CIO, twenty-three thousand voted to join the breakaway UAW-AFL, and fewer than 2,500 voted "no union."[11] After nearly twenty years of organizing battles, led mainly by assorted socialists, Local 600, UAW-CIO had been born and baptized.

But its tumultuous history had only just begun. Rouge was to become one of the few enduring focuses of class-conscious industrial unionism in the nation. Despite the UAW's cleansing itself of Reds and the CIO's expulsion of eleven so-called Communist-dominated unions in 1949 and 1950, Local 600 continued, long after the purges, to be a bastion of the left—and of a working-class socialist ethos—in organized labor and an independent voice in Walter Reuther's UAW.[12]

The Rouge local was a continuing base of militant, radical opposition to Reuther's goal, which he proclaimed in June 1950, of replacing "industrial warfare" with "maturity" and "stability in American labor relations." Carl Stellato, who (with Reuther's backing) narrowly won election as the "right-wing" candidate for the local's presidency in May of that year, made sure—both in his campaign and subsequent policy statements—to denounce not only Communism but also "monopoly capitalism" and "the greed and ignorance of capital."[13]

Local 600's credo might well have been, in Paul Boatin's words, "In a struggle with corporations, you've got to fight every day, every hour, every minute, every second, because their promises don't mean anything. They have no country, they have no god, they have no flag, they have no heart."

This sort of dedication had its personal costs, especially in the burdens it imposed on union activists' family lives. The company (or maybe even an activist's union opponents) would, in Orr's words, have "women call your wife at home and tell her. . . 'He's in a bar with me.'" George Pluhar, Jr., says that his dad's union activities at Rouge so upset his mother that she had two miscarriages. His father was away so much on union affairs that it "created a lot of problems" for them, and "they ended up getting divorced." As Shelton Tappes puts it, "Our wives married factory workers, but got us instead. Meetings all the time. Never home. And we were pioneers of a kind, 'radicals'—that meant they had a hard time from other wives. I lost my first wife, so did Woodcock, so did Fraser."[14]

For all their differences, however, Local 600's "progressives" and "right-wingers" were often unified (except for a tiny minority) in opposition to Reuther's leadership of the international. Indeed, Local 600's "right-wing" caucus sometimes took positions on union issues much to the left of the UAW's executive board.

Rouge's left-wing organizers were committed, in principle, to rank-and-file participation of its members in running the union, in making and carrying out the local's policies whether in daily shop-floor battles or major strikes against the company or in staking out and fighting for its positions on national and international political issues. The local's constitution, ratified in 1942 after often fractious debate, established an extensive system of representative government.

The local's members annually elected a president, vice president, recording secretary, financial secretary, sergeant-at-arms, and guide; they also elected three trustees at different, staggered intervals. These officers sat on the local's General Council, its highest governing body, which had both executive and legislative authority, along with delegates elected through proportional voting by workers in every unit at Rouge. Each unit elected a chair, who was a delegate ex officio, and one delegate for every four hundred workers in the unit. For example, in 1947, the General Council included 209 delegates from 20 building units.

The General Council, chaired by the local's president, met at least once a month. Its executive board, consisting of its seven top officers and the chairs of the building units, met at least twice monthly to attend to union affairs between meetings of the General Council and subject to its approval. Special meetings could also be called by a two-thirds vote of the council, a majority of the executive board, the president, or by petition of a quarter of the delegates representing at least a quarter of the units. Local members also elected delegates to the UAW international union convention, the Wayne County CIO Council, the

Michigan CIO Council, and to special and standing committees of the union, as well as voting on recurrent referenda that could be put on the ballot by a vote of one-quarter of the General Council's delegates.

The constitution of Local 600 based its form of representative government on the industrial organization of the plant itself. The workers in every unit were represented by their own elected delegates to the General Council; this assured them that their specific needs, grievances, and demands would be considered by the government of the entire local union. But the local's constitution also guaranteed the workers in each unit "a full measure of self-government . . . within the confines of Local 600." In each unit, the workers adopted their own unit bylaws and elected their own officers and delegates to three unit elective bodies: a set of nine regular officers (unpaid except for the chair, who got the same pay he was earning before his election); an executive board (of at least fifteen members); and a council (ranging, depending on the size of the unit, anywhere from fifteen to a hundred members). Each department and unit also elected its own committeemen.

Ford had designed the production regime at Rouge to make it the epitome of technical perfection and optimum profitability. But it also became, by design of the workers themselves, the bedrock of their industrial union's formal system of self-government and contentious, democratic political life. A campaign of some sort for some office or over some issue, with the local's rival factions vying against each other, seemed to be going on all the time. These were workers electing workers, not remote union officials. In this alert and active rank-and-file political milieu, militancy and democracy were inseparable. If their officers or delegates were no good, as Moore puts it, "They didn't last but one term, and they were gone and forgotten. . . . For a worker to see you smiling, as a representative, and a foreman got his arms around you, that was the kiss of death."

Highlights of
Local 600's History

Ford Motor Company fiercely resisted any and every effort by the workers to organize a union in its factories; it had its "own private underworld to terrorize the workers . . . and [a] highly organized terror and spy system [to quell] . . . disturbances."[1] Terror unquestionably was a formidable weapon against unionization. But the American Federation of Labor (AFL) was not much of an antagonist anyway; it made little serious effort to organize the auto industry (or the Ford plant at the Rouge river) because few automobile workers were craft workers.

■ RED UNIONISM

Only with the formation of the CIO was a major and successful drive to organize Ford launched. Long before this, however, the Communist-led Trade Union Educational League (TUEL) and its successor the Trade Union Unity League (TUUL) had been fighting to penetrate the plant and to bring to the Rouge workers the league's then-radical vision of industrial unionism and class solidarity rather than craft exclusionism. From the mid-1920s on, the TUUL targeted Ford plants as a "concentration point" in its drive to organize all of basic industry. Communists started agitating for an industrial union in 1925 and soon were printing and distributing shop papers to a dozen of Detroit's major auto plants. "These little four-page sheets, sold for a penny or given away by Communist distributors at plant gates . . . provided the only news of conditions and grievances inside the plants available to workers."[2] Despite its heroic attempts, the TUUL's Auto Workers Union (AWU) never managed to establish much more than a skeleton organization at the Rouge, however, let alone actually win union recognition or bargaining rights.

"Brother Bill McKie" came to be the embodiment of the Communist

organizing activities at Ford. Born in Carlisle, England, he was already
fifty-one when in 1927 he first stepped foot in the Rouge plant, bringing with him years of organizational and political experience. Once inside the Ford gates, McKie immediately began union organizing efforts.
At first he organized for the AWU by meeting with Ford workers away
from the plant in their darkened homes and basements to escape de-
tection by company spies. Then, in 1933, he led the effort to obtain a
"federal" local charter at Ford from the AFL, and when it was granted,
McKie actually became the AFL federal local's first president.[3]

The next year, Ford fired McKie for writing a series of articles that
criticized top company officials. But he went right on holding secret
organizing meetings in workers' homes. In the wake of the 1937 sit-
down strikes in Flint, when the UAW initiated a campaign to organize
the Ford workers, McKie headed up the drive.[4]

Many foreign-born workers were drawn to Detroit by the high wages
paid in the automobile industry, especially by Henry Ford's announcement of the $5 day in 1913.[5] Although Ford attempted to mold foreign-
born workers into a cooperative and dutiful work force through its
sociology department and paternalistic community programs, in the
end these efforts "failed, and perhaps even proved irrelevant."[6] One
reason for Ford's failure was the grass-roots organizations that the left
established among Detroit's various immigrant nationalities. The Finnish, Hungarian, Polish, Rumanian, Ukrainian, and Lithuanian communities all had organizations in which Communists were influential.

Many of these nationality organizations were affiliated with the International Workers Order (IWO). Formed in 1930 as a result of a left-
wing split from the Workmen's Circle,[7] the IWO was led by "avowed"
Communists.[8] The IWO focused on delivering various welfare, educational, and cultural services to foreign-born workers, and it also acted
as a political conduit to all workers. Some IWO lodges ran AWU leafleting campaigns. The Ford plants had a heavy concentration of foreign-
born workers, and the IWO influence was especially great there. "That
is really the secret, the key secret," as Saul Wellman told us, "of why
the Communists were able to make the contribution that they did in
the organization of the basic mass-production industries in the United States that other radical groups were not able to make."

In the face of unprecedented unemployment among Detroit wage-
workers during the depression, Communists built an impressive Unemployed Council movement there. McKie "found that he had become
a double organizer—of the employed auto workers into the Auto Workers Union, of the unemployed into the Unemployed Councils."[9] The
Unemployed Councils held rallies and protests and organized neigh-

borhood battalions to resist the eviction of workers and their families
from their homes.

■ THE FORD HUNGER MARCH

The peak of the Unemployed Councils' activity in Detroit came in
1932, when they joined forces with the Auto Workers Union to organize and lead the Ford Hunger March. They targeted Ford because he
was the largest employer in Detroit and had shut down in the middle
of the depression. If Ford was known as the man who brought Detroit
the $5 day, he was now paying wages two-thirds of what he'd been
paying in 1914 and was "pressuring his workers to tend 'thrift plots'
in their backyards and on his Dearborn acreage." If he was known as
a benefactor of blacks, he was now "employing Negroes at $1 a day
plus subsistence."[10]

On March 7, 1932, three thousand unemployed equipped with a Detroit parade permit and police escort marched toward the Rouge plant.
"Led by a handful of Communists, the band represented a cross-sec-
tion of Ford workers, former Ford employees, and above all, the miscellaneous unemployed."[11] Demonstrators prepared a formal petition
"embracing the demands of the unemployed for jobs or relief." At the
Dearborn city limits they confronted "about fifty Dearborn and Ford
police," who ordered the marchers to turn back.[12] When the workers
refused, Dearborn police fired tear gas at them, and firefighters hosed
them down with freezing water. But they kept right on coming.

Harry Bennett, Ford's "labor relations" man, personally confronted
the marchers outside the Ford gates. When someone threw a piece of
slag at Bennett and hit him, the "police and Ford service men at the
gate opened fire. Shots slammed into [Joe] York, marchers, and spectators along Miller Road. Workers, responding to the echo of the shots,
arrived to look at a score of dead and injured, screaming and twisting
on the cold, wet pavement," among them four young Communists. A
few days later, tens of thousands of men and women marched in a
funeral procession honoring and mourning the dead, and at graveside
the band played The International.[13] For many of the men who became
Local 600 leaders, the Ford Hunger March in the spring of 1932 was
one of the major formative political experiences of their lives.

■ UAW ORGANIZING AT ROUGE

It took another nine long years before the Rouge complex was finally organized. Some of the delay was fostered by Ford's paternalism,

some by repression: spying, intimidation, and beatings, as well as firings at the slightest hint of prounion activity, were carried out by Ford's three-thousand-man force of service men, a mix of ex-pugs, ex-cops, and ex-convicts.[14]

When the UAW's Ford organizing drive began in May 1937, the organizers at Rouge, led by Bill McKie, assigned most of the union's leafleting to women in the hope of avoiding attacks by the service men. But they attacked the leafleters anyway. As Dearborn police looked on, Ford's goons twisted the women's arms to force them to drop their leaflets and shoved, kicked, and punched them. Their attacks on union men resulted in several serious injuries; one man suffered a fractured skull, another a broken back, and a third severe internal wounds.[15]

UAW officials, including Walter Reuther and Richard Frankensteen, were not exempt from these attacks; they, too, were brutally assaulted in what is remembered as the Battle of the Overpass in May 1937.[16] McKie had warned Reuther that Ford's security men would probably use force to prevent leafleting in certain sections of the plant, including the Miller Road overpass, but Reuther reportedly insisted on leafleting there because he thought doing so would give the UAW "good publicity."[17] The union got the publicity, but it was less for the union's effectiveness than its casualties—and for the defeat of the UAW's first major leafleting campaign at Rouge.

A few months later, UAW organizers were back at the Rouge plant—this time accompanied by several outside observers. If this leafleting campaign was somewhat more successful, however, its success was short-lived. Soon afterward, the Dearborn City Council passed an ordinance forbidding leafleting around the "congested areas" of the city—which, not incidentally, happened to include the Rouge gates.[18] In the following months, nearly a thousand unionists were arrested while passing out leaflets. To avoid court tests of the ordinance, the city jailed arrested leafleters briefly and then released them without filing charges against them. Although no trials were held, this effectively ended the union's leafleting.[19]

In response, the UAW launched a formal Ford organizing drive late in 1937 led by Ford Organizing Director Richard Frankensteen. The drive involved five UAW organizing departments: "1. Concerted action by field organizations under the direction of Zygmund Dobrzynski. 2. Educational work among the foreign-speaking employees of Ford. 3. Colored and minority group organizations. 4. Distribution of educational leaflets. 5. Extension of general information concerning the campaign through publicity, periodicals, educational and welfare mediums." The focus of UAW's Ford organizing was the Rouge plant. The union dispatched "30 orga-

nizers, each assigned a certain section of the Detroit metropolitan area"
to begin intensive organization of their districts.[20]

The UAW distributed forty thousand copies a week of a special newspaper aimed at Ford workers. Organizers called in to radio programs
to describe the atrocious working conditions and arbitrary discipline
within the Rouge plant. To target black workers, they used special
appeals intended to dispel the myth of Ford's beneficence to the black
community.[21] But most blacks rejected their appeals, sometimes vio-
lently. When, for instance, eighteen organizers tried to distribute UAW
newspapers in the black community of Inkster in late 1937, a force of
some forty black Ford service men drove them out.[22]

As one means of derailing the organizing drive, Ford established four
company unions to compete for the workers' loyalties and lure members away from the UAW and other bona fide unions. Ford service
agents or company supervisory employees fostered each of the four
company unions. "The iron rule forbidding organizational activity at
any time on company property was waived in the case of solicitors for
one or the other of [these] 'opposition' unions."[23]

Ford also maneuvered to try to split the union. In fact, the UAW provided fertile ground for Ford's splitting efforts because its internal factions were sharply divided over a host of political issues. To try to
consolidate their own power in the international and thwart the ris-
ing influence of the left, then President Homer Martin[24] and Ford Organizing Director Frankensteen established the Progressive Caucus.[25]
In response, the Communists and Socialists formed an unlikely alliance
and organized the opposition Unity Caucus.

In a gambit designed to consolidate his control of the local, Martin
met with Father Coughlin. With Henry Ford's blessing, Coughlin had
(in June 1938) established the Workers Council for Social Justice, which
excluded "non-Christians," with the aim of turning Ford workers
against the "Jewish" UAW and CIO. Coughlin, acting as an emissary for
"kindly, old Henry Ford," told Martin that Ford would not object to a
union if it were purified of the Communists and "international Jews"
who controlled it.[26]

Martin began secret negotiations with Ford and Bennett in the summer of 1938.[27] The company offered its verbal, not written, promise
to suppress the Liberty Legion (one of Ford's company unions, which
was, in reality, already dead), submit to collective bargaining, and re-
hire all fired National Labor Relations Board (NLRB) complainants
(which the government had already ordered the company to do). In
return, Martin was to drop the UAW's NLRB actions (which would have
taken away the union's legal leverage against the company) and, with

Martin continuing as president, take the UAW out of the CIO into the AFL.[28]

When word of these secret talks got out, the opposition to Martin escalated, and, desperately trying to hold on, he suspended several left-wing UAW officials, including executive board members, who opposed his policies. In response, the executive board ordered his impeachment in January 1939—and the union split asunder.[29] Later that month, Martin called one UAW convention, the left another. But Martin, "discredited by his behind-the-back dealings, . . . was able to command the loyalty of only one out of every seven union members. Taking his splinter group into the AFL, he was financed by Ford and offered a union building by Coughlin."[30]

With the split, the UAW-CIO Ford drive lost its momentum. The UAW's fund-raising to carry out its organizing at Ford had netted no more than a fraction of the goal set at its convention two years earlier.[31] Still, inside organizing of Local 600 by workers employed at the Rouge plant went right on, mainly led by Communists and other left-wingers headed up by Bill McKie in cooperation with Reuther's Westside Local 174.[32]

The UAW-CIO's regional director, Richard Leonard, appointed Percy Llewellyn[33] as Local 600 president and put him in full charge of Ford organizational work.[34] Now, "with the prestige of the international behind him," as an internal ACTU memorandum reported in late 1939, Llewellyn "asked a small membership section meeting of the local for the authority to appoint a re-organizational committee with the announced purpose of selecting members to fill the vacant offices on the local executive board. He had no difficulty getting this set-up and immediately proceeded to pack the executive board with Communist Party members in order to off-set the influence of [Paul] Ste. Marie. At the present time the opposition to Ste. Marie on the executive board is thirteen to six."[35]

The core of leading activists in the local were on the left. In 1940, for instance, some eighty to ninety Local 600 members elected Bill McKie as a delegate to the 1940 UAW convention. "We voted for McKie and he was elected," as one of these activists recalls, "over the president [Llewellyn] and the secretary [Ste. Marie]." McKie told them that he would "go down there and see what he could do about getting some real organizing for the Ford workers."[36]

He got some "real organizing." At the 1940 convention, the president, R. J. Thomas, announced that the UAW had made an agreement with the CIO to set up a new joint Ford Organizing Committee.[37] Both the UAW and the CIO would contribute $50,000 to the initial fund to organize the Ford workers. Michael Widman, a former coal miner and United Mine Workers officer who was now the assistant organizational director of the CIO, would head the drive "under the supervision of the president of the CIO and the UAW-CIO."[38] The agreement called for "joint prosecution" of the drive.[39] It was this drive that culminated in the successful organizing of Ford workers in April 1941.

During 1939 and 1940 the NLRB had repeatedly served Ford with cease and desist orders, which he steadfastly ignored while trying to overturn them through the courts. On February 10, 1941, the Supreme Court turned down his appeal. Ford had to comply. Posters went up in the plant announcing that the workers could organize without management interference, and union buttons soon began sprouting on workers' shirts. Shop stewards started negotiating grievances with foremen and other supervisory personnel.

When Widman came to Detroit to set up the new organizing drive, only some nine hundred Ford workers were UAW members. He met with the presidents of the UAW's four Ford locals to "map out a program of action." "The Ford campaign," he told them, "is your problem, I can't organize Ford alone, nor can the CIO. A big part of the job will be up to you."[40] This set Widman's organizing strategy apart from that of many CIO organizing heads in other industries. Unlike them, he "kept strictly to his role as a nonpartisan, concerned solely with getting everybody's cooperation for Ford organization. He could not have carried on otherwise in the auto union."[41]

At the Rouge plant, "the machinery was there waiting for him." Tightly knit cadres in Local 600 were employed in many of its major building units—men who had fought for the union "through all the inglorious, silent, and deadly years" before this new joint drive was launched. "Steeled in years of long, underground struggle," their time had now come.[42]

Bill McKie went on Widman's staff as a paid organizer, and Widman put him in charge of the organizing there. "As long as you build the union," Widman said, "that's all I ask."[43] Norman Smith, Widman's assistant, worked with McKie to devise a strategy to "crack the fort," and he was "impressed by the way in which the old man brought out facts and figures, pointed out to him the strategic areas, laid out the plan of attack, defense, and eventual victory."[44]

Every local union office became a sub-office of the drive, and its members became organizers. The drive also included citywide "Negro, Italian, Polish, Hungarian and other nationality committees [consisting of] one person of each race or nationality from each local."[45] The campaign to reach Polish workers—who were among the most numerous

of the foreign-born nationalities in the Rouge plant—was exemplary
of the organizing among nationality groups.

The UAW had specifically targeted Polish auto workers in 1938 in a
campaign that Stanley Nowak organized. One of his innovative tactics
had been to get a regular talk show on a Polish radio station in Detroit.
As it turned out, not only Poles but also many other Slavic workers,
including Russians, Ukrainians, Czechs, Slovaks, and Serbs, listened to
the same station and to Nowak's talk show, providing him with a "terrific audience" among them.

Nowak also used the electoral process as a way to reach and organize workers. With the UAW executive board's approval, he ran for the
Michigan state senate on the Democratic ticket. This gave him a legitimate forum from which to address Ford workers who would have
been afraid to attend union meetings. But, unexpectedly, Nowak won
the race and was actually elected. When the new Ford organizing drive
began, there was State Senator Nowak canvassing house-to-house as a
union organizer in the downriver communities among Poles and other Slavic workers in the Ford plants.[46]

Overcoming black workers' loyalty to Ford was a crucial if not decisive task for the UAW organizers. When the new Ford drive began,
many blacks at Rouge as well as in other UAW locals wanted "a chance
to participate" in it.[47] At their insistence, the Ford Organizing Committee established an independent black committee to try to reach Rouge
blacks. The committee wrote and distributed its own leaflets and set
up a booth with union material for black workers outside the Rouge
plant. Meanwhile, Martin's UAW and the AFL launched their own Ford
organizing drive, which company officials endorsed publicly.[48] They,
too, targeted black workers for special attention. Don Marshall, Ford's
"'Negro Boss' let it be known that the AFL had Ford's blessing. Ford
Service cracked the whip inside the Rouge. Foremen and other supervisory employees became AFL solicitors on company time."[49]

The fight between the AFL and CIO to win over Ford's black workers centered in the Rouge production foundry, where most of them
were employed. Supporters of the AFL in the foundry outnumbered
the "CIO men" by far and often harassed and beat them. One CIO man
who refused to be cowed was Nelson Davis, a Communist, who "insisted upon wearing a UAW-CIO Local 600 cap at all times during his
shift in the Foundry. There were occasions when groups of anti-CIO
people surrounded him, threatened him with bodily harm, and on at
least one occasion, marched him out of the building. . . . Brother Davis
always returned with a new cap on the following shift."[50]

In March 1941 a series of sit-down strikes at Rouge halted production in one department and building after another. In the last two weeks of March alone, more than fifteen thousand Rouge workers sat down. Short, solid, and successful in winning immediate demands, the sit-downs were the prelude to the final wave of organizing and the major strike on April 2 that broke the company's resistance.[51]

On April 1 Bennett fired eight grievance committee members in the rolling mill at Rouge, and 1,500 men sat down and paralyzed production in the mill. The Dearborn police, at Ford's request, surrounded the plant, and a pitched battle seemed imminent. Reuther, mindful of the recent Supreme Court decision outlawing sit-downs, promised the police that the workers wouldn't occupy the plant, and they withdrew. In the early morning of April 2, Rouge's fifty thousand workers struck the plant, shut it down, and sealed it off to keep scabs out. The workers put barricades of cars, junk, railroad ties, and telephone poles across every road and took control of the railway tracks to the plant and the drawbridge across the river from Rouge so neither trains nor ships could get in or out of the plant.

Ford demanded that the governor and President Roosevelt send in the National Guard and federal troops. If that happened, the CIO retorted, all of Detroit would be paralyzed by a general strike.

Some four or five thousand men who supported Ford, most of them Bennett's service men, plus a few hundred in Martin's UAW-AFL and Coughlin's Workers' Council, were still in the plant. Also inside were a thousand or so blacks, a mix of recent migrants from the Deep South and long-established Detroiters. Despite Ford's repeated slashes in their pay, payment of wages below whites', and fierce speed-up in the foundry where most of them worked, these blacks were still loyal to the "old man." For years, their ministers also had preached in favor of Ford (many were on Bennett's payroll). The local NAACP also favored Ford, but the NAACP's national executive secretary, Walter White, came to Dearborn and used a megaphone to call on the black workers to leave the plant and join the strike. So did John Dancy of the Urban League. But they stayed in.[52]

On the second night of the strike, the AFL arranged a meeting in "Paradise Valley," the black section of Detroit, at which Homer Martin urged three thousand blacks to defy the Rouge strikers and "to 'march back in a body'" into the plant. Walter White, John Dancy, and other black leaders opposed Martin's call and firmly supported the UAW strike, and the AFL's black back-to-work movement collapsed.[53]

The strike was solid, and, with President Roosevelt applying pressure and threatening that Ford wouldn't get a single government war contract, Ford agreed to allow the NLRB to hold an election. Four years earlier, right after the Battle of the Overpass, 98.3 percent of the Rouge workers, when polled by Bennett's service men, had signed a loyalty oath to Ford.[54] But now, when the NLRB election was held on May 21, fewer than 3 percent voted for "no union," another 27 percent voted for Martin and the AFL, and the rest, an overwhelming majority of 70 percent, voted to join the "UAW-CIO."[55] On June 20, 1941, Henry Ford signed a historic contract with the same UAW that he'd fulminated against as a "Communist-Jewish conspiracy." He agreed to pay Ford workers the highest wages paid anywhere in the industry and also to make Ford a union shop.[56]

■ FORD LOCAL 600

Local 600, so long in coming, was to be a deeply democratic union. The political divisions present before and during its birth throes also continued to nourish and shape its lively and contentious political life for a long time. Organized caucuses of left and right regularly opposed each other in the local's elections—and they could compete in plenty of elections, both at the local level as a whole and in the various building units.

But less than a decade after its birth, Local 600's internal democracy was endangered by external attempts to subvert and overthrow it. In the Reutherites' battle to purge the UAW, and later the CIO, of Communists, their radical allies, and any and all other opposition, Local 600 took center stage. Walter Reuther had been elected UAW president in 1946, and his faction defeated the center-left coalition led by Secretary-Treasurer George Addes a year later.[57] In 1950 Reuther sought to bring Local 600 to heel and threw his weight behind Carl Stellato, known as a right-winger and anti-Communist, in the elections for the local's presidency.

Stellato barely won, defeating incumbent four-term president Tommy Thompson by 559 votes out of the 30,075 votes cast in the run-off election.[58] Once in office, Stellato immediately began an internal purge of Rouge Communists and their allies. By a narrow margin, the General Council voted to implement his new policy that "all elected and appointed representatives of Local 600, in whatever capacity, . . . [have to be] loyal Americans and union men." All officers of the local were required to sign a "pledge of allegiance to the government of the United States and no other" and swear that they didn't belong to the Communist Party or "support the policy and program of Soviet Russia and its satellite nations."[59] Officers who refused to sign were to be put up on charges of "conduct unbecoming a union representative or member" as well as for "Communist Party membership or subservience to the Communist Party."

Stellato put five elected local officers on trial: Paul Boatin, president, motor building; Nelson Davis, vice president, production foundry; John Gallo, recording secretary, motor building; Ed Lock, president, plastic unit; and Dave Moore, vice president, gear-and-axle unit.[60] They were tried under authority of a clause in the UAW constitution that had lain dormant until the Reuther faction took power in the international. The clause barred from elective or appointive position in the international, or in any local, any union member who was "a member of or subservient to any political organization, such as the Communist, Fascist or Nazi Organization which owes its allegiance to any government other than the United States or Canada, directly or indirectly."[61]

An eleven-man trial committee (a subcommittee of the local's highest governing body, the General Council) carried out a lengthy investigation, then rendered a unanimous verdict of guilty as charged.[62] It was now up to the General Council as a whole to consider, and accept or reject, the committee's verdict. But in the interim a new election for the General Council was held. Men supported by the local's left-wing Progressive Caucus took a majority of the seats, and on June 11, 1951, the council voted 94 to 21 to overturn the trial committee's guilty verdict. As a reporter for *The Daily Worker* noted, "The eleven members of the committee voted for the verdict and could only muster 10 others to back it." Stellato also voted to support the guilty verdict.[63]

This setback, as the result of the left's resurgence in the council, was also accompanied by Stellato's close call in that year's presidential election in which he barely defeated the Progressive Caucus's candidate Joe Hogan. As Ken Bannon, a long-time ally of Reuther's, told us, "Joe Hogan almost knocked the living hell out of him. And there's a question as to whether or not Joe Hogan won or not. As the result of that close election, Carl Stellato began to play games with the left-wing."[64] He now allied himself with the Progressive Caucus.[65] Indeed, over the following years, Stellato was to become a leading left-wing critic of Reuther's policies in the international union, earning himself the sobriquet of the "thorn in Reuther's side."

Reuther now launched another attack on the local that coincided (whether by design or coincidence is disputed) with the arrival in Detroit in early 1952 of the House Committee on un-American Activities (HUAC). Between February and April 1952, HUAC subpoenaed twenty-three officers of Local 600 to testify about their political beliefs and associations.[66] Most of the subpoenaed officers refused to answer the committee's questions, invoking their Constitutional rights. But two former Local 600 leaders, both of whom had moved onto Reuther's UAW payroll, testified as friendly witnesses. UAW officials were quick to take advantage of HUAC's assault on Local 600's leaders: "On March 12, 1952, the officers of Local 600, UAW-CIO were notified by telegram that, because of certain alleged violations of the Constitution of the UAW-CIO and other violations, the officers of Local 600 were directed to appear before the international executive board on Friday, March 14, 1952 . . . for 'the purpose of showing cause—if there be any—why an administrator should not be placed over Local 600.'"[67]

Reuther's executive board made three major charges against Local 600: First, that the local's publications failed to comply with the policies of the international union; second, that the local failed to remove Communist Party members from office; and third, that the local's president failed to enforce the international constitution.

Local 600's officers wrote a careful formal response to the executive board, denying these charges, but the board immediately put them under an official "administratorship." Reuther's staff then took control of the local and its newspaper, *Ford Facts*. The board removed the five elected officers whom the local's council earlier had failed to impeach and prohibited them permanently from running for local office. It also fired several elected shop committeemen and sent them back to their jobs in the plant.

The UAW's constitution allowed the executive board to impose a maximum sixty-day administratorship on an errant local, but the one installed in Local 600 lasted six months. The local's repeated requests to lift the administratorship were ignored, but when its officers finally demonstrated at the UAW's Solidarity House, the international scheduled special local elections for September of 1952. In the elections, the pro-Reuther faction was roundly defeated. Stellato ran "unopposed, . . . a last minute attempt to line up opposition failed," and his entire slate was reelected.[68] The local's nineteen units elected ten Progressives, three "middle-of-the-roaders," and six "right-wingers" as their presidents. At the regular election nine months later in June 1953, Reuther's allies were again defeated. "The right-wing slate, headed by 3 candidates on leave from the International UAW payroll," as the ACTU paper reported, "took a drubbing at the giant Ford Local 600."[69]

■ "OPERATION RUNAWAY"

With Local 600 wounded but still full of fight, and the local's leadership's continuing militancy and dissent from the newly fashionable era of "labor statesmanship," Ford went full-steam ahead with the decentralization of its huge Rouge complex. Ford's "Operation Runaway," as the local called it, gradually broke up and transferred various operations that had been part of Rouge's uniquely self-contained automobile production process to other plants in other states. Not incidentally, the building units that were the left's most durable strongholds were especially hard-hit. For instance, Ford sharply cut the operations of both the motor building and production foundry, where the Progressive Caucus regularly won elections, so that the number employed in the motor building fell from nine thousand in 1950 to fewer than half of that in the following decade. During the same period, the eight-thousand-man production foundry was gradually eliminated.[70]

Ford's decentralization was deliberately aimed simultaneously at undercutting Local 600 and thus weakening the UAW in the greater Detroit area *and* at finding a more docile work force where wages were lower, fewer workers were organized, and the unions were more accommodating.[71] The company's 1949 decision, for instance, to build its new body stamping plant in Buffalo, New York, reflected both of these concerns. An internal memorandum to Henry Ford II and other top Ford executives warned that the UAW's "position in the Detroit area would be further strengthened" if the company built its new plant in Detroit.[72]

If the strength of the UAW in Detroit was crucial in Ford's relocation decision, so, too, was the strength of working-class organization as a whole (and not only that of auto workers) at other possible sites for the new plant. In Chicago and Pittsburgh, as in Detroit, in the words of a Ford consultant's study of the "best location" for the new plant, this was the

one consideration that deserves special emphasis. . . . the ominous mixture of the United Mine Workers, the United Steelworkers and the United Electrical Workers in the Pittsburgh area; the combination of the United Steelworkers, the radical Farm Equipment Workers and the United Automobile Workers in the Chicago area; and the entrenched position of the United Autoworkers [*sic*] in the Detroit area, should cause any company considering the establishment of a new plant at these locations to pause. There is no question but that the union influences in these areas at these locations are much more powerful than in the Buffalo area, where the C.I.O. has not been able to establish a dominating position against the old, traditional A.F. of L. building trades unions and the railroad unions. . . . Introducing aggressive United Auto Workers unionism into a community that is the stronghold of the United Mine Workers and the United Steelworkers, and where the radical United Electrical Workers has one of its strongest units, in the turbulent Westinghouse local, could result in the combination of these explosive forces which over a period of time could well create an atmosphere of tension and strife in which industry could not hope to progress.[73]

All in all, Local 600's leaders estimated that half a million persons— Ford workers and their families—throughout greater Detroit, in Dearborn, in the downriver cities of River Rouge, Ecorse, Wyandotte, Melvindale, Lincoln Park, and in adjacent communities would suffer directly from the break-up and mass transferal of Ford's operations to other states. Indirectly, it would hurt many more people as the result of its "grave economic consequences [for] the communities heavily populated by Ford workers."[74] Yet Local 600 was unaided—if not actually hindered—by its international leadership in its resistance against Operation Runaway.

In mid-1950 the local formed a special Committee Against Job Runaway, headed by President Stellato (then still in Reuther's camp) and consisting of the local's other top officers and a number of chairmen of the production units in the Rouge plant. Stellato wrote Henry Ford II, president of Ford Motor Company, to request that he meet with them to give "straightforward answers" to questions about the company's plans. On June 1, 1950, they met instead with John S. Bugas, Ford vice president.

But the answers they got to their simple but profoundly important questions—How many jobs did the company plan to move out of Rouge, and when would the transferals start? How many of Rouge's workers, in what buildings and departments, would be affected? Would the company bring in other jobs to replace the jobs it transferred?— were "evasive" and "devious."[75]

Local 600 had no assistance from Reuther in trying to get these answers from Ford; worse, while the local was in the throes of trying to mount an effective resistance to Ford's pending decimation of Rouge, Reuther—over the local's vehement opposition—signed, on September 4, 1950, the UAW's historic five-year contract with the company. "We raised hell with him," as Walter Dorosh, then one of the local's officials, told us. "We said he had no right, without a convention decision, to sign a five-year contract. . . . 'Who the hell made you God?'"

Local 600's leaders opted to look to the courts for relief. Stellato and other Local 600 officials tried to meet with Reuther, but (as Dorosh, one of the officials involved, told us), they only got to see Reuther's secretary because "he wouldn't see us." On October 30, 1951, Stellato wrote to Reuther, again denouncing the five-year contract and informing him of the local's proposed suit. "No member of our union or any union would consciously sign a 5-year contract which would leave him helpless while his employer moved his job from under him. We owe it to ourselves, to our members and to the surrounding communities, to prevent this disastrous result." Local 600 would, he told Reuther, now file a "legal complaint to obtain an injunction to halt the decentralization of the Rouge plant." On November 11, 1951, at Detroit's Cass Technical High School, 2,500 of the local's most active members voted unanimously for the international's trying to abrogate the UAW-Ford five-year contract, pushing for a thirty-hour work-week for forty hours pay and bringing suit in the U.S. District Court to seek "an injunction against further removal of operations from the Rouge plant and against further farming out." The suit, as Stellato wrote Reuther the next day, had "the unanimous approval of every member of the Local and of the chairmen of all 17 building units. There is no difference of opinion on this issue." He again asked that the international join the suit but also said, "If the international refuses, we will go ahead anyway."[76]

In the judgment of the UAW's associate general counsel Harold A. Cranefield, the proposed suit was "novel in its conception," and if the UAW proceeded with it the suit would be unprecedented.[77] As he informed Reuther on November 8, the suit rested on the legal theory that the UAW's contract with Ford "should be construed as carrying a commitment by Ford against such practices [i.e., removal of operations and farming out jobs] or that the Court should reform the contract in accordance with the actual understanding of the parties though it was not written into the agreement."

The "usual pat answer to such a theory," Cranefield advised Reuther, "is that collective bargaining agreements are not contracts of employment:—that the employer . . . remains free to withdraw employment for any reason whatsoever (except one that would violate the National Labor Relations Act)." But Cranefield considered the theory "though novel, . . . very carefully thought out." It was "within the realm of possibility that the court might entertain the complaint." Indeed, he was "sure the suit would be taken seriously and would attract national attention among labor lawyers on both sides of the table and in the labor press and trade [i.e., employers' associations] journals."

Most important, Cranefield concluded, it was "undeniable" that if the court could be persuaded "to move even an inch in the direction of the theory of this complaint it would be a great gain for labor. It is equally undeniable that such advances are usually generated in the courts in such circumstances as these rather than legislatively."[78]

But Reuther and his executive board were not willing to support the workers of this recalcitrant "Red" local.[79] Not only did he reject their program, but in a speech at the UAW convention later that year he also charged that the local was "dominated by the Communist Party" and that its program was "Communist-inspired." "Brother Reuther evidently forgot," *Ford Facts* retorted in an editorial on January 19, 1952, "that 30,000 members of Local 600 sent him cards requesting the immediate negotiation of a 30-hour week with 40 hours pay. In his opinion, he believes that 30,000 of us in Local 600 are members of the CP."

On November 14, 1951, without its international's support, Local 600 filed the suit against Ford.[80] It charged that the company had perpetrated a "fraud" upon the union and asked that the UAW-Ford contract be either reformed to prohibit the decentralization or declared null and void because the company had falsely assured the union that it had no plans to decentralize.[81] The suit was "perhaps unique in the history of American labor-employer relations." At "the very heart of this case," as Ernest Goodman, counsel for Local 600, told the court nearly two years later, was the question of "the rights of workers under a contract with an employer extending over a long period of time to have some security in the retention of the work processes on which they are employed for the duration of the contract, and the accumulation of the rights which they can only acquire if the employer continues his operations at that particular place where they are employed."[82]

On June 5, 1953, the U.S. District Court ruled against the local. It declared that the local's allegation that Ford committed a fraud upon the union was "render[ed] doubtful" because Reuther and the other UAW officials who signed the contract with the company were not parties to the local's suit "complaining of the alleged fraudulent conduct on the part of the company." The court also ruled that the contract had no implied commitment against decentralization because it "unequivocally vest[ed] in the company, and only in the company, the right . . . 'to manage its business, including the rights to decide the number and location of plants.'"[83]

Thus, because Reuther ceded this "management right" to the company and refused to join the local's suit, the "realm of possibility" of "a great gain for labor" never had even a fighting chance to become a reality.[84] Instead, in the coming years, Ford's decentralization would sharply cut employment at Rouge. By the 1960s, the company had shipped away the jobs of more than half of Rouge's workers. The number of hourly rate workers would drop from around sixty-five thousand in 1950 (already down from eighty-three thousand in 1941, when the local was born) to fewer than thirty thousand. Many of the fifteen thousand workers at the Ford plant in Detroit's northern suburb of Highland Park would also lose their jobs.

So, with Ford and other corporations retaining the unrestricted right to dispose of their property (and their workers) freely, Detroit and the downriver communities soon became, as Local 600 leaders had foreseen and tried to prevent, "industrial wastelands."[85]

Working

■ JOHN ORR

My father worked in the motor building on a crankshaft line. Now, he never weighed more than 135 pounds in his life, and he used to come home at night so darn exhausted that he would just about go wash up come down and eat; and he would lay on the couch and listen to "Amos and Andy" and Kate Smith, who were the tops in radio at that time. Up to bed, to get ready for work. And my mother kept saying, "You two boys" (I have a brother a year and a half older than me) "are never going to suffer what your father did. When you are fourteen, I'm going to take you" (or twelve, the application age was twelve) "to Henry Ford Trade School," which she did. As each of us reached the age of twelve, we went up to Highland Park, adjacent to the Ford factory in Highland Park on Woodward Avenue, to the trade school.

Why did your mother take that route, in sending you to a trade school, to work at Ford's? Was it sort of assumed that you would be at Ford's at some time?

No, she didn't mind us going to Ford's, but she didn't want us working on a production line like her husband, coming home so physically beat every night. She knew some skilled tradesmen among her friends, and what not, who lived a normal life. Now, my dad had a hard way. . . .

I came here, my citizenship papers show, January 25, 1924; and I was nine on January 2. At any rate, my brother and I both went to trade school. He went at age fourteen, and I followed a year and a half later at age fourteen. . . . I went to Henry Ford Trade School. It was very good. . . . You worked four years. You worked in the shop end of the school two weeks, and then went to school one week. So, we got very little schooling, and I have always been ashamed of my grammar, and what not, on that account, because we had so little of it.

I went to the Henry Ford Trade School until the age of eighteen. They operated in violation of the law, because trade schools were allowed with industry if the products they made were not used in the industry that was sponsoring that school. Well, it was so blatant what he [Ford] was doing. . . . We had a trolley repair department; and if you ever saw kids work repair, oh, my God! I myself worked on valves, and they were from stead valves, with gates that big, that operated in the powerhouses and what not, to little things, very little, on rubber valves, like you change a washer at home. Most of them were metal. Some were so small. . . . It was quite evident where the leaks were, and you had to sand those out: hit them with a red lead and blue lead, black lead into each other so they made it—it was a male and female part. Your fingers were like sandpaper. I'd come home with blood oozing out of them. I got bitter in there, although I learned a lot, I'll have to say. I was learning to operate lathes and milling machines. . . .

Everybody that came through the Trade School didn't get into the factory. It depended on whether they needed you. . . . We got an increase if we kept up with our shop work and our school work, a penny every six weeks or whatever the term was.

I served an apprenticeship as a toolmaker in 711X. It was in the foundry machine shop. What you know now as the tool-and-die unit then used to be just the tool-and-die building. It was a tool-and-die building, with about four thousand people in it who built all the new tools and dies. But then there was a tool room and a die room in every building where there was many machine operations.

When I left the trade school and went in the factory, I was more impressed than ever what my mother meant by saying, "You boys are going to be tradesmen not production workers," because they were like animals, my God. Even today everybody thinks it's easy in a Ford factory, even today if you can get a trip through the Ford assembly plant and see those guys, they are like robots themselves—putting nuts on, putting bolts on, doing this and that. How the hell they stand the pace, it would drive me nuts. I couldn't have ever worked in there on production. They do it. Sometimes you ask a guy why and he says, "I'm not doing that, I'm building a home or a cottage or something." He says, "My mind is far away." He's just doing this automatically. I don't know how they can robotize themselves like that. But anyway, we were surrounded by good union people, the production workers were the ones who knew they needed a union. Don't forget by that time we had many examples of what we were suffering.

■   PAUL BOATIN

The word got all over the world, and even got to New Castle, Pennsylvania, where I was living: $5 for an eight-hour day was better than anybody else was paying. Nobody stopped to analyze the fact that an eight-hour day meant twenty-four hours' continuous work. . . . He would only work you eight hours, because eight hours after that somebody else took over on the midnight shift; and another crew took over after you on the afternoon shift. People came from all over. . . . during the depression years of 1920, '21, and '22.

There were parking lots for the salaried workers and the office people and the others for the general workers. Those parking lots, for that entire stretch of two miles, were full of people who came there at twelve o'clock and one o'clock at night to wait for the employment office to open at eight o'clock in the morning. So, I spent five or six weeks there [on the employment line] meeting people from all over. . . . And I was ridiculed. I was still an intellectual. I had studied English in Italy and I had gone to . . . what is known as the Gymnasium, which is the next step after high school. . . . I had a superior attitude, the attitude of a half-baked intellectual who thinks he knows more than the ordinary worker who may be inarticulate, and so forth. [Looking back,] those workers . . . they knew a hell of a lot more than I did, even though I had read a lot of books and they were barely able to sign their name.

I remember one case in particular, a young Mexican who couldn't speak English. I knew more Spanish than he did English, even. . . . We met there [on the employment line] at one o'clock every night. You have a tendency to try to get back to the same spot; so, you've got people there that you know. You form a union right there, so to speak. Somebody has to hold the place for a guy who goes out to get coffee or get peanuts. . . . They came there to wait for the employment office to open; and that went on for five or six weeks, an interminable period of time, and this was July and August. [Laughter.] I remember this young Mexican trying to convince me that I should tell the company that I was twenty-one years old, because otherwise I'm not going to get full pay. There was no work permit needed at that time. I said, "I'm not going to lie to Mr. Ford." But inside of me I recognized that I was going to have to lie. I was going to have to tell him I'm at least eighteen, otherwise I won't get the job at all. That much concession I would make. So, my name had become "Mr. Dummy, Big Dummy" from this young Mexican. "How old you today, Big Dummy?" Well, the irony of it all is that we both wound up on the same job on the same shift in the same place. He was getting the top wage, and I was getting only half of it. After working there six or eight months, I forget, I was getting $3.20, and he was getting $6.20. So, you learn, you learn very fast.

■ THOMAS YEAGER

I came here to Dearborn [in 1928], and I got a job—imagine, with one
shoe on and one bedroom slipper [I had my toes broke in the coal
mine], and they still hired me. They needed men. You can just imagine this big Rouge plant, at one time eighty thousand. (Now, I don't
know, its fourteen or something.) But, anyway, I got a job right away,
and I worked in production, [in] the B Building. I worked in there off
and on. . . . In those days, there was no union, and you had a job and
you didn't have a job. . . . The old model goes off and the new one
follows it. Sometimes you are off three months, five months out of a
job. There was no unemployment compensation. There were no benefits of any kind. You never knew where your next dollar was coming
from. . . . then after the union got in, it wasn't long, . . . everything got
straightened around.

■ MIKE ZARRO

I got interested in mechanics, so I signed up with the Ford Motor
Company to get into the Ford Trade School. That was back in 1929. I
was in the trade school for about a year and a half; and they were more
or less teaching you the fundamentals of running tool shop machinery. You know, such as automatic grinders, shapers and lathes and all
that. Just enough experience to work with lathes and equipment within each tool room which was supplied to all of the units in the Rouge
plant. (I think that at the time of the origination of the union . . . in
1941, there was eighteen units). . . . After a year and a half, [in 1931]
they sent me to the Rouge plant, to the glass plant. . . . I was a small
guy. I couldn't pick up that glass. That was three-quarter-inch glass. That
was before they had the thin plate. "Well, we . . . are going to use you
here for a couple of days," he says, "because we are short here. You
go back into the department." So, I tried to stick it out for three days,
and then I finally told him, I says, "If you can't do better than this, I'm
going to have to get out of here." So I went up and I saw Mr. Brown,
who was the superintendent at that time, and I told him, I says, "I come
here with the idea of going into the tool room. That's my respected
type of work." And he says, "We're going to set you, if you want to wait
a few days." So I got a little crazy-like, and I just got mad, and I went
to the employment office and cleared out. Then I quit. So, then I went
into Briggs [Briggs Manufacturing Company] in the body shop, and I
was instrumental in organizing over there back in 1937. Finally Ford
Motor sent me a card. They sent me a card to come back to work. My

job was there. You know if you quit, they'll bring you back. But if they lay you off, you're never going to get back.[1] That's the way they operated in them days. . . .

I went back to the glass plant. So, I says, "Well, what have you got to offer?" You know, I was a little upset about what happened previously. They said, "We're going to put you in a good job, 'final inspection,' and then you can go up in 'floor inspection.'" So, that sounded pretty good to me, so I took it. . . . and I kind of forgot the idea of working in machinery and stuff.

■ HORACE SHEFFIELD

My first job at Ford's was working as what they called a sander. . . . I fortunately got hired at Ford's in December of 1933. . . . Maybe it was 1934. I recollect it was the 28th of December. I went into what they called the B Building; that was where they made the bodies. They worked on the bodies and I worked as a sander. That's where the cars were primed; you had to smooth them down. That sort of thing. It was a very hard job. I had learned that job, [I had gotten hired,] at Briggs, [where] I worked for a short while sometime in 1933.

How did you get the job?

I don't recall. I just went out there two or three times and got hired. . . . I had to stand in line, no question about that. As I try to think back, I don't recall whether someone gave me a note to [Don] Marshall or what. . . .[2]

Were many blacks hired into the B Building?

No, there were fewer blacks in the B Building. The massive number of blacks were in the production foundry. But there were blacks dispersed throughout the plant.

■ ARCHIE ACCIACCA

I went to work at Ford's in 1935, January 3, 1935, at the Rouge plant, on production. . . . I got in, [but] not by going on a line. There's very very few people who are able to go on the line and go to work. I got in. My dad knew a realtor that was pretty well up on the West Side, a fellow by the name of Frischcorn [?], a nice guy, very nice. And this Frischcorn knew somebody at Ford's—I don't know who in the heck he knew, I don't remember, some wheel at the employment office, I think. He helped my dad get a lot of his friends in. So he gave me a letter, as he gave a lot of others, and . . . I brought it to the employment office, and I got into work at what was then known as the

"pressed steel," but now they call them "stamping plants." I worked
there for, well, my real physical work was only in the preunion days,
because after the union came in I was a union representative all my
life, all the rest of the time I spent with Ford's. But from 1935 to 1941
I worked there.

■ DAVE MOORE

A guy living next door to me said, "I got hired at Ford. I slipped in
through the line, and I got in the back door. They hired me. One guy
dropped his pass, and said, 'I got a pass here if you want to use it.'"
On January 17, 1935, I walked all the way from my home. I walked all
the way. I left home at 2:30 that morning, and I got out to Ford round
about 4:00. And that line looked like a million people. At 8:00 the
employment office opened up. They had all the Ford service people
there.[3] And they would let so many come through, and stop. One guy
said, "All those who got a pass come up to the gate." I had this pass.
I went and I got inside. . . . "You're hired at 62 and ½ cents an hour."
Wow! 62 and ½ cents an hour. "You'll work in the foundry on the shake
out." Shake out was the worst job you could get. You pour that iron.
If you're making a piston, that mold is shaped in a piston. The iron
come out of the furnace just like water. Guys would come up, and pour
that iron in there, then it would set so long. They would spray water
over it, and the steam would come out, and it was hot, and you had
to go and shake it out. That's what you call a "shake out." All that fumes
coming up.
    What are you shaking out—the bubbles?
    Well, you would get that mold it was in, and just take it and shake
it, until all that sand come off it. . . .
    I worked in all that fumes there for about three days; and they took
me out of there, put me outside on the shipping dock, shipping motors. I was weighing 116, and the motors weighed six hundred pounds.
And I had to help a guy put the motors in a box car to be shipped out
to different parts of the country. . . . "I know I'm not going to stay here
long." . . . I would be struggling with this motor. But I began to get it,
there's a way you can handle it. We had a chain that, once we got it
on the platform, a hoist could pull it up and stack it. . . .
    Why did they take you out of the foundry?
    I think what had happened, that the guys that I was working along
with in the foundry . . . didn't want to go outside in the cold weather.
It was January, and it was cold outside on the shipping dock, and the
wind was blowing like mad.

I wanted to get away from that steam. I didn't know what to do when they said "shipping docks." "You got a chance to go out on the shipping dock." This supervisor was from a place called Columbia, Tennessee. I never will forget this guy, he had that real southern accent. "How about one of you boys come out here and go with me out on the shipping dock? I don't care which one. Just get your so and so over here, and come with me." So, nobody made a mad rush. But I wanted to get out of that heat. So, I went off. He said, "Son, how much y'all weigh? Now y'all come on here. You know you're gonna have to work with these boys out here on this dock, and put these motors up. Now, y'all understand that, don't you?" "Yes, sir." I was going to get out of there.

I worked out there until April, when the weather began to get a little better. And, lo and behold, they sent me to a place called the rolling mill. Back in the hell again. That's where they roll all the steel out of. I stayed there . . . for awhile.

I was working over on a place, what you call a "pickeling tank," where we'd get the steel, and put it in a big tank to set for awhile 'til it's pickled. And then they would get the fumes cooking up again. I went from hell to double hell.

■ JOHN MANDO

I started on the frame line. I used to work on the end of the frame line with three other guys, and as these chassis frames came off the line, assembled, we would straighten them up and put them on hooks, and they would go through the paint tank. And there were a lot of frames that came off.

And then they asked me if I wanted to serve as a utility man, a relief man. And I took that job. I used to do that as well as relieve other people on the frame line putting it together before the finished product. And that's the last job I held before I left. And when I came back I went to work in the rolling room. I went to work as a "hooker." A hooker is not the kind— . I was a crane hooker. One of the guys that would direct the crane as it came down, tie up the bundles or barrels or whatever, and give the operator the signals as to where to drop it and so forth and so on. And after some time at that, . . . it was like middle 1947 or the latter part of 1947, there was an opportunity for people to work—qualify—as crane operators, so I took a crack at that. And I worked as a crane operator from '47 up until—actually, I think, the first time I got interested to accept the nomination was in '49.

Was that a skilled job?

Crane operator? No, it's not classified as a skilled job as we consider skilled jobs. The skilled trades are composed of electricians, millwrights, tool-and-die workers, and that sort. And the crane operators were kind of in-between. They were semiskilled. [There] were a couple of drives on to try to get crane operators included in the skilled group but it never quite actually came about.

■ KENNETH ROCHE

At eighteen years of age I was hired in to the Ford Motor Company, and that was in 1940 in September. I was taken there by my mother, down to the city hall by Clarence Doyle, who was councilman, and Carl Brooks, [who] was the chief of police. . . . He was the stooge of the Ford Motor Company. This is the way things worked then. If you didn't know anybody you didn't get a job. . . .

I went to Henry Ford's school over here, and my education was all wrapped up in a nice ball and handed to me. There was nothing of classes of social studies or anything about socialism, capitalism—nothing in my curriculum about that at all. I went to Fullerton High School. Back and forth until the ninth grade there and to the twelfth grade in Fullerton. From Fullerton right straight to Ford Motor Company. . . .

They took me—my mother and Clarence Doyle took me—down to Carl Brooks's office. I sat outside on the porch of the police station. They went in, talked to Carl Brooks, and the next thing I know there's a Lincoln pulling up. Carl Brooks's secretary drove me into the [Rouge] plant. I was hired immediately into the plant and went to work in what they called at the time the "apprentice school." I worked there for three months. And then in December [1939], they put me out into the plant, into the gear and axle building, and I worked over there . . . for several years.

■ JOHN ORR

Well, of course, the women came out, women coming into the plants because sure in hell what the service men were paid [while fighting in World War II] then couldn't keep the woman at home with any kids. They had to go out and work. Don't you remember Rosie the Riveter? They were out making money.

They weren't just out making pin money—that helped hold the wages down. Women keep screaming about making, what, 58 percent or 65 percent of a man's wages. Many of them will take part-time jobs as pin money, and they're not too concerned about union wages or anything else, because their husbands are making money. Of course, that hurts the ones that really have to work and keep a home up because their wages are dragged down, too.

And that's never been true in the UAW. There was never a period when women didn't make the same wages.

They had equal pay for equal work?

Yeah. That was true then and it's still true.[4]

■ KENNETH ROCHE

Well, the women didn't come in until the war, and they started hiring women after there was a big fight with the Ford Motor Company. They didn't want to hire women, but they were forced to hire women because they picketed the local, they picketed the company and demanded that they be hired, and they did, and they started hiring a lot of them.

The women picketed Local 600?

Yeah, they picketed the local too, and finally put pressure on them, and they hired the women.

■ ARCHIE ACCIACCA

The war brought in women and people from outside the Detroit area. We had a woman as a committeewoman. They were a majority, and she got to be a committeewoman. It worked out pretty good, I'll tell you, they were happy to get in there and get equal wages. That's one thing we've never had any trouble, even a fight, today at this late date when I read about women not getting equal wages compared to men.

We'd had some bad layoffs as a result of the war ending, everything phasing out. . . . And then the . . . big layoff came, in 1947 or '48, somewhere in there, 1947 or '48. . . . A lot of men, a lot of women, laid off, and they went out in the street. No problem, nothing was heard. . . . They were getting unemployment compensation. And while they were getting unemployment compensation, everybody was pretty happy, they had a little income, sit home and having a little money coming in. When that started running out, the women started complaining about when are they going to . . . get back to work. They said, . . . "We hear that there's some men in there working in there with less seniority than we've got." They went down . . . to the local union, they went to the international union downtown, at Solidarity House, complaining about men working in there with less seniority than women.

Well, women I used to get along with real real good during the war,
everything was real nice. As a matter of fact, I think I got a majority of
their votes. But when this thing hit the fan about men working with
less seniority than them, I said, "Okay, we're going to do something
about this." First thing I did was call a meeting and publicize the hell
out of it and let everybody know what we had done.

There were three jobs on the loading dock; Ford used to load side
panels into box cars to ship to the assembly plants, it's a complete side
assembled with the components inside of it. . . . All the braces and
what have you. Three big healthy men used to handle it, pick it up off
. . . the conveyor and put it [down], they had two layers of cars,
understand? . . . Three big men used to do that. Another job, rooftops,
they were heavy; and another job was floor pans. . . . There's a front
part and a back part made separately, and when it's put together, it's
very heavy and awkward. So, when we were having these layoffs the
company got a hold of us and said, "Look we've got these men over
there that have less seniority than these women who are coming
through, you want to send those women over there to bump those
men?" They said, "They're going to get disqualified, they're not going
to be able to do the work." We said, "We don't want to do it that way
because here's what would happen."

I've got to explain this one. We had a lot of women with 1942 seniority. . . . They would be sent to bump the youngest in their group . . .
of classifications. They've got to bump the youngest. They don't have
a choice who they're going to bump, they've got to bump the youngest and the youngest were these big strapping healthy men on these
three different jobs. . . . That woman wouldn't go over there. She
wouldn't try. She wouldn't even look at it and say, "I can't do it." At
that point she's disqualified. Over here would be a 1944 woman working but she don't bump that woman, she bumps this one because this
one here could have 1946 or '47 seniority, understand? . . . So there's
where your disqualification come in, we thought that was an injustice.
We told the company we don't want it that way.

We had previous experience where Ken Bannon came from out of
Highland Park, where they disqualified a bunch of women out of line
of seniority, and we didn't do that. So, we said to the company, "Oh
no, we're going to separate those three jobs. We're going to separate,
take and leave that side panel, rooftop and the floor pans alone, these
women don't bump there. If there are men who come through that
can handle that job, they can bump there. These women will bump
the youngest on the jobs that they can do." We got the company to
agree to do that. So, we called a meeting, man, over this issue. . . . I

made a big bulletin. They went down to the Solidarity House complaining about being laid off, splashed it all over the building, big big turnout, men and women, good, man, that's up my alley. So I says, "Here's our problem. Women are working with more seniority than some men on these certain jobs. If these women went over there they would be disqualified and they'd go out in the street."

We assumed that they don't want to do that, so we said, "Okay, you want to go strictly contract. Do you with 1942 seniority want to bump the youngest in a building, and go that way? Where over here could be somebody with 1944, '45, or less seniority than those men? Oh no, no." That hall was jammed. We explained the whole thing to them. I said, "I want a vote. Either you're going to agree with what we've done in the building or you want to change it and go the other way." One hundred percent, not one person voted against us, that we done the right thing. Everybody says we're doing the right thing. But what happened, some politicians there (I don't want to name any names) got a hold of it and started hollering about women being laid off on the line of seniority. We were called down to the Solidarity House. We explained everything we done. We got a clean bill of health, everything was fine, no comment. But these shysters I talked of, they were going to do something, they got up, and went outside, and got a lawyer. They had a lawyer with 110 or 11 signatures. I don't know what they paid the lawyers, or what have you. I'm sure that the lawyer took a little advantage of them. They take the case to court that these women got laid off on the line of seniority, they went all the way to the state Supreme Court. The state Supreme Court looked it over and I got a copy of this, that's one thing I'm going to keep. I throw a lot of junk away because I accumulate a lot but I keep this one. When the state Supreme Court got it and looked into it, they threw it out. They wouldn't even hear it, and that was the end of it. Oh, our politics got rough, yeah, I went through a lot of things.

■ MIKE ZARRO

Right across the street from the glass plant they had a tire plant. My God, that was all women. Oh boy, yes. They were pretty good workers too.

After the war a lot of the women in the other plants that got hired during World War II got laid off, but in the glass plant they maintained their employment there?

Well, we had a little trouble there. We had to go through the General Council and through Local 600 and meetings with the top management.

They wanted to lay them off. So we said no, we can't go for that. You can't keep people for six months and lay off women with two or three years. It took three years. So we had a big fight. We almost had a strike over it. And we finally won out where the women could exercise their seniority as they were being eliminated from each unit, why they would exercise their seniority in whatever unit that carried them within the eighteen units. So the women got a good break out of it. They've still got a lot of them working there yet, right in the glass plant since I've left. There's women there with thirty-five years' seniority.

What kind of work did the women do in the glass plant? Did they have easier or lighter work?

Well, the glass plant was always considered a good place to work. And it wasn't really heavy work unless you got a backbreaking job. Yeah, they fit in pretty good. Some of them tried to take jobs which they weren't really adapted to. They'd take it and then, "Let me off, let me get out of here." We let them try it out. So, yeah, the women did all right in the glass plant.

Some of them they always leaned a little to the boss, but most of them were all right. They didn't care much about coming to meetings though. I always, man, I'd bawl them out for that.

Did any of them get elected to positions in the glass plant?

Yeah, I had one elected, Irene Johnson. She was my secretary, recording secretary. We always had a woman on the slate.

■ WILLIAM JOHNSON

A lot of the men felt that with the war over, and a lot of the guys coming back, those jobs [held by women] were needed for them. Well, of course, they had prior seniority rights anyway, so they could bump those women. They could displace them, because the women only had seniority starting in maybe 1942 or '43, and the average guy that had left the plant had seniority prior to that. So, . . . they could bump a woman.

So, it didn't matter how many years you were in the plant, just mattered what year you entered. Is that right?

He had seniority greater than she did because he had military service counted. Yeah, coupled with his actual seniority. So, using that method, they got rid of, not all the women, but they got rid of a substantial number of women, until finally, I think, enough of them went to the international union and began to raise hell, and then there was a change in attitude on the part of local unions. That was not only true of Rouge, it was true of all the plants; and they decided they were going to accord women the same seniority protection that they gave to men.

There was a change in policy?

Yeah. After that, sometime in . . . the late 1940s or the early 1950s, they began to hire women on the same basis, pretty much as they hired men. See, by a state law in Michigan women were limited to the hours they could work. . . . The state law was changed, too.

The Depression

■ JOHN SAARI

I was a depression youth. . . . I left home at a very young age. I rode the boxcars. I left home without a penny—well, beg your pardon, [with] 3 cents. . . . I had another fellow with me, and he couldn't take it, and he didn't even know the way back home. . . . So I took him back home, and then I left again, and I went from city to city, state to state. I always say, "I travel first-class boxcars."

How'd you get along with food and all during that time?

I used to do odd jobs, and then I used to just bum it. . . . When you got hungry, you went to a place and you asked people for something to eat.

Now, a thing happened which had a very big influence in my line of thinking. You know, a lot of people felt that, "Well, let's go to the wealthy section [of town]." And they couldn't get nothing. In fact, one fellow comes running back to us, and he said they pulled a gun on him. So, we went to working-class sections, and they were just as hard up as probably I was, but we got a sandwich. They always made a sandwich, or we got a banana, or a few ears of corn. Some grocery stores, they were quite understanding, and they would give us a loaf of bread.

And you had the jungles them days. What they called the jungles were all the hobos. . . . They congregated. Some of it was disease ridden. It was terrible.

And another thing happened to me. I never had no experience with blacks until I hit the road. We had one black man up in my hometown, and well I didn't have much to do with him but everybody liked him. So one day (I just forget what town, somewhere in Wisconsin) . . . I happened to be sitting down all by myself. And three blacks came, . . . and they sat down, and they looked at me and they said, "Hey, what're you doing out here?" I said, "Same thing as you," and they said, "How old are you?" "Oh, fifteen." "Geez," they said, "why don't you go home to your mother?" I says, "Well, I'm looking for a job." I had a lot of il-

lusions in them days. They sensed that I was hungry, and they told me,
"Now, you stay right here till we come back. We're going out and get
something to eat." One of them said, "We're going to have a harvest."
I waited, and sure enough they came back and they had everything.
They had bread and butter and lunch meat and fruit and milk and
whiskey and everything. They gave me some of that and they gave me,
even, whiskey. They just gave me one, and they said, "Now that's
enough for you," and I'll never forget that. . . . I never dreamed that I
would become involved like I am, like I have been. If I would have
known that, and anticipated it, I would have gotten their names, and
where they were from and stuff like that. But I imagine they're probably dead.

I saw some terrible sights. . . . We went to the jungles [in Indiana.]
There was men there; they had gonorrhea, they had syphilis. I'm telling you, it was terrible. . . . They were older than I was. . . . Another
thing that was a big influence on [me], [in] all towns them days there
was a lot of people on the road bumming.

In the 1930s, the depression, various cities, they made ordinances;
. . . they didn't want us people in town. So the whole police force,
when a train would pull in, a whole police force from that city would
gather around that train and anybody try to get off, they clubbed him
back on. . . . You talk about slavery. Now, a lot of people felt that the
slaves were freed. . . . This was a lot of baloney. During the last depression, for instance, they used to work a racket. If they caught a couple
of hobos, they passed a law, they passed ordinances that unless you
had 60 cents on you, it varied, different amounts in different towns
and if you didn't have that amount on you, then you were put in jail.
. . . They worked you, see, they worked you for nothing. So, what
happened, these politicians, no doubt, they was getting money, free
labor, and they got a cut from somebody else, because they brought
you over there to work, and the county was paying your fare in jail. . . .

That was a tremendous influence on me, which told me that, gee,
something is radically wrong, that all is not well, all these things. Now,
even in fact I happened to be a victim of it, what they call a kangaroo
court, . . . Well, it's rather comical in a sense the way they work it. They
gotcha. For instance, I was picked up . . . for trying to take a train, right
out of Grand Rapids. The detective—well a funny thing. I carried two
pair of pants with me, one was corduroy and the other one was a little dressier pair, and so the train was pulling out, and I was running
along the station. I was trying to get my corduroy pants on. There was
a fellow in the mail car says, "Hey, towhead, there's a dick in the cab."

I said, "Ah-h-h." No sooner than I'd jumped in the first coach on the train, and the damn thing, I don't think it went five hundred feet and come a crunching stop, and somebody grabbed me and threw me on the ground with a gun. So we ended up, there was three of us, we ended up in jail. . . . A fellow . . . talks to me, and he said, "Hey, how old are you?" I said, "Fifteen." "Where you from?" I told him. . . . He says, "I'm getting out today. I'm gonna get a hold of somebody. . . ." So sure enough he did. They let him out that day. Pretty soon the sheriff comes in. . . . "Now look," he said, "that kid he's only fifteen years old." They let us go.

Sometimes what used to happen is, if they caught you, if you happened to get into Illinois, which was bad . . . they would take a hobo, and they'd sentence him, and they'd work him for—maybe give him a sentence, I don't know—maybe ten days, thirty days, something like that. They'd work him for that length of time, and then they used to tell him, "Don't come back into this town, because we're going to get you again, and it'll be maybe ninety days before you get away." . . . One fellow was telling us, he was a hobo, . . . [that] he got caught in that, and he was [in] for about six months. And there was nothing he could do about it, see. And I almost got caught in it myself. . . .

I says, "All right, . . . I'm going to head on up north." . . . I ended up in Detroit, in Dearborn. That was in 1936.

■ MARGARET AND STANLEY NOWAK

Stanley Nowak: I worked at [Hart, Schaffner, and Marx] until the Great Hoover Depression. When the depression started, the section, as we called it, all the workers, all of those who did the same work, we divided according to the union agreement, one part worked one week and another part worked another week. Well, it got so bad that we would have one day in two weeks to work. And I said to myself, 'Well, what's the use?' I had a little savings, and I thought I would catch up on my education, that I needed it badly, or see the country a little. So, I quit. And a month later, before I decided what to do, the *Chicago Tribune* . . . came with a screaming headline across, "Seventeen Banks Close in One Day." One of them was the bank where I had my savings in there. It [stayed] closed for three years, if not more. So, I was left without a job and $50 to my name. [Laughs.] . . .

Margaret Nowak: He laughs about it today.
Stanley Nowak: But—
Margaret Nowak: He survived.
Stanley Nowak: I survived. I joined the unemployed movement.[5]

In Chicago?
In Chicago, yes, and I took a very active part.

■ DAVE MOORE

I don't think you ever have witnessed people eating out of garbage cans. . . . Where 90 percent of the population of a city as large as Detroit was out of work. There wasn't any work. Where families, whole families, were on the move all across the country. I'm coming to New York to get a job, people in New York coming to Detroit, and there are no damn jobs. And when shanties out in the boondocks are built for whole families to live in, people living in cars and people going around to these markets where there was a possibility of food, picking up rotten potatoes, cutting the rotten off to salvage some part of that potato that may be good. And they would bring them home and put them in water to cook. No meat in them, just cook them in water. I have seen this happen. And you see people don't have any clothes to wear. A guy will wear—you wear a pair of shoes to go someplace and you come back and let your brother have them. I did this with my own brother. . . . We had three or four pair of shoes for nine people . . . .

If Roosevelt had not been elected there would have been a different form of government here. If Roosevelt hadn't beat Hoover. If Hoover had stayed in, it would have been a different kind of political system in this country. Because people were ready for it and they didn't give a damn what it was—they were going to get it. He did a heck of a job. I'll have to say Roosevelt saved this country in my opinion. I don't know what form of government it would have been, but I'm damn sure it would have not been the one we exist under today. I don't know whether it was the Communist government, I don't know whether it would have been a Socialist, I don't know whether it would have been a dictatorship, I don't know what it was. But they were damn sure ready to scrap the one we had, and the only reason why they voted for Roosevelt was Roosevelt said what he was going to do. . . . And these were the things they wanted to hear. "I'm going to create jobs. I'm going to have the federal government provide jobs for you and your family. If you elect me I'm going to guarantee you a job and if you don't have a job, then you vote me out at the next election." He kept his promise. He wasn't getting a hell of a lot of money for it. But they went to work. CCC, WPA, PWA, everything it was.[6] Artists, actors, just common workers they had something to do. They were getting paid. But before they didn't have a damn thing coming in, and nowhere to go to get anything. Nothing. . . .

You want to see mass suffering, if you want to see some real indignities as far as human beings concerned. . . . Whole families lined up. Big open fire hoping somebody around would give them something to eat. They didn't have any place to stay. And you could just imagine what it was to be able to buy a whole slab of smoked bacon like that wrapped up for 35 cents? A whole slab. But where the hell were you going to get the 35 cents? You could ride the street car here for 6 cents anywhere all over the city. Where were you going to get the 6 cents from? You could buy any kind of property you want for $500 but where in the hell were you going to get $500 for it? You could go in one of the most beautiful restaurants up in downtown Woodward Avenue here and get a steak dinner, rib steak dinner and mashed potatoes, apple pie, coffee for 20 cents. A steak dinner. But where in the hell was you going to get that 20 cents? . . .

If you live under a major depression where everything is down, the money that is available, only a few people got it and they will not let it go. Money it's available, they got it. Women going to do housework for 50 cents a day, they scrub floors and cook meals for these people, wash their clothes and iron them, take their kids to school, and come home with 50 cents. That happened right here in the city of Detroit. Well, 50 cents was better than nothing. Some people ask, "Why are you so bitter?" "Well, what in the hell do you want me to be? Do you want me to laugh about it and say I'm happy this way?"

I know damn well that if that condition comes again, I don't think that the American people, not this generation of people, will stand for it. I don't think so. When Roosevelt got elected, the revolution was in the making. The whole country was on the verge. . . . To give an example, people who fought in World War I, who the government had promised they were going to give them a bonus, and the administration under President Hoover refused to give it to them. They marched on Washington.[7] These are guys less than ten or fifteen years, or a little longer, had been out of the Armed Services of their country. They went to Washington, and what happened? They turned soldier against soldier. Some were killed—they were ran out. They ran over [them] with horses. And here are people who had committed themselves to give up their life for the events of the country by an order of a president who had never been near a damn gun or none of his family had ever picked up a gun to defend the country. He was turning another soldier against the other to keep these rousers out of Washington.

You could see misery and deprivation, hunger and everything that makes life uncomfortable was plentiful around the city of Detroit. And I used to shovel snow in the wintertime, and pick out ashes in the summertime, and cut grass, and do whatever. Not only me, but every-body in my neighborhood. Whatever way you could make a few pen-nies, we tried. But instead of getting better, it got worse. At that time Hoover was still president, and "a chicken in every pot and two cars in every garage" was a slogan at that time. But we never could find the chicken or pot to put the chicken in. Damn sure we couldn't find a car to put into two garages.

Things went to happening here in Detroit, but people began to get together and discuss their plight, and as a result of that, especially those who had been working and were unemployed, the unemployment councils were formed. All kind of agitation took place. You could see at the time some of the best people, I thought, come forward who had not been given the opportunity to do so by speaking and debating about what should be did, how it should be did, who should lead and what not. And I was going around these places, listening to everything. With unemployment councils. And I began to get acquainted with guys, women, and everything. So, I found myself deep involved. Evictions was taking place. I would join up with a bunch of guys. They would just for example, set [some woman] and her family out. No sooner than the bailiffs and sheriffs left, we'd go and put them back in.

How did they arrange those? How did you know when people were being evicted? Did you have neighborhood watches?

Well, the news was spread: "Howard Jones is going to be evicted in the next block."

At that time it seemed like the depression was not always bad. It brought people . . . closer together. And they shared the common, I would say, bad things with each other. And the good things also. It seemed like more unity at that time. It was more unity among the black and white people here in Detroit at that time than it has been here lately. . . . But during the time of the depression, the whites and the blacks was closely knitted. The working-class people, those who were working in the factories, were doing the hard cold work. . . .

How did they know that the bailiffs were coming? Sometimes they didn't know. They just come and set them out. Sometimes . . . they'd chase the bailiffs away. Then they'd go and get the police and here come two, three, or four cars of police, went in to back them up. Then we had to back off. But they couldn't stay forever. When they would leave, we'd put them back in again. And nobody would tell them [the bailiffs] who put them back in again. They couldn't keep [watch] twen-ty-four hours a day, forty-eight hours a night. So, we'd put them back in. Sometimes they'd get so damn p.o.'d by the many trips they'd have to make. "Is it the hell worth it?," you know.

But as time went on, I began to get more involved in things. So, I found myself deep involved in the unemployment councils. And we did many things. Demonstrations, leaflets, argued with each other, debated what should be did, who should do it.

■ JOHN SAARI

[The depression had] a big influence on me, you see, in all towns, them days, in the 1930s, there was a lot of people on the road bumming. They had no homes, no nothing, and I saw where families were out on the street. I saw a woman with her baby sitting on a couch not knowing where to go.

And so at this time I was sitting up there, and there was another fellow, he was an easterner by his brogue, and he had a package on his lap. . . . Three or four fellows . . . started to get off, and they went down, and the police went after 'em, and they instructed them to get back up there. Or, "You're going to end up on the rails."

So this easterner, he gets up and he goes down and he confronts these policemen and he tells them, "Now, look, we didn't ask to be here. We're here of necessity." He said, "These fellows don't like your town anymore than they probably like any other town but they have a right to come in here, whether they're rich or whether they're poor, they had a right to come here." Now he told them fellows, "You go on and I'll watch here. If anything happens to you guys, I'll take care of the situation." And he had a gun in that package, and so . . . they let them fellows go.

Now, no doubt they picked 'em up later.

■ THOMAS YEAGER

In 1932 that's when the depression came, remember? The depression came along, and I got laid off. By that time I think we had three or four children. . . .

My brother-in-law, my wife's brother and I, we decided, we both had cars, we decided we were going to go into the trucking business. "What are you going to buy a truck with?" (I went all over trying to borrow money, even went to Ohio to try to borrow from my other brother-in-law; and I went back to Pennsylvania. But no one would loan me the money to buy a truck.)

So, . . . you know what we did? We turned our cars in, and we got a dump truck. We were doing all right, my brother-in-law was working up at Ford's, where they were making those Stout airplanes.[8] And I was working with the truck. What happened was, winter set in. See, in the fall they were making new roads and new streets, and all these subdivisions, and things; and so it was cement, just cement, that was all we hauled, cement, cement. When they folded up, there I was.

So, I said to my brother-in-law, I said, "Well, I'm going back to the coal mines. Its the only thing left for me to do. I have to leave my family here, and go back, and I got to make a dollar somewhere." So, I went back.

And I was never so glad in my life, when I got back out of there. I stayed about six months, and then I came back home. But the reason I came back, I finally got a notice from the Ford Motor Company to report to work.

Coal Miners

■ KENNETH ROCHE

My parents came from Pennsylvania. . . . My mother was the daughter of a coal miner, and my father was the son of a coal miner. Their fathers were killed in mining accidents, cave-ins in the mines. They moved to Detroit, and both got jobs working at Robert's Brass. They moved to Dearborn from Detroit, and my father couldn't find a job. He changed his name from Zezecki [?], which is a Polish name, to Roche, which is an Irish name, but very few people realize it.

■ THOMAS YEAGER

I had a brother and sister, and had relatives, that worked in what they called Crucible, in Pennsylvania, and there was a big steel outfit and they had their own coal mine. So, I had a half-brother there that took me in the mine with him. And I got my first taste of it, and I was scared to death.

Were the mine workers organized there?

Not at the time when I was there. They had been organized years before then. . . . So, after I was there for awhile, I met my wife. She was staying with an aunt there in the coal mines. Her uncle worked in the coal mine there . . . [and her] father and a number of people worked for the Oliver Snyder Steel Corporation, which had three big mines outside of Uniontown, Pennsylvania. And after about six weeks of the clings, we got married. This marriage has lasted, it will be fifty-nine years coming this April. We have had five children. And the oldest son was born in Crucible, Pennsylvania. In fact, we got married in a little town along the river by the name of Fredericktown, Pennsylvania. And then we stayed there about three years, and I started learning how to cut coal.

But there was no union. And we worked all hours. You go in some nights, and you had a bad night you could be in there all night, come out the next morning, you would meet those guys going [in]. The coal loaders would go in the morning, and you would meet them going down to the mine. About three years and I got scared. They had a big mine explosion down about maybe seven or eight miles from where I worked in the mine. I worked where they had a big explosion in what they called the "mother mine." It was about 289 miners got killed. I went down there for rescue work, and I saw all that down there, women and children. I came home, and I told my wife, "Hey, I'm going to get out of here." "Where are you going?" I said, "I'm going to Detroit.". . .

I started working for Ford in September of 1928. Just before this, I left one part out. I went in one afternoon to cut coal, and the place was bad. We put up some props, thought we would hold a slate up. The cement slate came down and you had to wear rubber boots there was no such thing as [steel] toes or anything like that; . . . and that rock come down there, and that slate come down there and caught my toes. They had to haul me out of there with a motor that night.

■ WILLIAM JOHNSON

A large contingent of people from Appalachia—Kentucky, Indiana, Ohio, Virginia, West Virginia—who had come out of the mines . . . had been in the mine workers' union. . . . When they came to Ford, attracted by the $5 a day proposition back in the late 'teens and early 1920s, a lot of them had had previous union experience. . . .

You think the ones that had come from the Appalachias were active in the coal miners' union?

Oh, I would suspect they were mostly, if they were active at all it was at a lower level, maybe job stewards. . . . [Tommy] Thompson himself had been what they call a check weighman in the mines, and he had left the mines because of the cyclical unemployment in the mines, I guess. He came to Detroit, and one of his outstanding features was that he had been a check weighman in the mine workers' union before coming to Dearborn and getting hired at the Rouge plant. . . .

Were the southerners who came up during the war also previously coal miners?

Well, it depends on the part of the country they came from. A lot of them had been farmers. Well, I guess you'd have about an even split between coal miners, people from the Appalachian region, and people from just the South generally and who had been mostly farmers, small farmers.

■ THOMAS YEAGER

These miners, when they were trying to get the unions in, these miners were fired by the company. When they got things straightened out,
these people were on the black-list, and never got called back. That's
why so many miners were migrating into Michigan. They came here
to get jobs, and you got jobs at Ford's.

■ JOHN ORR

I would give a lot of credit to the mine workers. . . . [There were] a
lot of layoffs in the mines, and most of those guys headed for Detroit,
because the automobile business, for awhile, was booming, and they
hired in there. Pennsylvania, mostly. You will find among the old-timers many of the original organizers in Ford were from the coal mines.

I'm sure you have heard of Percy Llewellyn who died in April of this
year. He was a member of the United Mine Workers but he never
worked down below. He worked upstairs on the depo. I gave the eu-
logy at his funeral, and I told the story that he told me. "I belonged to
the mine workers but I was never down in the mines in my damn life,"
he said. "I didn't put that coal down there, and I'll be goddammed if I
was going down there and dig it." No, he worked upstairs as a check
weighman, working for the union, checking the boss's weights.

Mack Cinzori [was also a coal miner]. (Mack, that's his first name.
That's his legal name.)

Did he actually work in the mine?

Yes, he did. Hey, they all did except Percy, as far as I know.

■ VICTOR REUTHER

Were a lot of coal miners involved as organizers?

Not in the Ford organization. Miners were used as occasional speakers who would come in. I was director of organization in the state of
Indiana during the tail end of the great General Motors strike after the
Battle of the Running Bulls in Flint, when I had to get out of town;[9]
and there were some miners that were assigned to my staff in Illinois;
and there were some who were sent in to speak, like Powers Hapgood
and John Brophy and others. They were top people, but they were sent
in much as the Amalgamated sent in Leo Krzycki, and Rose Pesotta
came in from the ILGWU, and these early people. That was a part of
their contribution to the national CIO, but the Ford drive came so late
in the great wave of unionization of CIO. Steel and rubber and auto

were already well underway. . . . I don't recall any mine worker organizers having been sent into Ford's. Now, this is true, that many auto
workers came out of hill country where the miners had some unionization, and they brought that union experience with them. That was
true in Flint; it was true in Anderson, Indiana; it was true in River
Rouge, too. Well, they knew enough about unionism to know that
that's what they wanted. They wanted a strong organization, and they
knew what solidarity meant, sticking together. And those were important lessons to be learned in those days. The corporation was so bent
on dividing the workers through fear and intimidation and open brutality that anyone who had the experience of fighting mine companies
in the hills knew what was involved. So, it gave them a degree of seasoning, so to speak, preparing them for a very difficult struggle. It was
important.

Paternalism

■ JOHN ORR

A lot of things that the old man [Henry Ford] was given credit for... weren't quite true. Maybe he meant well. I don't know. That was always the thing that kept the Ford workers from organizing until four years after GM and Chrysler were organized. "If only the old man knew he would do something about it." [They believed] it was the lesser bosses and whatnot that imposed all these indignities and all this mess.

■ HORACE SHEFFIELD

But Henry Ford really had built up a relationship with the various ethnic groups. The old man gave the churches coal and that sort of thing. You had to go through many areas to get a job or when you're laid off, you buy a car. All that sort of thing. But anyway, he'd built up initially through a core leadership group that supported Ford's. Of course, this made the conflict even sharper as far as the various ethnic groups were concerned because you not only had to fight Ford, you had to fight these groups in the community. . . . The thing that had the greatest impact, really, was Ford shelling out the hard dollars. I mean really the tremendous amount of money that he gave these folks. Now clearly, it affected, this leadership . . . because . . . really they were subsidized. I mean he did things for them that retained their loyalty. . . . But by and large, Ford relied heavily on mercenaries . . . and all these various groups to weld support for his movement.

■ PAUL BOATIN

I think it is important to take note and to remember that even though workers in other plants were organized earlier than the workers at Ford's, a lot of educational work and a lot of militant activity was carried on in connection with Ford workers going back to prior to the 1929 economic crash. There was a certain feeling of paternalism in the families and in the minds and in the homes of the Ford workers. . . . But that should not be misunderstood, because workers were playing safe because there were spies all around. So, if you saw the picture of Henry Ford hanging where the Madonna and Child might be otherwise, that worker was a thinking individual who was merely trying to protect his job security because he knew how dangerous it was to do otherwise. . . .

People . . . got slugged, got beaten up, got arrested distributing literature on Miller Road to the Ford Workers. . . . The expression in their eyes indicated that, buddy, they were with you and they admired you for your courage. There were many obstacles that were overcome. The Bennett "Spy and Gangster Department," and the Dearborn police carried on a process of intimidation. If you distributed leaflets on Miller Road, you were arrested. Some of us went in and out of jail almost every other week. Finally, this ordinance was challenged, not just by the pressure of the workers but by the understanding of some of the judges that that ordinance against the distribution of literature should be taken off the books, and it was so taken.

■ JOHN SAARI

Some [workers] didn't want to offend the church. . . . All during the 1930s, the Catholic church, the priests, and that, were preaching antiunion: "Don't join. Don't join." But if we didn't have the Catholic worker voting for the union we'd have never made it. So who did the Catholic worker believe? He believed us. And that's a historical fact.

■ WALTER DOROSH

The church played a role too. I'm a Catholic. I belong to the Catholic church, and when I went to church . . . they opposed CIO—called them "Red-dominated unions." They encouraged the parishioners to support and vote for the AF of L. I know a number of Catholics who wouldn't listen to our church and said, "Well look, if you want to preach you go on and preach." I had a big fight with my minister. I just told him, "You just go jump in the lake. I happen to know who is organizing the plants." I told him, "I'm an organizer. I'm working with John L. Lewis, the coal miners, and don't tell me about that." They had always labeled John L. as a radical in that period. He was very radical; [in] the 1937 strike in Flint, he shut the whole city of Flint down. The battle, when it started, was a long battle.

■ PAUL BOATIN

You had to buy your job [at Rouge]. You had to buy a car. You had to
do all of these things. There were even charges made that "so-and-so
let the boss sleep with his wife"—and that type of thing. Those were
signs of desperation. My own little brother, in 1933, paid $300 on a
car in order to get a job. . . . He worked a couple of weeks, and then
he got fired. He owed additional money—I forget how much. So, he
had no job.

■ ARCHIE ACCIACCA

A lot of poor guys (and I knew some of them) bought cars to get a job;
and they'd work a little while and get laid off and lose the damn car.
They didn't care, that's the way it was. A lot of guys bought their jobs,
a lot of guys paid $75 back in those days. Well, it was just recently the
big depression went through. They paid $75 to get in there and work
a little while, and out they went.
    *Was this money being pocketed by somebody like the guy who'd
hire, not the company itself?*
    I think it would be the individuals at the employment office. That's
my guess, but I don't know. I knew guys that paid. Where the money
went, I don't know. It was rough.

■ WALTER DOROSH

The Ford Motor Company had two independent unions called the
"Ford Brotherhood" and the "Ford Liberty Legion." (The president of
the Ford Brotherhood was Judge Leo Schaeffer of Dearborn. And the
president of the Liberty Legion was a top company official.) When the
union organizing became very strong in there, and everybody started
talking about unionism, the Ford Motor Company was encouraging
people to join either [of these] company-dominated unions.
    How many workers did they get to sign up?
    The only way to get a job at the Ford Motor Company, you had to
buy it. . . . We used to go to the city hall, and you'd pay the company
official or you bought a Ford product. You go and buy a Ford car and
you tell them, "I'll buy a car if you give me a job." "No problem." They
give you a letter, and you go get the job. And then if your payments
were done, you got laid off; your car was paid off, you got laid off. The
only way you could hold on to your car or job is to go back and get
another car. We used to have the thing so well timed that when your

last payment was due, the boss came up to you, "Hey, it's about time you get a new car." I said, "I got a payment yet on my car." He says, "That's okay. They want you to go out and get another car."

That was the way you had your jobs; and so when the boss come up to you, and told you to join the Ford Brotherhood, he was signing you up [for] the union. The guy wanted his job, so he signed up.

■ MARGARET AND STANLEY NOWAK

Stanley Nowak: I introduced a resolution [in the state senate] to investigate job selling at Ford's.

Margaret Nowak: They had quite a racket going there.

Stanley Nowak: Yes, quite a racket. . . . There were women who had small restaurants or bars or small hotels where the Ford workers, single workers, lived. One woman who was out of the business told me that she sold, probably, over five hundred jobs like this. The process was that somebody would come to her and leave eighty, ninety, or a hundred dollars and his name and address. She next would submit it to somebody, and she got a percentage of it. And the next week they would get a job. And he worked for two-three months and then he was fired.

Margaret Nowak: And then sell it to another person.

Stanley Nowak: And it went on and on.

Margaret Nowak: When he introduced that resolution, he showed it to some of his colleagues in the senate, so that they would know what he was going to do. One of them said, "Would you hold it awhile, and let me get in touch with the Ford Motor Company? Hold it for a couple of days and see if I can get a statement from them." So, he said, "Sure." Well [Stanley] didn't get a statement from them, but he found a representative from the Ford Motor Company sitting at his desk the next morning when he went in. It was a typical football-type figure that Ford loved to hire. In fact, he was one of the famous stars of football, Newman, Harry Newman. So he tried to persuade Stanley that it was all a mix-up, and said Bennett would like to see him. Stanley said, "Well, alright, if he wants to see me. He can come here. Here's where I see all of my constituents." And he was unhappy about that, this fellow, because he said, "Well, he wants to see you there." Stanley said, "No. I make it a practice to see my constituents right here in the office. Particularly since its a big company, I don't go to them; they come to me if they want to see me." Well, he finally bothered Stanley until Stanley threatened to have him thrown out, and he didn't come back any more. Ford was obviously disturbed about it.

The thing was announced in the press. He talked about it on his radio program—that he had introduced the bill. There was a lot of press publicity, so the racket sort of stopped temporarily for a year or so. Then in the next session, two years later, he introduced one again. And the senators finally told him, no, they weren't going to release it from the committee. . . . They said, "What you need is not an investigation but you need legislation." So he said, "All right. Suppose I draft a bill on this, would you support it?" They said, "Sure." Not only that, one of the prominent Republicans, Senator B. L. Drake [?] said, "I'll help you draft it." So, sure enough, they went through the statutes and they found one that prohibited job selling. But it did not spell out the terms so that they could trace the people who did it [the selling]. So, by offering a simple amendment—and Drake agreed to even introduce it with him, become co-sponsor—that would take care of it. Well, it didn't get released from committee. They voted it down. But by that time it was obvious that there was going to be a full strike. Stanley knew he had done what he could to publicize it. Now, if the union were established it would end it anyway.

The legislation was going in 1940 or 1941?

Margaret Nowak: Yes. The first one he introduced was in 1939, and then the second was in 1941.

■ WALTER DOROSH

Some of the older guys, older people became acclimated to the Ford conditions, you know what I'm talking about. They have already learned, and they have become kind of susceptible, they become very milktoast. The younger guys that come in there . . . they were raising hell. But what [the company was] doing is getting rid of these guys . . . fired, that's all, with no questions asked.

■ DAVE MOORE

One of the important factors [that kept Ford from being organized earlier] was Ford had jobs that were more liberal toward the blacks. I shouldn't use the word liberal. There was nothing liberal in the bastard. He had a strategy that was much different than General Motors and Chrysler. He built homes for blacks out in Inkster. I say homes, they were shacks. He would give them land. They could go out and farm a garden. You could go to his stores and buy food. It was something like the old concept in the South, the company store. I guess you heard this song about the coal miners, "I owe my soul to the compa-

ny store." Well, in this case you owed your soul to the Ford Motor
Company if you participated in his plan. . . . After he gave you all this,
he said, "Now, you got to pay."

But anyway General Motors and Chrysler, they didn't have blacks
on any machine. The best you could do was work cleaning up the
floors, mopping in the restrooms, in the men's restrooms and things
like that. But Ford had a sprinkling of blacks here and there in the
different buildings, and he showed a little more, I would say generos-
ity and understanding, by not just completely, this is all white and this
is all black, because he even had whites in the foundry. Most of them
were foreign-born. Italians, Poles, Ukrainians, things like that. He had
a sprinkling of blacks in the motor building. That's where all the motors were assembled and what not. He had them on some pretty nice
jobs.

They had one black guy—Don Marshall—who did all the hiring of
the blacks [at Ford's]. No white man would hire blacks.
Was he connected with some of the churches before?
Yes. And all the blacks were confined to the foundry. So, he says:
"How much you weigh?" I was weighing 116 at the time. I said, "I
weigh 150." He say, "You must have rocks in your pocket." I never will
forget that. "You're hired."

■   ARCHIE ACCIACCA

The company had misled—somehow got to—the black guys, and there
were some good black guys. Oh, some of them they really stuck their
neck out, but the biggest percentage of AF of L guys were in the black
units, the foundry, production foundry was the worst. . . . That was
because they figured that they owed Ford something because Ford gave
them a job. It's understandable. . . . And, man, we had some good guys
in there that had their heads banged a couple of times. Because they
were UAW guys but . . . after we got a union, they, the blacks, today I
think are more prounion than whites.

■   WILLIAM JOHNSON

*Was the production foundry a strong CIO building when the union
was doing its organizing drive against the AFL?*
Well, you probably had more people that stayed in the plant during a strike in the foundry than in any other unit, because blacks basically were suspicious of unions. They'd never belonged to unions be-

fore. What few had, had a lot of misgivings about unions, because the only unions they had come in contact with were AFL unions. They [the AFL] had a structure set up, where they have separate locals for blacks and whites. And most blacks did not trust the old line AFL-type unions. And they didn't know a great deal about this CIO. . . . We had a large concentration of people that stayed in the plant during the strike, during the whole period of the strike. Ford brought food in there, armed guards and all that thing, and took care of those people that stayed in the plant.

So those people were probably supporting neither union, neither the AFL nor the CIO?

Well, they were loyal to Ford, more so than any union because most of them felt at that time, too, Ford . . . had larger numbers of blacks. . . . Ford had blacks that hired blacks. They had blacks in the employment setup, and these people had extensive contacts to the black churches and black civic organizations, and that was just an outright plain loyalty on the part of the large number of blacks toward the company. . . . The company paternalism fostered that type of allegiance to the company, and they had a great deal of mistrust for unions, because blacks as a whole had never gotten anything like a square deal from any union.

Did that change once the union was voted in?

Oh yeah. Yeah, that changed rapidly. In a period of two or three years you could notice almost a complete turnaround in the attitude.

■ JOHN ORR

Ford had another problem [organizing] that Chrysler and GM didn't at the time. We probably had the largest percentage of Negro employees (the decent word to say then was *Negroes*) than any of the others; and they were infiltrating jobs that were only held by whites throughout the years. And very few of them were in GM or Chrysler's. They had been relegated to foundry work, shoveling sand, pouring steel, cleanup jobs in the other production buildings, dangerous things . . . . Finally, Ford started to put a few in the tool-and-die rooms as models. And infiltrating the assembly lines and whatnot with them.

Well, what do you think his incentive to do this was?

Help break the union, I think, because most of them looked at Mr. Ford as their emancipator, not Mr. Lincoln. He was hiring them on jobs that they had never had before. They never did have a vote or never did give a breakdown on how the whites voted and the blacks. The NRLB doesn't conduct the elections like that. But we could have told

if they would give the figures by buildings because we knew the build-
ings that were predominantly black like the foundry.
  The production foundry? How did they vote in that?
  Nobody ever revealed it.
  What's your impression?
  I say about 50-50. Because the overall vote in Rouge plant was two-
thirds for the UAW. Of course it probably wasn't all black either. Most
of the whites [in the production foundry] were foreign-born, Italians,
Maltese.

■ WILLIAM JOHNSON

During the war they brought in a handful of women. Prior to the war
there were no women.
  Was that because it was basically heavy work?
  No. It was because Ford didn't believe in women working in the
plant. The only way a woman could get a job in a Ford plant was if her
husband was killed in the plant; out of consideration of an employee's
death, they would occasionally hire a woman. . . . You could almost
count the number of women on two hands in the Rouge plant—in the
production, in the hourly-rated people. You had women clerical . . . and
you had very few of them.
  Right after the war, . . . for a period of time, there was a concerted
effort on the part of the union and the company to get rid of all the
women. Finally, we recognized that we have to give them the same
rights that we gave men, seniority rights; and so it began to change.
That was in the late 1940s before that happened, because the company just had an out'n'out policy that women belonged in the home. . . .
They didn't belong in those plants . . . . The union felt the same way
basically as the company.
  There had been no women in the plant prior to the war and it wasn't
an atmosphere where you were accustomed to seeing women. You just
didn't see women in the plant.

Thugs, Spies, and Stoolies

■ MARGARET AND STANLEY NOWAK

Margaret Nowak: Don't forget about your two organizers that were murdered [in the Chicago packinghouse strike].

Stanley Nowak: Yeah. . . . in the 1920s, in the packinghouse, most of the workers were either Poles or [other] Slavs, like Russians or Czechs, or Lithuanians. Lithuanians are not Slavs but they are a big group there. There were three locals. Two of them spoke at their meetings in Polish because they didn't speak English at all. Polish-speaking locals. That's how many of the labor unions in the early days were organized. That way. There were Polish organizers; and one of them, first, was slugged and killed on his way home from a meeting. Then someone else [was] hired in his place; a few weeks [later] he was killed, in the early [part] of the day, by sluggers who were never apprehended. These were things that I was introduced to at a very early age.

■ DAVE MOORE

During the time of the organization of Ford many people were beaten, and they have the scars today to show for it. Some people were murdered. I'll give you an example, this hunger march. And you could take the Battle of the Overpass, when Walter Reuther, Dick Frankensteen, and Dick Leonard and the rest of them were beaten openly, with the police standing right there. . . . But that's just one example.[10]

■ MIKE ZARRO

Well, we had a hunger march, yeah. We organized the hunger march. . . . We went to the Ford Motor Company over on Eagle Street, and

Harry Bennett, he just unloaded his gun there, and killed four of them. About ten, eleven of them was wounded. And he got away with it.

■ DAVE MOORE

A big thing happened in my life. It was when we had the hunger march back in 1932. . . . And on that day, the Detroit contingent got a permit from the city council of Detroit to march through the city limits of Dearborn. And they said we couldn't come any further. . . . You see all kinds of versions of how many people were involved in that march. Newspapers had their version. Each individual had their version. In my own version, I would say at least eighty to one hundred thousand people.

When we got to the city limits of Dearborn, a place called Baby Creek Park, that's where we had to make our decision whether we would go on. We decided to go, and we went down Dix until we got to a place called Miller Road. There were people coming from south of Dix—from Wyandotte and the others, Inkster, River Rouge, and whatnot, and Detroit. . . . We merged then. We started to move, they turned the fire hoses on us. Words were exchanged. We stopped and decided to go on again. And the police started to use tear gas. . . . And on that day, that's when I grew up to be a man. I was in that march. . . . We got down to the place called Gate 3 on Miller Road by the employment office. And that's where all the fighting began. First some shots rang out. Tear gas was going. I saw five good guys, three of them were good friends of mine, killed. Joe York, Coleman Lenny, and Curtis Williams, a black guy that got killed. He died later on. But one of the guys almost died right there in my arms. And Joe Deblasio, a guy that was shot and fell right across a cop. . . . And I saw blood. Black men, white women, black women all pulling together right down Miller Road. . . .

I was the honor guard at the funeral for the guys. One of the honor guards at the funeral. One of the biggest funeral marches since I've been here in Detroit—I don't know what happened before we came—that ever took place in the city of Detroit, took place when they buried the guys. . . . Come all the way from Ferry down to Woodward and down to Grand Circus Park. And you couldn't budge for the crowd there.

■ ARCHIE ACCIACCA

Anyhow, they heard of this march, and they come out (and this was in the wintertime) with hoses, guns, and to stop this march at the

Rouge. They pinpointed it as being "Communistically controlled," the Communists were running this show. That's where they started with, "The Communists are the union guys, the leaders in the [AWU] are a bunch of Communists." As a matter of fact, when the campaign was going on they were trying to put out [that] the AF of L were the good guys and the [AWU] guys were the Communist guys, see? So in this march five guys were killed. Good unionists, five of them were killed.

■ HORACE SHEFFIELD

Oh, spies were critical. My God, yeah. . . . I ran into that myself. . . . They reported on the activities, and they instilled fear in people. Yeah, yeah. There was no question about it. It wasn't something that, your imagination got the best of you. Ford actively employed spies. And I guess those outside were professionals as well as those in the plant, snitches.

■ ARCHIE ACCIACCA

It's almost unbelievable the way Ford was run. It was a real gestapo set-up. . . . For some people it's hard to believe but I'm putting it in on facts, and I know. This guy Harry Bennett used to have his service men. Most of the service men were guys that he got out of jail, and he controlled with an iron fist. He had something over them. They were rough. You had to toe a real line in those days. Oh yes, their job was just walking around in plain clothes; you didn't know who they were. They watched. If a guy was loafing a little bit, they thought, or goofing off or stalling. And they'd go to the toilets and check the toilets. If they see somebody is staying too long, or smoking (you couldn't smoke in those days), they were turned in. They had the authority to fire. . . .

   In 1940, the big drives started coming on at Ford's. Well, let me back up a little bit. General Motors and Chrysler were already organized. They organized, I believe it was in 1937. They were already organized, and Harry Bennett and his goons were doing a terrific job in Ford's, oh a terrific job. They put the scare, the fear of God into people, that "you join a union, you're going to get fired" and all that kind of thing. A lot of people believed it; they had me believing it for a while. But then we got going, and the momentum looked real good. So, most of us started joining up. This is about 1940 when most of us got going, and started talking to people, and seeing meetings getting bigger and a lot of people participating.

■ KEN BANNON

One of the problems [we had,] you never knew who the hell was a member of your organization who was also a member of the service department.

So you had to be very careful. . . . The only way you would get to know people is by working side by side with them and giving them false information in this way and that way and see if it bounces back.

You know, we were hearing many different things, for goodness sake. When you become part of an organizing drive, you have to be careful and so on and so on. But, be that as it may, meetings as such for organizing purposes, no, we would meet amongst ourselves, people who were active in the—how should I say it?—people who were close to Walter [Reuther,] and what Walter stood for, and people like Walter.

■ WALTER DOROSH

We [were] suspicious of individuals . . . who participated in all activities but never say nothing. . . . The kind [who] would go to the meetings . . . to the strike meeting, the meeting of some groups [and] want to know what's going on. We used to have [a] guy in the plant who was an electrician, and he used to go all over. He used to attend meetings. . . . At that time, we had eighteen units and he used to be at all the eighteen unit meetings. They would say, "What the hell are you doing there? You don't have a right to go in that meeting." You could just sit there, nobody would stop you. And we found he was a company paid agent. But we are foolish if we don't think in the union, that a corporation, a billion dollar corporation like Ford, doesn't have any agents around. They may have them right in the board, you don't know, but they are pretty smooth.

■ SAUL WELLMAN

What I want to get across to you is that if people are hiding, or they're not revealing, their Communist Party membership, it's not because they're cowardly or unprincipled. The American workplace isn't protected by the Bill of Rights. The power of the employer to hire and fire was absolute. I mean, you're dealing with a very dangerous place in which you're going to get protection from nobody. Until unions were recognized, there was no protection for workers. The workplace is hardly an environment where people can freely express themselves. In 1940, for example, Johnny Gallo was fired by the Ford Motor Company for *laughing*.

■   MARGARET AND STANLEY NOWAK

Stanley Nowak: The first real pioneers, the first people who actually risked everything they had, . . . they distributed a lot of material, leaflets. And how did they do it? The workers would bring them with them, and they would put them on the machine, on the conveyor, those leaflets would go out through the whole plant. They did that kind of work. Now how many of them were involved in it, I couldn't tell you. . . .

Margaret Nowak: That's how Tony Morandus got fired. They caught him, he put a little stack of leaflets on the conveyor belt and they'd go down the line.

Stanley Nowak: So that's how the work was done for years. But it was a very risky business. You see the Ford Motor Company had well-organized what they called security guards, or whatever the hell they were. And they had stool pigeons everywhere. (They did it for the money.) You appeared at a union meeting, public meeting, even in the days of the CIO. And the next day you were fired. . . . The Ford Motor Company had its own. You see, Ford had a highly developed method of dealing with workers. Not for their interest but for the company's interest. For example, in the black community he would have individuals who were able to give jobs [to] black people. . . . Ford did that kind of a job. . . . [A stool pigeon] would also report to the company whatever he found. . . . He was sort of a link in a chain through which the Ford Motor Company kept track of [things]. . . . We would call a meeting, and if it was in a public hall, people wouldn't come. And for a very good reason, because somebody would report who was there at the meeting, and he would lose his job, and very likely be put on the blacklist. And in those days it was very difficult. And we would call small meetings in homes. And then we would have ten, fifteen at private homes. . . .

Margaret Nowak: All the workers on one block would meet in homes.

Stanley Nowak: And we would have somebody in front of the house in summer watching; if any stranger appeared nearby, a message was sent to us and we'd immediately put beer, a case of beer, some cards and make it a party at home. . . . The Ford Motor Company . . . actually controlled the municipalities: Dearborn, all of Lincoln Park, . . . Ecorse, River Rouge, . . . all of the municipalities down the river. Because that's where the Ford workers lived. They controlled it—well, they had all kinds of municipal acts against distributing leaflets, against organizing meetings, and in Dearborn particularly. So to get in front of the Rouge plant, nearby where workers were going to work, it was impossible. You'd be arrested for the violation of a city ordinance, in the early days. (They later broke up that violation.) But at first . . . it was absolutely impossible to get anywhere. . . . Like a military camp. . . . Like a fortress.

■ DAVE MOORE

We went to one hell of an organizing drive at Ford. I was fired. I was caught with UAW literature inside my shirt. I got the hell beat out of me. They took me to the "desk." That's what they called it. They took you to the desk. They said, "Nigger, if you ever be caught around the Ford Motor Company again, we'll kill you." And they got me to the gate.

But anyway, through the NLRB cases, we got back. But in the meantime, we were still pushing for organizing. Finally, we organized GM. GM went on a sit-down strike in 1937. Chrysler was being organized. Then I, Shelton [Tappes], and some of the other guys out at Ford, we were planning, 'cause that's where the big activity was going on. Gas was 6 cents a gallon at that time. Where you going to get the 6 cents to get the gallon of gas? Anyway, we'd throw in our pennies and whatnot, and we'd go up to Flint to help the guys out there in the sit-down strikes. And after Chrysler, GM was organized.

Activity centered around Ford, and it was just awful. So many things had happened to guys who was involved in the Ford set-up. Ford was— GM was supposed to be rough—but out of the three, the brutality and the death, the company went to prevent the union from coming in. I mean, beatings, shootings, arrests, going to court. Ford controlled Dearborn. He had control of the city of Dearborn, economically. All the judges was on his influence, all the city politicians. . . .

The big point in organizing Ford, why it was so hard in my opinion, was because you had, number one, the brutality to force workers, on the part of Ford. Some people in my opinion was not raised to face the brutality. Number two, you had his propaganda going that, "If the plant is unionized we are going to close it down."

They had spies. They had all kinds of methods that were used by the company and not used by GM and Chrysler, such as guys visiting your home and going back and reporting to the company that "Judy had a meeting at her house last night. Joe Blow was there. Sally Rose was there. So and so and so." "So, well, Judy, we are going to have to lay you off. We don't have any more work for you." And they would send you out, and somebody else would come right in and take your job. They didn't have any consideration of how long you had been there, all they wanted to know is to find out what were your activities as far as pro- or antiunion. . . . But despite all of that, Ford didn't prevail. Through meetings and leaflets, propaganda, determination— I would say on the part of guys like [Walter] Dorosh, guys like Bill McKie, guys like Tony Marinovitch, they were determined—out of that came the real . . . [drive] to organize Ford.

■ JOHN ORR

We had suffered a lot of indignities. . . . "Do this, do that." If you protested it was either "Miller Road is the nearest street," that's where the employment office was, or "hit Miller Road." It was so evident to most of us, or not enough of us at the time, I should have said. You couldn't buck that outfit alone.

So, we were happy to hear about the UAW coming on the scene organizing, and that was late 1936 and '37. They organized Chrysler and GM in 1937 . . . the sit-down strikes, and all this and that. But it still took four more years to convince the Ford workers to join the union.

Most of [the organizing] was done from within. Because the city of Dearborn passed an anti-handbill ordinance. . . . So, unionists couldn't even come in the city gates and pass out literature and what-not. It was against the law. I'd just wait for them to come in. It was always known when they were coming. Off to jail they went. So that law was ruled unconstitutional, and that let more in, and they started having organizational meetings.

■ MIKE ZARRO

In the company in them days it was really bad. They had these goons. I was beat up before we got a contract. . . . I worked at Briggs Local 212, so I had one of the 212 hats. So the afternoon shift I was going out of the gate down Schaeffer and the lighting was bad out there, so these four goons they pummeled the hell out of me. They said "get that hat off there." They took the hat off and stepped on it and pounded me down in the cinders. And the other poor guys, well, they got scared and run away, and they left me laying there in the cinders. I didn't get hurt bad, but it was just the idea. I thought maybe they took my hat, but I found it twenty feet away. I had all kinds of [union] buttons there, so I was glad that I got my hat back!

I got interested in organizing after coming from Briggs, Local 212. They were the originators of organized labor as far as automobiles is concerned. I started—I got a hold of Marl Garshia [?]. And he was from the coal miners and John L. Lewis's group. So he give me these authorization books, pads to sign up members. So I signed up, oh I was getting about two, three books a day. And at that time you had to be careful. They were fighting the union, and they had the goon squads there. I got a little careless in the cloakroom. Whatever clothes you had, jackets, you had to put a chain on it and lock it up in them days. There was no lockers or anything, so as I went through these receipt books, why I put them in my pocket. As they were filled—I didn't want to carry them around during the day.

So the way it turned out, the sweeper, who was a stooge for the company, he went in there and he got those receipt books, and he must have turned them in to Lee Trese [?]. He was the building superintendent. He used to be a submarine commander during World War I. Boy, he was a tough guy. So he called me into the office there. I can't give you the specific date. But he called me into the office and he says, "Well, we don't need you around here." He says, "We don't like the kind of company you keep." And I says, "Well, it's too bad you can't say what's on your mind in this day and age." He says, "Well, we are going to get rid of you." I says, "Okay, but I'll be back." He says, "Not if I can help it."

So they discharged me. I was off three, four months, something like that, and finally through the National Labor Relations Act I was reinstated back in the glass plant. I went back to the same old supervisor. He says, "Well, we've got a job here for you. You just keep your nose clean, and we'll get along fine." I says, "Yeah, well, I'll do my best, and we'll see what happens here." So from that time on there was a continuation of organizing.

■ WALTER DOROSH

So, when the union came in, we took, Jesus, about a year until we were able to get what they call the personnel payroll records of all the personnel. And the reason we wanted this, we were threatening to strike them again unless they turned them over to us, because we want to know just what the hell kind of wage rates we would be asking for on our contract negotiation. . . . And when we got the payroll records and we pulled them out, . . . well, it showed you the company's operations, there were some guys who did nothing. They were just clerks in the department. They are making $1.50 an hour. The foremen were making 90 cents an hour. Oh, were they [the foremen] hot, when they saw these.

I delivered, I showed them, to the supervisor. . . . (I had what they call the body die division. Fender and body division die room came under me. I was the committeeman, what they call the district committeeman.) They gave the whole thing to the president of the unit. . . . And so he turned those records over to me, and I was supposed to go by and check each guy off and find out if that's his rate of pay. . . . I told him, "This is what the records show." Well, they started all looking at them, and then we found out that these guys who were getting $1.50, $1.60, were the stooges for the company—because the minute we got the payroll records, they disappeared. . . . Sweepers make more than the clerks. All they [clerks] do is like check in the payroll, and menial jobs for a foreman. . . . By looking at these payroll records, you were able to tell who the stooges were, who the agents were, and . . . we began to put two and two together.

Ford had an organization, the Ford service department run by Harry Bennett. He was a goon. They hired all the convicts from Jackson Prison in their service department. . . . There is many a guy got beat up and killed, and we never even found out to this day what happened to some of our organizers.

But it didn't do him [Ford] no good. We [the UAW-CIO] finally struck the plant. . . . It was a fight also with the AF of L. The AF of L was more conservative than the UAW or CIO. The CIO was considered a left-wing union, and the CIO won. We got sixty thousand votes, and the AF of L [got] twenty thousand. The Ford Brotherhood didn't even get on the ballot. They didn't get enough names. The Ford Motor Company saw they couldn't make headway there, and so they switched their support to the AF of L.

■ THOMAS YEAGER

[In] 1941, when the union come in [and struck the plant], I was working midnights . . . and I saw . . . these guys walking around, and the first thing, they had steel clubs, steel outfits just like knives, and you are all out there, and I was all by myself.

Who were those guys that you are talking about with the steel clubs?

They were the guys that the Ford Motor Company brought in to guard the plant inside.

■ VICTOR REUTHER

You had a sizable influence on the part of the corporation in the union, for . . . when the vote was finally taken on whether the UAW would represent the Ford workers, approximately sixty thousand voted for CIO and twenty thousand voted for Homer Martin and Harry Bennett's slate.[11] Now, it was an open secret that Bennett and Martin had made a commitment to try to get as many of Bennett's Ford service men in as committeemen in the UAW, once the UAW was recognized. Hence, it is reasonable to assume that in the local union politics on both sides, on both sides there was a corporate influence. That is difficult to measure, but one would be naive to assume that Harry Bennett suddenly gave up his intentions of penetrating the UAW from within. . . .

Several attempts were made on Walter's life. But one of them in particular, where two thugs very close to Harry Bennett, one on the list of his payroll, broke into Walter's little home and tried to waylay him. Some months afterwards when the contract was signed with the Ford Motor Company, one of those thugs phoned me and said, "You know, our boss is now signed. You're not mad at us any more are you?" He wanted a meeting to talk and what he was saying was so obvious— "If you can't lick 'em, you join 'em." And since his boss had just joined us, so to speak, these thugs felt, "Hey, we better get on board too." So that throughout the whole Bennett organization there was that feeling, "Okay now, the boss is signed with the UAW. We're going to get in and get involved there." So the union was confronted with enormous pressure to penetrate our ranks by company people.

The Rouge local union reflected this very complicated relationship between a company that tried openly with armed thugs to break us, and then suddenly embraces us to such an extent they put the union label on the car and you wonder whether it was the all-embracing bear hug of one who wants to suffocate you. Now, don't expect that under those kinds of circumstances you're going to have a clean, clear separation between left and right or militant unionist and pro-company unionist. It was a very confused situation and remained one for quite a few years.

Leadership: Bill McKie and Walter Reuther

■ SAUL WELLMAN

[Bill] McKie didn't come onto the scene until 1929. He came from England to live with his daughter. She had preceded him. While on a visit, he decided to remain. He got a job at Ford as a tinsmith, and shortly after began to organize an American Federation of Labor local union. . . .

Bill McKie was already an experienced Socialist activist and trade unionist when he came to the United States. He had been active in the labor movement of Scotland before and after World War I. He had been a charter member of the British Communist Party. He couldn't understand the absence of trade union organization at Ford; and so he undertook to change it. He had intelligence and guts—and the commitment of a Communist to the cause of working people. And, he was a skilled worker. Skilled workers have always been decisive to the production process and not always easily replaced. So, they're not as open to intimidation as the unskilled workers on the conveyor line.

He was a skilled tinsmith, and he had to travel all over the Rouge plant—and he made contacts for the union wherever he went. If he had been an unskilled worker, stuck in one department or one line, and couldn't move beyond five or six workers, he wouldn't have been as effective as he was. He concentrated his energies on organizing young people like Ed Lock, John Gallo, Dave Moore, and others who, within a decade, became leaders of Local 600.

■ PAUL BOATIN

Well, Bill McKie was a known Communist. He was one of the first people to help organize the union at Ford's under what was in 1927 a concentration point of the American Communist Party. They organized what they called the Auto Workers Union and put out an *Auto Worker* newspaper.[12] I helped to distribute that paper but I played only a small role.

McKie was one of the leaders, along with Philip Raymond, who was mentioned in that book [*Brother Bill McKie*], who died recently in California, who ran for mayor of Detroit and so forth. He was beaten up by the police many times. McKie was elected an officer at the local and refused to sign the Taft-Hartley Non-Communist Affidavit, and was therefore asked by the union to step down because the government put the union leaders in the position of clubbing their own brothers into line.[13] This was the—it wasn't the government that told McKie, it was the union officer, "you can't serve." But he always continued to serve on committees even though actually he was not a top officer in the local.

As a matter of fact, he never held top office. He was a trustee and served on the executive board. I envied him. Because of his age he didn't want to run for top office, he felt that he was more useful, I envied him precisely because I thought that was the correct way. He, being Anglo-Saxon, he was able to do things that other ethnic people could not do because the Anglo-Saxons were permitted privileges really and given considerations. I mean the company would fire foreigners from Moscow, but wouldn't fire a guy who was from Scotland who had been in the Salvation Army in Scotland and played the drums and all of that. And he was an inspiration to many and I know of nobody, not even rabid anti-Communists, who ever had a bad word to say about McKie because he was beyond suspicion, beyond reproach, and of course he didn't hide the fact that he was a Communist, whereas others, the cowards, wouldn't admit it. They played the Communist role, they were fellow travelers, they were stooges for the Communists but there's always ways of trying to castigate and cast aspersions. So among other things McKie was admired for the fact that he was an open Communist, and he served as a teacher for many of the younger people.

Well, I don't know whether if they were asked some of them that are still alive whether they would admit to it [McKie's influence]. But one of the officers, long-time officers of the local, W. G. Grant, was both president and previous to that financial secretary. I'm trying to give out people that actually worked in the same department with McKie, who were closest to him, Tom Jelley, John Orr, who would not admit it if he thought it was being publicized. John Orr refused to serve on a defense committee with, for the five of us who were indicted, who were on trial, because he was advised to keep his skirts clean. But he learned from Bill. Walter Dorosh, although much younger I'm sure learned something, although not as much as he could have. The present financial secretary of the local, Bob King, was in the same department with McKie. The present chairman of the tool-and-die unit, although much younger, Al Gardener, learned from McKie.

Now those are specific cases of people that knew him, knew of McKie's activity prior to the union coming in and after the union came in. But generally even though prior to the union days and even after the union came in, you were not permitted to go running around the plant. You would be asked what you are doing here, and with McKie he did not drive, therefore it was a little more difficult for him to be in access, whereas those of us that were top officers had passes. We could drive our car into the plant and so forth. That was a concession that [Harry] Bennett made. He said, "I'm going to give you the best union, better than anybody else," and [he thought he'd] put all of us on the company payroll. You see this was part of the process of winning the fight and they succeeded pretty much with a lot of the people.

But McKie knew and was in contact and had an influence on many others: James O'Rourke, myself, William J. Cooper, [Shelton] Tappes, Mack Cinzori. . . .[14]

I recall taking William McKie out in the country to visit some people. Usually, not usually but many times, he wouldn't let me come in. He went in by himself . . . because his argument was he spoke with a strong Scottish brogue, and he says they don't like to talk when there are too many people listening. Later on I said to myself, "McKie, do you think they'll suspect me of being a company stooge? I mean, let me come in." And many times I went in depending on the circumstances—if he thought these workers were already progressive, liberal and so on. . . . One time, when I went in with him, he walks towards the man, and they confabbed a little bit and then they went into the kitchen, and I'm just walking around. Nobody told me to sit down or stand up or nothing. I'm just watching. But from where I was standing there was a kind of an archway.

From where I was standing the living room was to my left and through a little hallway I could see a part of the bedroom. There was a picture of Henry Ford hanging over the bedstead in the bedroom. And yet I didn't ask McKie. That was not—it would not have been correct for me to say, "Did he sign up?" That's the wrong, you don't ask questions like that. But I'm sure that he signed up because McKie had been there before, and he wouldn't have gone back a second time if the guy hadn't given him a good reception. So what does that picture represent? The guy was trying to protect himself just as many innocent workers went and painted the boss's house. They brought wine to the boss. They made sausage and canned goods.

■ HORACE SHEFFIELD

I knew Bill McKie very well. Bill McKie was one of my good left-wing antagonists. . . . He came out of a great tradition of unionism. And very articulate. . . . He was kind of an ideologue but that's beside the point. He made a great contribution. . . . Ford had really balkanized that plant. McKie got the Italians, he got the Poles, and he had his fingers in all of them . . . to be able to pull all these forces together. We worked in the plant and obviously we just didn't have the leverage at that time. Now, actually, we were getting organized and we were beginning to get into meetings. We were beginning to develop that sense of solidarity. Now, Bill McKie, he, and others [on the left] contributed to that. Out of their ideological background. They knew the sense of what it meant, solidarity and that sort of thing, which really for the CIO, for blacks, and others out at Ford's was a new thing. Because they were talking about integration and solidarity in the ranks, that sort of thing. So, really, they contributed greatly to the spirit of the whole movement.

■ MARGARET AND STANLEY NOWAK

Margaret Nowak: [Bill McKie] was a sort of symbol—

Stanley Nowak: —because he was the first president of the first local that came into existence at Ford. And after that he was retired, that is, he didn't work. He was blacklisted. He would be in the front whenever he could.

Margaret Nowak: He had a shock of snowy white hair—

Stanley Nowak: And he was a symbol of that whole Ford drive for a long time, an individual that symbolized that whole, big struggle. Even when he got very old, . . . it was amazing how he still was able to go to these meetings and speak and argue.

■ JOHN ORR

[Bill McKie was] an avowed Communist. . . . That was part of it. Everybody liked Bill, and they hated Communism. Well, not everybody hated Communism. They knew what he was. He never pretended. . . . After the Taft-Hartley Law came in Bill was back in the plant, and he was elected local trustee, and had to resign because he could not sign the anti-Communist affidavit to retain local office. And he said he'd he damned if he'd disavow his Communist affiliation.

Why was he well-liked in the shop?

He was a lot older than most of us and he talked sense and he lived—you know, he wasn't trying to organize a union for his own financial benefit or this and that—if ever a guy lived frugal, it was Bill McKie. He never owned a car, to my knowledge, in his life, and he used to get his bundle of papers and peddle them in the neighborhoods.

■ SHELTON TAPPES

[Walter] Reuther almost learned what he knew from the knee of Bill McKie. When he was president of Local 174, Bill McKie was his mentor. So, how could he [red-bait]? Sure, he played the game of red-baiting and all that. But I don't think he meant it all that harshly as some of his followers did.

■ PAUL BOATIN

In relation to [Walter] Reuther, you know about his trip to the Soviet Union along with Victor? That he denied later on having written a letter from the Soviet Union which contained the salutation, "Yours for a Soviet America"?[15] That his wife was a Socialist? (I know that for a fact because I was a member of the same youth group with her, where she was trying to organize the rest of them. She was always involved in arguments, because some of the young people in the youth group started coming there for girls and having parties.) And that he himself, along with Victor, played a role in the Socialist Party to differentiate themselves from them? And [Emil] Mazey . . . considered himself a better communist than the Communists.[16] [He] considered the Socialists traitors because of the role they had played in Hungary [in the 1930s]. Mazey is of Hungarian extraction.

■ SHELTON TAPPES

Whenever there was a proposal made that had some merit to it, why [Walter] Reuther would be very quick to grab it. And when he spoke that was his program, . . . Reuther was sort of a loud mouth. He was considered a demagogue, because he was always coming out with a plan. Of course, this was all part of the strategy, let the people know you, . . . "I don't care how much you talk about me, just mention my name when you do." This was his thing and it worked. And I will say this, that although I was a rabid anti-Reutherite, once he became president, I had to respect the achievements that he made. It was just tremendous.

■ PAUL BOATIN

He [Walter Reuther] worked actively with Communists to get support to go to the 1936 South Bend [UAW] convention in South Bend, Indiana. He knew all of the time that he was associating with Communists. But when he saw things change and it was to his advantage to play with the un-American Activities Committee, the Senate Internal Affairs Committee, to red-bait and so forth, then he became pure. And when it was safe to associate with Martin Luther King, towards the end only, did Martin Luther King come to speak to UAW meetings. There is this terrible opportunism—which is not necessarily evidence of a flaw—in Walter Reuther's character. It is conditions that make the man, so to speak. You press from all points and you want to maintain the position of power. What is wrong is, when you pass the story on, that if he can only get rid of the Communists, get rid of the Reds, then the union will grow. Implying that the company will then be nice to you. That they will stop fighting you. Because that is not true. The class struggle goes on. It's eternal. It's a continuing proposition between employee and employer. And that's the fallacy of Reutherism. But we will outlive it. We'll outlive Reagan and all their—just the way we've outlived Mussolini and Hitler and all these other sons of a bitches. Well, that's not either here nor there.

■ KENNETH ROCHE

What were the general feelings of the workers during the war about the no-strike pledge?[17]
    That's how Reuther got his power. The workers during the war were against the no-strike pledge. The leadership of the union was for the no-strike, and that's R. J. Thomas. They were for the no-strike pledge. And Reuther was militant, boy he was a super-militant at that time. He was against the [pledge]. . . . "We got to have a right to [strike]." . . . He had the sympathy of the workers, all right. At that time he improved the wages. The government was trying to get everything out that they could. They couldn't afford the work stoppages. Then, immediately upon getting elected in 1946, Reuther started putting no-strike pledges in the contract, negotiating five-year contracts with no-strike [clauses].

■ JOHN SAARI

[Reuther] was a demagogue A-1. Now, after he was elected he comes out . . . and signs a five-year contract in peacetime, in peacetime. Who did that benefit? Why that curtailed grievances, that curtailed everything.[18]

■ JOHN MANDO

Did Reuther have authority over who could and couldn't run for office in the international?

Well, he didn't have authority over who could or could not run, but he had a great deal of influence. And the one thing about Walter is that he was very much the kind of a guy that—"Look, let's work together. Let's do this together, we've got an election here. Let's make this election, you go on about it in the most effective way you can. Try to gather the votes." He'll stay out of the way, you see. But at the point [you] get into the name-calling, and the point that you get into the mud-slinging, and at the point that you get vicious, and he views it as possibly being damaging to the organization, then he will intercede. "Look, if you can't do this on a high level, if you are going to campaign in the low row, so to speak, then we're going to have to do something about this." He was a very, very persuasive guy. So, naturally he would not get involved until it got into that kind of a dog fight. But at the point that he became displeased with the way the campaign was going, he would then exert his influence. Not necessarily pick somebody else, but start looking at other candidates. Select from those candidates rather than the two that was creating the furor.

■ HORACE SHEFFIELD

A lot of the left-wingers wound up on Reuther's staff. How did that happen?

Well Reuther made it that—I thought it was a wise decision. Reuther set out to try to unite the union, and all he asked is just that you come on the team, . . . "Let's play as a team member." By that you didn't have to tell him, "You just put Karl Marx on the side, his 'Manifesto' on the side." They knew enough to do that. And I thought it made sense. That it really helped the union, really, and it gave the union strength at times, and at a time that it needed it.

■ WALTER DOROSH

Oh, we [Local 600] had lot of support at conventions. But . . . Walter was always turning around on the convention floor. He would get some issue. I remember we had a conference in Washington, D.C., and that's when we introduced the resolution [for thirty hours' work for forty hours' pay]. (Originally, "thirty for forty" [was] instead of [Reuther's] "guaranteed annual wage.") Walter Reuther said the thirty-hour week— at that time we were involved in the war with Korea—the thirty-hour week was "helping the Communists," and we "must be Communists"; and boy he really reared. Took us to town in Washington, and we had the FBI in a conference. What a setting it was. They invited the secretary of labor [Martin P. Durkin]; . . . he was a pipe-fitter, remember, in Eisenhower's cabinet. He would come in; and he red-baited: "Anybody who would do this, would be stabbing soldiers in the back." We said, "What the hell are you talking about?" We had layoffs; thousands of unemployed; we had twenty thousand unemployed at the Rouge. We were down to sixty thousand then. And we were "agents of Moscow" by recommending thirty for forty.

Walter [Reuther] started getting friendly with me . . . in 1961, when I got elected to negotiate.

(I knew his wife before, well I knew Walter and his wife together, but I knew her before she married Walter. She used to be in the old [Michigan] Civil Rights [Congress] headquarters in the Hoffman Building, and she used to collect dues. She was a secretary in the office there. Her name was May Wolf, Wolfman. But we used to know her by Wolf. So, I knew her real good.) When I got elected to the Ford National Negotiating Committee,[19] Walter got worried about it, because we had Carl [Stellato], me, we had four elected from Local 600, and it was eleven on the committee; and we had two other guys. We had enough votes on the committee to stop Walter from doing anything. So, when we met the first time, Walter says to me he wanted to talk to me. He says, when he was young he would do "a lot of foolish things like you do." He says, "I did some things I'm sorry for," bla, bla, bla. He says, "Let's let bygones be bygones. Let's concentrate on helping the workers and the negotiations." I said, "Fine, that's all I'm here for. We got no problem if its on behalf of the workers."

This was in 1961?

Yeah 1961. Then, after we completed negotiations, he asked me to come work for him. I said, "No way, no way."

Going to work for Reuther at the international meant you had to adopt all his views?

His man, period. That's all. Reuther ran that with an iron fist. But he mellowed, in his latter years I know. He cut out a lot of this redbaiting and a lot of his divisive tactics. I got to know Walter very well.

I went out with him often. I was chairman of the Ford Negotiating
Committee, and then I was also chairman of the [UAW] Resolutions
Committee.[20] Walter appointed me for that job. And the next five conventions, we used to have a lot of fights. But then he began to support every resolution that I supported. He had mellowed. Well, we had
some private talks, and I guess he felt in his latter years, he was se-
cure in power. They needed no other techniques or tactics, and he was
all power. But I think, like I says, when you age you mellow sometimes,
too. . . .

About 1970, Walter was making all kind of concessions to us [Lo-
cal 600]. He called me up: we would sit down and we would talk about
different programs. I'm not saying he went along with me on everything, but he wanted to know our views, which was important. We
had a dialogue, in other words. . . . At least five conventions I went [to]
meet with Walter, and he wanted to know what our position in 600
was. I think it was the wings kind of disappeared. The right and left.

■ JOHN MANDO

Stellato actually . . . wound up on the international staff [after he
stopped being president of Local 600]. . . . [He and Reuther] patched
up their differences and, in fact, he was placed—he was selected by
Ken Bannon. Ken Bannon was the Ford director, and he selected Carl
to his staff with the blessing of Walter Reuther.
So he was on the Ford Bargaining Committee?
Well, when he was on the Ford staff, he was not on the Ford Bargaining Committee. He was on the Ford Bargaining Committee [from
Local 600] before he was selected to the staff. In fact, I think, that is
where they patched up all their differences. He was on the Ford Negotiating Committee a couple of times.

■ PAUL BOATIN

My contention is that he [Walter Reuther] would have become a very
strong anti-Vietnam person. He would have played a very very dominant role later on because he always wanted, for opportunistic reasons
or whatever, he always wanted to be out in the forefront. He had a
sharp mind and he didn't hesitate to call the capitalists names. He
would call Wilson of General Motors (who was then secretary of defense) a jackass—all that type of stuff—but with the same vitriol he
also denounced the Communists. That is, he was more concerned
about establishing the fact that he was not really a socialist of that type.

"I'm not that kind of socialist," or "I'm not a Socialist. I believe in the free enterprise system and the 3 percent formula," and the other things that came out. That doesn't mean that Reuther had not learned something, absorb[ed] some of the ideology of Bill McKie.

It was Bill McKie who brought the Reuther brothers, based on the fact that they had been in the Soviet Union, into the labor movement. Not only that, history, it's not easy to prove it, but Walter Reuther was not working in industry. They got him a job and then they set up Local 174. One of the things that McKie was sorry about was that he made the recommendation at the Cleveland [UAW] convention for Walter Reuther to be an official delegate and to be the spokesman of Local 174 and so forth. He said . . . it was a mistake.

When Bill McKie died, Walter Reuther [did not come] to the funeral, no. The international did not come to the funeral.

When Walter Reuther died, we went to the funeral. I even shed a tear or two, I don't mind admitting.

Organizing

■ JOHN ORR

I'm foreign-born. . . . I'm from Canada. I came over here at the age of nine; and the way we came, my father led an aborted Alberta strike in a rubber plant back in Canada. We lived in a house that was built by the rubber company. He was a bootmaker, and not a tiremaker. This was a bootmaker outfit. He started a union then that subsequently has become the United Rubber Workers Union. And he organized it pretty well, and they decided to go on a strike one day. (I believe this occurred in 1923.) The plant was built in four stories, and he worked on the top making boots, and at a given signal they were supposed to go from the fourth floor down the stairs, no elevator, and each succeeding floors join in the walkout. . . . But when he and one other guy started down the aisle, the other workers started looking at each other, and some started to follow—bosses were looking—they ran back to their job. My father and this guy started down the stairs; the other guy got to the first step, and he ran back and went to his job; and my father walked down. When they saw him alone at the third floor, second floor, nobody joined. He walked out, and walked home. Our "home" was owned by the rubber factory. Well, they offered to reinstate him if he would sign allegiance to the company, swear that he would never again join a union, organize, or walk out, and he refused. So, he was just about blackballed in the rubber industry in Canada. He came here and got in the auto industry.

■ JOHN SAARI

I was born of Finnish immigrants. . . . They settled up north in the copper country, and that's where I was born. My dad was a copper miner. We had a big family. . . . My dad was very strict, but along with that he was a very religious individual, but in a different sense than most religions. He was not an acquiescing type of individual, and he couldn't hold a job. He was a good miner and everything, but he'd get fired over and over, and they finally blackballed him. And he went into contracting: he'd go from farmer to farmer, and say, "I'll make your hay for so much," or "I'll pick your potatoes for so much."

So, when he was working in the mines, they were unorganized?

They were unorganized, yes, and it was terrible, terrible. . . . You had to buy everything from the company store. So my dad he had to buy his own caps and fuses and things like that. He could get them cheaper on the open market than he could buying it from the company store, so he just went ahead and he tried to get others to go with him, to not buy from the company store, and buy it on the open market. But, of course, people were fearful of losing their job. But he stuck his neck out, and he went and bought his equipment in an open market. And they fired him for it. . . . So there was no, what you call, "real freedom" as such.

Every place I went, I used to wonder . . . well, why people would [say to] me, "You're a good man" [when I told them] "I'm Finnish." . . . I wondered what did they mean. How do they know I'm a "good man?" What they were talking about was that the Finnish people, for instance, [in] the copper mines up there, were organizing it. The Finns played a tremendous role in developing a trade union culture in this country. And they were all socialists, pro-socialist. When the Socialist Party kinda split up in 1919, and the Communist Party was organized, . . . 7,500 Finns [left the Socialists and] joined the Communist Party. So . . . when they find out I'm a Finn, well, gee, I used to get invited, "Hey, hey, come on over here."

By the other Finnish people you mean?

Well, not only that but the other people, non-Finns, non-Finns.

■   PAUL BOATIN

My father [and uncle] . . . were fired [for trying] . . . to organize the cement workers. They were working in New Castle, Pennsylvania, for the Lehigh Valley Cement Company and the union was not organized. The AF of L stooge had come there. (The charge was made that [the stooge] ran away with the money, but actually that was more suspicion than proof.) All the workers who were involved were given the opportunity of apologizing and explaining that they were misled, and the ones who wouldn't bow were terminated. And they decided to come to Detroit. . . .

I was left in charge of the family there—my aunt and children and so forth—and my father and uncle came here, and two or three months later I came.

■ WALTER DOROSH

[My father] was an employee of [Ford's], and they discharged him, and
he was blacklisted [for being involved in] "bloody Monday" in 1932.
The Ford Hunger March they call it.[21] Thousands were blacklisted, and
they could never get a job anywhere. He could never get a job. Any
time he got a job in another location, after a week or so they would
trace him down. . . .
Was he in the skilled trades?
No, just in the regular production. I think he worked in the foundry.
And was he interested in the start of the union?
Oh, most certainly. We used to have the Ford Organizing Commit-
tee meetings in our home [in] 1931–32.
This was the Auto Workers' Union?
No, that wasn't it. I can't remember the name of it. It was a long
time ago. It was more than the Auto Workers' Union.
So, he was organizing for them?
Oh, absolutely. When I was young, about twelve or thirteen, I used
to stay and act as a lookout [for the organizers], because the city of
Dearborn was Ford city. Mr. Ford owned the city lock, stock and barrel. He owned the police force, the city council, the mayor, John L.
Carey, and they passed any ordinance that Ford wanted. . . . You
couldn't distribute any leaflets in the city, organizing leaflets.[22] We'd
go out to the gates, [and] pass out leaflets for organizing purposes. The
police would come there and arrest you, take you to jail and harass
you, and they would let you go, but after you had gone before a judge
(and the judge, Leo J. Schaeffer, was the company's judge). They had
everything, and they just had this constant harassment.

■ KEN BANNON

My dad was not involved in the union movement as such. He was a
member of a union, but he wasn't active in it. My grandfather Gaffney
was a member of the Socialist Party, and very, very active in organized
labor up in Scranton, Pennsylvania.
Was that a coal mining town?
No, my grandfather Gaffney was tied in with the city workers. As a
matter of fact, he caused a strike up there in the early 1920s, and he
was fired. . . . So, he had some pretty rough times there for a while.
He finally got back to work, but not in the job he had, but as a person
who would be hauling ashes. This was back in the hard coalfields. . . .
But, anyhow, my grandfather Bannon was quite active in the United
Mine Workers in Scranton, Pennsylvania. So that's the background. . . .

[I got involved in organizing] . . . as a result of some of my activities back in Pittston, Pennsylvania. After I graduated from school, why I worked in the coal mines and we had a bad situation up in Dupont, Pennsylvania, one of the mines I was working in. The air was bad, and so I and another person, Patty Nardel, we shut the mine down. And at that point in time the CIO was getting very very active, and Tom Kennedy, who was then secretary-treasurer of the United Mine Workers, lived in Hazelton, Pennsylvania; I think Mike Kosic [?] was the regional director of Region 1 of the United Mine Workers. They said, "Well, if you have that kind of piss and vinegar, we could use you out in Detroit to help organize the CIO." Not the UAW at that point in time, but the CIO that I was sent out here to do, to organize.

And so my wife and I got married very young and . . . came out to Detroit in 1936. At that point in time you could buy a job at Ford Motor Company, Harry Bennett and his group. And the United Mine Workers . . . bought a job . . . for me—at the old motor building in the steering gear department—at the Ford Rouge plant. . . . So I worked at the Ford Rouge plant from 1936 on, and helped to organize . . . there. You were not allowed to talk . . . union. If you had a button on or anything else you were automatically discharged. I was fired in 1938, on New Year's Eve really, 1937, 1938 you might say because it was New Year's Eve. . . . Well, they wouldn't say for union activity back then, what the devil. Of course, it was quite obvious; and then I was fired again in 1940, but I got back through the NLRB on both occasions [in 1938 after, I would say, about nine months; in 1940, I would say about three weeks].[23]

So in the meantime you continued your organizing activities outside the plant?

Well, no, I had to get some work, at that point in time I had a child and my wife: you need bread and butter to put on the table.

■ DELORIS AND KENNETH ROCHE

Deloris Roche: I grew up with it [unionism]; and then I married it. . . . If you're involved, you may get tired of being alone with the kids all the time. But you realize the cause and principle. It would be extra hard for the wife who didn't understand this. I had a union background. I'm not saying we didn't have our arguments over it.[24]

Do you think that caused a lot of marriages to—?

Deloris Roche: Oh, I'm sure it did.

Kenneth Roche: Gone seven days a week. You got meetings at night, emergency meetings, caucuses, you put a leaflet out in the day, bring the leaflet home, proofread it and run over and print it and distribute it by the next morning.

■ GEORGE PLUHAR, JR.

[My dad] had a family, a young family. It took a lot of courage for him to become an organizer and get fired from his job. And knowing what the result would be, my mother was high-strung. . . . She had two pregnancies and lost two children. They shifted shifts on him, they did everything to him. He had to work midnight shifts sometimes. They messed with him there. Seniority had nothing to do with it, in the plant, you were just shoved around. Just being shoved around, I think, had a lot to do with him becoming a right-wing, excuse me, left-wing. . . .

[Union activities] actually probably created a lot of problems for my father and my mother, because they ended up getting divorced, . . . because a lot of the activities took a lot of time. There was a lot of time that he spent on his own time out in the field. He went to conventions, . . . negotiating conventions, and to Atlantic City for the annual [UAW] conventions. He spent a lot of time away from home. . . . And he was very set in his ways. He was a very dedicated man. . . . He felt that the union was the greatest thing that ever happened. Well, it was the workers' way to organize and to be able to compete against the company, . . . He was whole-heartedly into it. That was really his only activity.

You mentioned that you walked the picket lines with your father during demonstrations or strikes. Was that common? Did a lot of the men and women working in the plants bring their children to the lines?

Not really. It wasn't a very common thing. I think that my father spent time with me, a lot of times, because he wasn't home. So, he took me with him. I got to know all of the guys that were connected with the local in the different plants. I got to know them as a kid, as I grew up.

I think wives coming down, supporting their husbands, was very common. They came down to bring them food and things. And that was just an accepted thing, that that was the way to go.

■ DAVE MOORE

I have seen families divorce, separated [because of working to build the union]. Me, I didn't have a problem. I wasn't married, and at the time that I got involved, I was on the verge of getting married, but I had two young ladies tell me, "Whatever you are involved in, you love it better than you do me." I don't know. I got so deeply involved. I never have run away from marriage, but I never did get around to it. I have seen the effects [organizing] has on some, and then I have seen some survive. You take a guy like [Walter] Dorosh, he and his wife have raised a family, and he and Rose are still together. A guy like Johnny Gallo, he and Anita stayed together until he died. Take a guy like Bill Johnson, he and his wife are still together. They reared kids. They have got grandkids and great-grandkids, but it all depends on the individual. . . . I think a lot of women whose fathers had been involved in the union movement and married, they understood because their fathers . . . gave them a lot of education on it. And when they got involved with a guy and married a guy who is involved in the union. "Well, that man is out there taking care of union business, so it will make it possible for you and his kids to—they are going to have a good wage." This was the attitude.

Yeah, [union activism] did have some effect on families. Some who were not prepared for it, some women were not willing to accept their husbands being away for long periods of time and not coming home when she got dinner ready, instead of being home at five o'clock he didn't get home until eight o'clock. And he's in a meeting and some of the guys they were leaving, and some guys would use it as an excuse.

I think now that a woman understands better because a lot of women got involved in union activities, in war work, at that time.

■ KEN BANNON

You weren't on the CIO organizing payroll?

No. I wasn't a full-time organizer, I was just an in-house, in-shop organizer. . . . You know, the best way to organize anything is get on the inside. Most of the organizers were members of the Communist Party. Because of my background, my dad, as I mentioned, my grandfather was a Socialist, so I had pretty good ideas, and I knew about different things. I was never a member of the Communist Party.

But . . . who helped us to organize Ford more so than anyone else [was] the Ford Motor Company by their behavior. You couldn't go to the john, that was a pretty deplorable situation. You had no place to sit down at lunchtime and it was pretty hectic. You had the service department there, and you had new people coming in working next to you (and particularly those of us who were kind of vocal); and you had to watch what you said, and it was a kind of a harrowing experience. Then you had many, many people who were unable to, who, well, we used to call them "foreigners"—I never called them "foreigners." But people who had come from the Old Country, so to speak, and who were unable to speak English in a clear manner. They were somewhat fearful of losing their jobs, and you would see the advantage the company, the foreman, would take of these people. You know, call them "Polehunks," and it was pretty, pretty, pretty, bad. And you would see people, for goodness sake, fired for no reason, and many of these people had no idea what redress they had. So, words like that, well, activities like that, all throughout Ford, particularly in the Rouge plant—[this] was the key to organizing. So, the activities of the Ford Motor Company and the organizers as such were the people [who organized]. The best organizers were members of the Communist Party.

How important do you think that the efforts of Reuther and his Local 174 were in the early Ford organizing period?

Well, I think it was important that we had a base, we had a place to go to. We were members of Local 174 way back then; and then when we began to organize, we put up our own little offices up on Michigan Avenue there. We got money from the CIO for that of course.

Was that when the formal organizing committee was set up with Mike Widman?

Yeah, well, Mike came aboard I think in 1937 or '39.[25] The one who really did the job as far as Mike Widman's organization was concerned was Smith. He . . . had kind of a big, paunchy stomach, and he chewed tobacco and dribbled all over his shirt, but I can't think of his first name now.[26]

Smith, where was he from?

CIO headquarters. He worked for Mike Widman. . . . [Smith] did a masterful job in organizing at Ford. Widman, as far as the CIO was concerned, [was] from the outside. But Mike . . . was more of a, you know, Mike was kind of a sophisticated guy. He was a sophisticated person. Dick Leonard helped too, I might add. Dick was on the payroll. He was in Local 227, which was the Chrysler local, the DeSoto local really.

On the inside, [were] Bill McKie,[27] who was a member of the Communist Party, Ed Lock, who was a member of the Communist Party, who worked in the same department I worked in. . . . Johnny Gallo was also instrumental. Johnny Gallo was the person who was fired for laughing by Superintendent Bayes. Johnny Gallo worked next—well, for about a year and a half Johnny Gallo and I worked side by side. But be that as it may. I think I mentioned Percy Llewellyn. Shelton Tappes was about the only real great Negro, black, leader that we had.

Where was Horace Sheffield at this time?

Well Horace wasn't that active in the foundry back in the early 1940s. He did a little bit, he did some work. Don't misunderstand me, he was helpful. But the ones who were outstanding, I thought you were talking about the outstanding people.

I am.
Okay. Shelton Tappes who was black.

■   SAUL WELLMAN

Many radical groups were really dedicating themselves to organization. Yet the Communists distinguished themselves more profoundly than the others, and it wasn't because . . . they [had] a better policy, but rather because they had certain tools and certain instruments at their disposal which the other groups did not have. One of the tools was [their] connection with a vast network of sick and death benefit societies of the various ethnic groups.

Now, this is a nation of immigrants, and immigrants in the main come to a strange place dealing with a strange culture, and have many problems; and the early waves of immigrants were mainly men with no family. . . . So, there were some very practical problems they had to deal with, like what do you do when you get sick? What do you do when you die? Who disposes of your body? That's how these sick and death benefit societies came into being.

One of the unique features of Detroit is that at the turn of the century when it began to emerge as America's auto city, . . . the highest number of national groups settled there and in the greatest numbers. So, it was no accident that you had the largest grouping of Maltese Americans, Arab Americans, Rumanian Americans, as well as other groups. . . . The real picture of Detroit is embodied in the Diego Rivera mural. . . .

[On] the assembly line you see tall men, short men, skinny men, fat men, black men, white men, yellow men. . . . The genius of Ford was that he could assemble a group of illiterate and unskilled people who couldn't communicate with each other, but who could build this complicated piece of machinery with three thousand different moving parts that really worked. It was also a way to keep a work force docile and controllable, because they couldn't communicate with each other.

This vast network of sick and death benefit societies existed as various ethnic groupings. Their members were to be found in many of the basic industrial towns.

What I'm saying is that in steel, in mining, in auto, in glass, in rubber, [in] these small one-industry towns, which were typical of industrial America, in the main the very large part of the industrial work force from 1870 on was made up of these immigrant workers. . . . They needed the sick and death benefit societies. In the main these organizations, in the 1880s through the turn of the century, were under the

influence of social democrats and Socialists. When the split took place
in the socialist movement in 1919, that split went right through everything, including the sick and death benefit societies. They also split.
Out of that split came a left-wing of sick and death benefit societies.
By 1929 or '30, they decided to come together and organize what they
called the International Workers Order.[28]

[The other factions] remained independent, on their own. They still
exist, many of them. . . . For the left and the Communists, what it did is
it brought them together, so IWO eventually became an organization of
about 165,000 members. It had a lot of influence, because it had a lot
of money, and it was able to provide an important service. And it had a
politics, that was prolabor, pro-New Deal. In a word, "progressive."

Young radicals came on the scene in the 1960s, with the idea that
all that was necessary was to have a correct line and a correct policy
and workers would follow you. All that was necessary was to write a
leaflet or issue a manifesto, and that was baloney. In the 1930s, we had
links to organized foreign-born workers who were in the plants. In a
place like Detroit there must have been about twenty-five or thirty
different IWO lodges. In Michigan, the IWO had about three or four
thousand members. Now, they were not all in the Rouge. . . . But there
was a substantial number there. . . . Ford brought people from all parts
of the world actually, and that's why it was no accident that the city
of Detroit had the largest concentration of ethnic-group people. . . . The
most remote groups were brought together, and in a sense that's the
character of the automobile work force. So, what you had at Ford was
tens of thousands of foreign-born workers. And the left and the Communists had an influence among these people that preceded the 1930s
and the '40s. It went back to the 1920s. That's the link really. . . .

IWO also had a politics. Not a socialist politics, but a politics that
related to current political struggles. As an organization, it had to deal
with the question of social security and pensions and health insurance
and stuff like that.

*The people who run these IWO campaigns are workers in the
shops?*

Right.

Are they usually labor leaders?

No, people very much like church activists. I mean you need dea-
cons and you need secretaries and treasurers and committee chairpeo-
ple and so on. It was run the same way. There must have been about
twenty or twenty-five such IWO chapters in the city of Detroit, Jewish, Armenians, Maltese, Arab, Russian, German, and others. I don't
know what the figures were but in Detroit, I think the IWO must have

had two to three thousand members if not more, mainly working class. They also . . . had about five or six IWO centers, so that these became places that union organizers could use.

They also had choruses, dance groups. They were dealing with the problem of how an immigrant generation passes on its culture to its first generation of native-born Americans. Some of them had schools, I went through Jewish school. My people were Jewish—atheists, but fiercely Jewish—heavy into the cultural implications of Jewish tradition and experience. There were Jewish schools, and my parents made sure that their kids learned how to speak, read and write Yiddish. I could read Shalom Aleichem in the original when I was fifteen. They had Finnish and Russian schools and they had Maltese schools and Polish schools, and choruses and publications.

Culture was a very valued thing and very important. But the most important thing they did was to provide a doctor when you got sick. I think for $2 you plugged into a doctor system and then you got a plot when you died, there was someplace to bury you.

You paid the dues to a neighborly organization to hire a battery of doctors. It was the early forerunners of health [maintenance] medicine and things of that type. . . . The Social Security System we now know wasn't begun to be set up until the middle or late 1930s. They [the organizations] fell victim to the McCarthy assault and were smashed in the late 1950s.

The national organization was chartered in New York and when the New York state superintendent of banking withdrew its charter, the organization was no longer able to finance its sick and benefit function. That was its end.

About how many IWO members were in the Rouge plant?

Well, strictly a guess, somewhere in the neighborhood of 1,000 to 1,500, because in the Rouge there were Poles, Arabs, Maltese, Rumanians, Ukrainians, Italians, and many were members of IWO lodges. . . . Most of the union activists were not active in the IWO. The folks active in the union were many of the younger guys. They belong too because you need a doctor, you have to worry about what's going to happen when you die. IWO was far more important in the organization of steel [than auto], because in steel, you had a greater number of foreign-born workers than you did in auto. And the steel towns were really small, one-industry towns. They had nothing else but that, and so the IWO played a very important role not only from the point of view of organizing it, but from the point of view of giving cultural sustenance and ideological sustenance to the people who lived in these towns. They were a vehicle for radicalism. . . . in steel. I don't mean radicalizing for a revolution, but radicalizing to overcome the enormous power of the steel owners, to keep the union out.

■ PAUL BOATIN

The point that has to be remembered, and this was all preparatory to the building of the union at Ford's, is that even though the workers in the Rouge plant (and when we say Rouge plant, we're talking about the bastion of the Ford Motor Company) were of a foreign ethnic composition, and there were many attempts by Father Coughlin and others to divide these workers along religious lines, along color lines, and along nationality lines, it didn't work. Ultimately the best organizers of the union were of foreign ethnic origin. In fact, when the CIO sent its organizer here to begin the main organizing drive in 1940 he was of Italian extraction, recognizing precisely that the workers in the Ford plant were of ethnic extraction, and many of the rank-and-file organizers were Polish, Ukrainian, Italian, generally ethnic. This shows the influence and the courage and the understanding both at the top and at the bottom.

I'm not saying that an exact count was ever made. But in the building of the union, it was [men with] Slavic names [who were] the voluntary organizers. I mean in the dozens. The other large group were the Italians. The smallest groups were the American-born whites.

How about blacks?

Blacks? There was only a few, and they all worked in the foundry. [When] the organizing drive picked up steam . . . leading black and ethnic priests and pastors were won over to help, in spite of the fact that the papers carried on a campaign that CIO meant "Communist International Organization." That didn't scare Reverend Hill [a black minister]. It didn't scare Monsignor Chiarocchi—and it didn't scare others. Paul Robeson, denounced as a Red, was welcomed by the union organizing committee, along with the NAACP [National Association for the Advancement of Colored People], to help bring about the organizing drive.[29]

■ MARGARET AND STANLEY NOWAK

Stanley Nowak:The vice president of the Amalgamated Clothing Workers, by the name of Leo Krzycki, . . . was assigned here by [John L.] Lewis to come and help to organize the auto workers, once the UAW decided to work with the CIO committee at that time. And Krzycki, who was of Polish background, a former Socialist from Milwaukee, knew enough that—he knew first that this is a big Polish community, and that to win the Polish worker required two things: . . . to do quite a bit of work in their language, and, second, by someone in whom they would have some confidence, especially was one of them. It's just like black people, in a sense, he knew this much. When he came here, I accidentally met him at a meeting of the Polish workers' paper here. And we both were to speak, and Homer Martin who was then elected president of the UAW—

Margaret Nowak: It was a picnic.

Stanley Nowak: —was also speaking at that picnic. So, the first thing he asked me was, "What are you doing?" Well, I was by that time selling paint for a living, because I had to do something. So, he said, "You shouldn't sell paint. Why don't you come and work with us?"

He engaged me to come before the UAW board, and talk to Homer Martin. So, I came before the board, and the question was not whether we should organize, but how to organize.

Homer Martin was letting radicals do his organizing?

Yes, you see—

Margaret Nowak: They were the best organizers.

Stanley Nowak: —as a result of that [UAW] convention in—

Margaret Nowak: South Bend.

Stanley Nowak: —South Bend, in the early part of May in 1936, the union got its independence, and it elected new officers. He was fully in agreement to work with the left. And when Leo Krzycki told him of this problem of Polish workers—"We need somebody to attend to this"—he fully agreed to it. . . . There was a brief discussion at the meeting of the board, and they assigned me to come with a plan, how to organize. They gave me a few days' time. I went over to some friends who had worked together, thinking how to do this. In the past, when you were organizing language locals and small shops like clothing, there was not much of a problem. You'd find people who were Polish workers or Italian or whatever they may be, and they would do most of the job. They would have contact with people. But here you have a new industry. You have shops where tens of thousands of people are employed of all nationalities, all over the city. And . . . you'll find Polish workers and other Slav groups in every shop. So, how do you approach them? Do you go where it is necessary to approach them in their own language? That's one thing. But what do you do, go by the gate with your own [language,] when there are workers of a variety? Should we have local language-speaking locals when that's such a mass industry? So, we debated and prepared a plan. We suggested that we do not organize language locals, but we do have ethnic committees

[and] a Polish organizing committee; [it] would carry on the organizational work of the Polish workers, in both Polish and English.

Second, the question was, how do you get them? Well, I knew that there were nine radio programs at that time in Polish. What they did—they would buy time for one hour or two hours. They would give news, they would give Polish music, some serials, and advertising. That's how they sold it and made money on it. But people listened. The Polish people listened to these programs. So, I found— . . . there's always a piece of luck in it—so in these nine, I found someone I knew from Chicago, a former Polish actor who had a program like this. So I went to him and got an agreement that he would sell us ten minutes, twice a week, for certain sums of money (I forget now how much, not much, very little), . . . [on] a Polish program.

Now in relation to this radio program, we learned . . . that many of the Slav groups, like Czechs, for example, or Slovaks, Ukrainians, Russians, even some Serbians, listened to this Polish program because they didn't have their own program, and listened to the Polish music. They learned enough to understand the language. So, when I got to speak on it, within a few weeks I had a terrific audience, thousands, not only Poles, but all the Slavs.

Margaret Nowak: All through Wayne County.

Stanley Nowak: Then we had meetings, open air meetings at street corners, parks, both Polish and English.

And so that's how I was hired [as an organizer]. Our great pay was $40 a week and $10 expenses. Actually, each week what I returned to Margaret, to our home treasury, of my earnings was about $30. . . .

We organized General Motors. We organized Chrysler. But we couldn't touch Ford. We did, but we had so little [to show] until the strike at Ford took place in 1941.

Both GM plants that we had were mostly on the east side of Detroit. Chrysler was all east side. (The big General Motors plant on the west side we had not touched at that time yet. We couldn't get to it. Ternstedt. They employed mostly women there.) So, Walter Reuther, who was the president of that newly organized local [Local 174] went to Homer Martin, that I should be assigned definitely to the west side of Detroit. On the west side was the Ford local. So that's how I was then transferred over with exclusive attention to the west side. But I still had my regular program. That's the background.

■ VICTOR REUTHER

The ethnic community groups played a very very important role in the unionization of Ford. We had special leaflets and papers distributed in various Slavic languages—Yugoslav, Polish primarily, Italian. There was a great collection of ethnic groups at Ford's, much more so than was true in Chrysler and General Motors, and certainly much more so than in Flint, Michigan, during the sit-down—which was heavily a southern-oriented work force. Anyway, these foreign-born groups brought with them some trade union experience, but much more a political experience. And they tended to support the Unity Caucus much more, or the more militant group, the so-called left group, . . . as against the right, the [Homer] Martin forces.[30]

■ DAVE MOORE

I got involved in the union, and I got fired. It was the UAW, Local 212. That's what it became later on. It wasn't in the local at that time. I didn't work at Briggs but four or five months, at the most. I got fired there. It wasn't regulated at that time. You'd go in, they'd send you home. Lo and behold, I was told that they were hiring at Ford's, 1935. And, in between that time, there was much activity going on around organizing. . . . The real movement began to organize here. It began to make the drive on GM and Chrysler, and in 1936, about a year after I'd worked there, . . . I ran into Bill McKie again. "Look," he said. "We're going to organize—we're going all out this time. So, come on. . . . Come to the meeting over on McGraw tonight. We're gonna have some of the guys tonight, and we got some plans." So, I started going back and forth to these meetings. . . . I got involved with McKie. I got involved with a guy named Percy Llewellyn. Of course, he's dead now. Johnny Gallo. He's dead. And Paul Boatin, he's around. And we set up what you call the Ford Organizing Committee. And things went to happening. Shelton Tappes and Walter Dorosh were involved. Dorosh especially. Dorosh was deeply involved in it. I guess Walter and I've been friends over the years. When you mention his name, that's why you see me beam like I did. Some of the others had some real outs about them later on, during the McCarthy Era. I haven't got to that part.

■ MARGARET AND STANLEY NOWAK

In 1938 you were first elected to the state senate?
Stanley Nowak: That's right.
Can you explain a little bit about your campaign and how you came to run for the office?
Well, as Margaret mentioned to you, it came as a part of a Ford drive. Since we encountered very, extreme difficulties to get to the Ford workers, much more than in General Motors or Chrysler. At General

Motors or Chrysler we went on to the factories, with leaflets, amplifiers, speaking and so forth, but at Ford we couldn't because—

Margaret Nowak: Union men seen attending Ford meetings were beaten. Read Keith Sward's book. There's a lot of information on that.

Stanley Nowak: So, in that struggle, how to get to Ford workers, I probably with my radio program did quite a bit [to reach] Polish workers. But outside of that we had no mass way. Somehow, you learn. You struggle with problems, and you learn something. I observed (and others observed) that many Ford workers who were afraid to attend union meetings attended the Democratic Party picnics, clubs, a variety of them. So, the idea was that if one of us was a candidate for public office, he would have a right to speak at these meetings. That was one thing.

And a second thing, too. Why we selected the state senate [to run] a candidate is because the individual who served in the Michigan senate at that time was, in a sense, a stooge of the Ford Motor Company. He was a Ford worker before he was elected to the senate; and when he was in the senate he would return and do some odd work at the Ford Motor Company. His name was Joseph Roosevelt. That was not his name. He changed that name.

Margaret Nowak: His name was Capola.

Stanley Nowak: Yeah, he was of Italian origin. I have nothing against that, of course, but it was mentioned. But he changed that deliberately in 1932, because he felt that that was a name that was—particularly on the Democratic ticket—he could be easily elected. He was right. He was [elected] in 1932, to the [lower] house; and then, in 1936, I believe, he was elected to the [state] senate. That's where he was. And we learned from Governor [Frank] Murphy, who was the governor at that time, that he was a most reactionary senator in spite of he was a Democrat, and a big business senator because he was a Ford man.

Margaret Nowak: He was killing some of Murphy's rural electrification programs, for example.

Stanley Nowak: Friends who participated in that meeting suggested that I go into politics. Also John L. Lewis wrote to Detroit here and suggested organization of the Labor Nonpartisan League. So, between the two there came an idea, "Well, we should have somebody running for public office. Who would fit that?"

In general, I had certain hesitation. I had never run for public office. I had no knowledge what to do. It was completely new to me. . . . But they said, "You have the best chance because there is a large group of Poles there." Second, because of the radio program that I had for the union. So, I accepted that. There was also a great deal of democracy within the Dem-

ocratic party. In what sense? The only thing that was required if you wanted to be a candidate was to deposit $50 at the secretary of state, and a
certificate, your birth certificate or your citizenship, and that's all. And then
you were already a candidate in the primary.

Margaret Nowak: Or, in place of that, you could get . . . signatures
filed in a certain order. But, we didn't have time to do that.

Stanley Nowak: Either you pay $50 or you had petitions. Well, I
didn't have time to collect petitions. I didn't have any organization.
So, some people donated in the campaign immediately $50. I deposit-
ed the $50; and I had a little card like this. At the Democratic Party
meetings, in that district there, I would show that to the chairman, and
he would grant me the right to speak. Well, what I did, I tried to link
together the question of election and—

Margaret Nowak: Before we get into that, I want to tell them the
part that the women played in making sure that you got on the ballot.
There was a group of women, they called themselves "The Eleanor
Roosevelt Democratic Ladies American New Deal Club." Great big long
name. [Laughter.] And these were all Polish women who had worked
with him in Polish work, and at many of these meetings where he
spoke, and all this. And so when he needed the money to file for that
petition, he went to them as an experiment, told them what he needed and asked them if they would make a contribution. Well, they not
only made the contribution, they advanced the entire $50 for his filing
fee, and endorsed him, and went out and actively campaigned for him.

Stanley Nowak: Yes, that was the beginning of it. I had audiences.
People would have two, three meetings a day on Sunday, weekends.
We would have, on Sunday, five picnics—just a huge audience. . . . It
was on the west side. Most (many of them) were Ford workers. So, I
would linger. I would tell them that it was not enough to gain conditions in the shop, but you have to protect them with some laws. And
you have in Michigan something like a Wagner Act. Actually, my message was, "You people have to organize. You have to have a union."
That was the message. There were quite many candidates for that office, you see. That district was a Democratic district. The fight was to
get the Democratic nomination.

The district included which cities?

It included two wards in Detroit, Dearborn, and all the downriver
until the end of Wayne County, all the municipalities, and Lincoln Park,
Wyandotte—that was a big community. In all of these municipalities,
there were quite many Polish workers, and most of the Ford workers
lived either in these two wards of Detroit or in these municipalities
and downriver.

So, a committee was organized to carry on the campaign; and the committee grew very rapidly. I was surprised. My fellow Democrats looked at me funny, and they said, "You expect to win the election that way?" I said, "Yeah." "Do you think you can defeat such a name as Roosevelt on the Democratic ticket?" I said, "Well, I'll try." [Laughter.] Actually, I had my doubts very much. But that was not my objective. My objective was to get this union message to the Ford workers. To get around this whole difficulty. So, when we came to the close, a week or two before the primary election, I was offered money to withdraw. Well, I thought to myself, that looks good. That looks good.

Who offered you the money?

Well, somebody not too well known. But he was only an agent put on by someone else, I imagine. So I said, "No, no." "Hey look, you are not going to win the election, so why can't you? You have a chance to make some money?" I told him very friendly, whether he believed it or not, I told him, "I'm not out to make money. And I don't intend to withdraw now."

On the day of the election, we had to cover three hundred precincts with campaign workers, workers with leaflets; and, later on, when they closed the voting booths, and the counting took place, to have watchers to watch them how they counted. It required a tremendous amount of people.

Margaret Nowak: And we had them. All of these nationalities' groups. Every single one of them sent many, many people to work in the campaign. Ford workers came by the hundreds. They managed the campaign. They raised money. They made speaking engagements for him. They knew he didn't have the money to do it. We couldn't have done it otherwise.

Stanley Nowak: After the Hoover Depression, working on $40 a week. How could I? When the returns were broadcast on radio, "Roosevelt" and I were running head-on. Sometimes I would be a few votes behind, next time he was ahead, next time I was a few votes ahead, and he was behind, because there were other candidates, quite a number of them. Then, around two o'clock in the morning, the news came that I was two thousand votes behind. So, I said, "That's the end of it. I made a good showing."

Margaret Nowak: We tried to console ourselves.

Stanley Nowak: "We better go to sleep, and get some rest." I had some union negotiations for the next morning, so I had to get some rest. And then the next morning I went to do my negotiations with the company; and around three o'clock in the afternoon when I was through I decided to go to the county building to find out what was the final results, because I never had found out. And then I met one of the—

Margaret Nowak: Mort Furay.

Stanley Nowak: Yes, who was in charge, of the Labor Nonpartisan League, a big Irish fellow. "Senator, congratulations!" I didn't do it, but he congratulated me. "I didn't get nominated." "Like hell you didn't. And now I'll take you in to your office." I said, "Look, how could I catch up, being two thousand votes behind?" "You'll see." So he went into his office and there they all said, "Yes, you got elected. You got the nomination!"

Margaret Nowak: They all started greeting him as "Senator." . . . He had about 190 some votes margin in the end, but he was the nominee.

Stanley Nowak: And then the press began to publicize my picture; and they wrote a lot about this strange fellow, about how he got to be nominated.

Margaret Nowak: Ford had a bitter editorial about it. That was among those papers that I had up in [our friends'] attic. And the FBI got up there into those papers and that thing disappeared. But *The Ford Independent,* the old man's newspaper, bemoaned the fact that their district was represented by a Communist.[31]

He said that?

Stanley Nowak: Yeah. I had to run against a Republican, a fellow by the name of [Orville] Hubbard. I knew nothing about him. And the news came to me that he was a member of the Black Legion, and that I should be on the watch out, because they may use some physical attacks.[32] "Be careful of them." Well, I was careful. (Actually there was a period when not only they were doing that, but before that, when union people were being slugged, union organizers were being slugged. So I was careful.)

Margaret Nowak: He was well protected. The boys took good care of him.

Stanley Nowak: Sure.

Margaret Nowak: Always sent a bodyguard—in the group, he was well guarded.

Stanley Nowak: Sure. And then just before the final election took place, I thought to myself it was rather quiet, everything was quiet. "Something is being planned for the last minute." So, I thought to myself, "I better be prepared for it." But how could I prepare? Well, I had ordered, and paid in advance, for radio time, political time, on the Canadian station. [It] was the only place I could get. . . . So, I had the print shop ready, and radio program reserved. Saturday afternoon, early afternoon, one of our men brings in a leaflet to show me. It has my picture [with] Stalin's picture, all in red. And a clipping showing that churches have been closed in the Soviet Union—

Margaret Nowak: Implying that's what he was doing to do.

[Laughter.]

Stanley Nowak: —and underneath names of a variety of clubs, names of individuals.

Margaret Nowak: And they were all fictitious.

Stanley Nowak: All fictitious, because the people who prepared it knew that there would be libel.

Margaret Nowak: They had to be careful. They were very careful of planning this.

Stanley Nowak: So, at that time [Henry Kraus] (he was previously editor of the *Auto Worker*) was ready to immediately write a reply— got their printers to print at night. Sunday, early morning, we had something like fifty thousand copies of these people's names—

Margaret Nowak: And there were several hundred men ready to go to work.

Stanley Nowak: Yeah, and we had men, cars. So what we did, two things: first, we knew that they were going to concentrate on church- es, in the community, particularly Catholic churches, big churches. We found, not men distributing [the opposition's] leaflets, but boys. These boys had been given 50 cents or a dollar; and they gave us all those leaflets.

Margaret Nowak: And then our men would pass ours out.

Stanley Nowak: The other group would pass house to house, on porches, Sunday. And they found these leaflets on porches, so they picked these leaflets out of the door.

The election took place on Tuesday. That was a Democratic district. I think our vote was two to one. Both the congressman and I ran from the same district. So, late at night, who appears at the door of our house?—this Mr. Hubbard.

Margaret Nowak: He came early in the morning, before I went to work.

Stanley Nowak: Oh, early in the morning, I guess.

Margaret Nowak: He didn't come up the stairs. I told him that you were asleep, or that you had gone to negotiations. And he said, "Tell him I want to congratulate him on his victory," and he introduced him-self. And he was a big, athletic-looking type of man, typical football player guy. He was some character. He was mayor of Dearborn for many years. Many, many years.

■ JOHN SAARI

[When I got to Detroit] there was a lot of ferment developing about Ford's. There was a hunger march here. I wasn't here. I was about a year and a half away from that. I came to Detroit in 1935, '36, and that hunger march happened in 1932. (I first hired in at Ford's in December of 1936, in the old spring and upset building.) I know several fellows that were in it. I got acquainted with them and, of course, I picked up a lot of good things from them. Like I say, the environment, it's all (I believe a person develops lines of thought from his environment, depending upon his conditions of life). I became active and I went to meetings. There was a Finnish hall on 14th Street. We used to have meetings, and them places were packed. And agitation going on.

We had several agitators. A fellow by the name of Taylor was one of them. Oh he was tremendous, a tremendous speaker. . . . I was awed. "How come that guy remembers all that stuff? He must do a lot of reading." I started reading, and once I started reading, I spent almost as much time in the library as I did anywhere else. I read labor history. I read about some of the labor [leaders], like Eugene Debs. I read about the Haymarket trio. I read about [Tom Mooney], and I read about this lawyer, oh, what the heck is his name?
Clarence Darrow?
Yeah. I read about him, and I says, "What a remarkable man that Darrow was. . . . What a remarkable individual to go through all that. He was a good lawyer. They offered him a big job on the railroads, and he turned it down to be with the lowly guy down there, trying to defend him." And so this led on and led on. . . .

I became involved and I got to learn a little bit about Ford's. I met a lot of the Ford workers. Some of them were right wing; some of them were left wing. I played ball, I went on a softball team. I was unemployed for a long time there. . . . A lot of fellows talking to me, wanted me to join organizations. And one of the organizations was the John L. Lewis Nonpartisan League.[33] "Nonpartisan?" Well, that didn't strike me right. I said, "How can one be a 'nonpartisan'?" I used to argue about that issue. . . . You can't. That's an impossibility. . . . If you're nonpartisan you never make a decision. And once you make a decision you're no longer, you're a partisan. [Laughs.] That was my attitude. . . . I learned a lot through the John L. Lewis organization.

I only lasted one year [at Rouge], not even one year. I got laid off, and I just couldn't get back to save my life. . . .

I got a job in Square D, which was organized. Square D was the United Electrical Workers.[34] And I had quite an experience over there.

I turned that place upside down agitating. . . . The fellow in the shop got ahold of me and says, "Hey, you come down with me." He says, "There's a fellow from the United Electrical that wants to see you." Well, I met him [Jim Matles] in downtown Detroit. . . .[35]

Square D was organized at the time but, oh, the conditions there. For instance, the women, there was a lot of women working there, and they got paid, they was getting for the same type of work a fellow was getting 85 cents an hour and she was getting about 50. And I started agitating on that, and I ended up on the bargaining committee. They had a contract, and negotiations were coming up; and so the dominant forces in that local, of course, they ganged up on me. They was involved in some shady stuff. The union guys, some of the union guys. . . . I was elected on the committee because I made a speech at a meeting. And I really agitated on these issues. And so the chairman and some of the other members of the staff they kinda wanted to get me off of that platform; and so several fellows came to the platform, I guess they were going to handle me physically.

But the workers came to my defense. [A guy named] Newman was the president at that time; and Eugene Ladd, he was a tool-and-die maker, he was the head steward. They wanted me off the committee, so they went around and everybody resigned. Then they came to me and said, "Look, everybody resigned from the committee except you and so we're going to have new elections but you have to resign too." I says, "No, I'm not going to resign." I said, "If the workers want me off of the committee, call a meeting and let 'em vote me off, but I'm not going to resign."

So they did call a meeting, and through parliamentary trickery which I didn't understand very well then, they got me off of the committee. But as soon as they had to have nominations again for a new committee, I was the first one nominated. And I got next to the top vote and then a big fight ensued. We used to meet in the Hoffman Building and Christ, guys was falling down them stairs and windows were breaking, but nobody came at me. I think there was a lot of Finns working there (and I'm a Finn), a lot of Finns working there, and boy I'm telling you it was something.

So this guy then, this Matles wanted me to come, he wanted to talk things over with me. . . . I went to meet him and he said, "You know," he says, "I've been hearing about you. You got the right angle. You're all right. But you need some help." I didn't have a caucus. Because at one of the meetings then, they, the rank and file, they revolted against the president, and they yelled my name and said, "Get up there, you're the president, you're the president." So now what the hell do I do? [Laughs.] What am I going to do? I'm by myself, so I went up there and

I says, "Well, it looks like I'm going to have to open up nominations for chairman." I was just put in there, but if I would've had the knowledge that I have now I never would've done it. I wouldn't have pursued it. I would've used the authority the rank and file gave me, and I would have done the job. But then I felt I was talking about democracy.

But anyway, I talked to Matles, and he told me, he said, "Look," he said, "you stick with us." He said, "We need to clean up a couple of locals there." That was an amalgamated local, various different shops were bunched into one. . . . So, Matles told me, he said, "Look," he says, "you stick with us. We want to talk with you some more. You're gonna need help. We want to help you and you need help. You can't do it alone. So you stick with us, and you're gonna be all right." He said, "We like what you say, we like your action." He said, "You caused a lotta, the workers are with you, the workers are with you. That's the big thing."

That was the time when I run into this guy, . . . [Robert] Lieberman. . . .[36] The World War II started. . . . "Hey," he says, "why don't you come back to Ford's? Now is the time to do it, they're hiring.". . . But I was on the committee over there [at Square D] and everything, and I didn't know whether I should leave up there. Jesus Christ, I didn't know what to do. I was leaving the [Square D] workers flat. . . . He said, "Look, we need you here. [Rouge] is a big place, a hundred and twelve thousand workers here." Well, that made sense, so I did. I quit over there [at Square D], and Bob gave me a letter. . . . I didn't read the letter. . . . I was told to go into Gate 4, and just give it to one of the employment people there. I gave it to the first guy I come to. He opens that letter, he reads it; . . . and he puts that letter back in the envelope, and he said, "You got to go to that first desk over there." . . .

The head guy . . . takes that letter, reads it. His brow wrinkled, and so he said, "Okay, come with me." I followed him, and he . . . [was] looking at that letter, and he says, "Well, looks like all the comrades are coming back to Ford's." I said, "What do you mean, 'comrades'?" What the hell's he talking about? I didn't quite get it. . . .

Did you ever find out what that letter said?

No. I never opened the letter or anything.

Who did Lieberman know that he could get you in that easy?

Lieberman didn't tell me, other than he recommended that I be hired.

■ VICTOR REUTHER

A crucial part of the drive at Ford's was reaching black workers. . . . Some of the early black workers . . . formed a committee and began working through black churches. . . . Harry Bennett used to hire most blacks through preachers in black churches and the Bennett crowd would subsidize some of these black churches with modest little gifts.

So we had to reach the black community; and I remember the day that I got Walter White, then the head of the NAACP, to come out and we made the rounds of the Rouge plant with a sound truck and he would speak as the workers gathered. The final breakthrough with the blacks was a very crucial victory in winning Ford workers, because Ford had a much higher concentration of black workers than did Chrysler and General Motors.

■ THOMAS YEAGER

When the union came in here, I was working midnights, and I was operating the electrical turbines. In order to get there, you have to go down the elevator, down the shaft, and you go under the river. So, when all this was happening, they struck the plant; and the Ford Motor Company brought in all those colored ones, truckloads and truckloads was in there.[37] And I was over in that big building all by myself. I saw those guys up there, and I wanted to go home, but there was nobody to relieve me.[38] And there I sat. Finally, I barricaded the door.

■ SHELTON TAPPES

Bill Bowman, he was brought down from Saginaw, he was a preacher up in Saginaw. But in order to get the ministers, black ministers in this town behind the union, they utilized his expertise. He had two brothers that worked in the Chevrolet plant up there, and had worked in there himself at one time. He had some good union background and they used him to make these ministerial contacts. And there's also John Miles. Charles Hill was another. He was very stalwart, in fact he's an honorary member of Local 600. [Then there was] John Conyers, Sr., father of the congressman. He's from Chrysler Local 7. He and I were a team that they used on a special radio program that came on every week. On this program we would have a little dialogue between us, why people should join the union at Ford's. . . . He was active in the union at Chrysler, and being black, why they wanted to make this special appeal to the black people.

■ WALTER DOROSH

They had Negroes, of course [who were organizers]. . . . Our mayor of Detroit, Coleman Young [was an organizer]. I have known Coleman for umpteen years. We organized together. Coleman [Young] was one of the prime organizers. . . . I think he worked in the stamping plant here. I knew Coleman very well. We spent many a night together running away from the goons.

■ HORACE SHEFFIELD

[The UAW] had set up a drive, about sometime in 1940, where they concentrated on the black community. I got involved in it. . . . We set up an office on Milford in the black community and it was a matter of ringing doorbells and really talking to folks in the plant. That sort of thing. Yeah, and as a matter of fact, I am, at the time of the strike, why I was president of the Detroit NAACP Youth Council. The senior branch opposed the organization of Ford and we in the Youth Council favored it. . . . At the time that they had the walkout, why I got a sound truck and went up and down the Miller Road urging these people that stayed in, these scabs to come out. And I was also involved, was also responsible for, helping to get Walter White, who was then the . . . national executive secretary of the NAACP, to come out to Gate 4 on Miller Road there, to speak and urge the scabs to come out.

Who would you say were some of the important individuals who contributed the most to the organizing attempt at Ford's?

Well I certainly would say, oh, I think of blacks, I think Walter Hardin who was black, Chris Alston, that was in the black community.

Dave [Moore] was more articulate, more well read than Nelson Davis. He was strong on the black liberation thing. That was almost his forte. Nelson Davis [was] a decent guy [and] rose to be the bargaining committeeman in the foundry, but really just didn't have all of the tools. . . . He parroted whatever the line was. But Dave Moore was certainly—he articulated much better.

■ ARCHIE ACCIACCA

The one that I know outstanding in there was Shelton Tappes, a ferocious guy. Didn't he tell you that he had a hard time in the black group at the time?

■ JOHN ORR

He [Shelton Tappes] was president of the iron foundry during the original organizing days. One of the first elected. He was on the original Ford Negotiating Committee. We got autonomy in 1942. He was the original secretary of Local 600.

Was he popular with the workers?

Well, a large segment of foundry was antiunion, and sometimes [in] certain quarters in that building, boy, [his] life was in danger, I'll tell you. I remember one time I went in that foundry, and was lucky a bunch of us did come out. Some guys had a rope out and were going to hang [him] from the nearest rafter for working against Mr. Ford. But he was a gutsy fellow, a skinny little guy. . . .

Those guys who were mad at Tappes, were they black workers or white?

Yeah, black. Well, now there were other black workers. There were those who would protect him. But his back was right against the wall, boy, and he was taking them all on.

■   SAUL WELLMAN

One of the things you have to know about auto that contributed to its ability to organize differently than in many other places—there were many factors that make it different but one of them is the fact that there was a cadre of trained people available as organizers in 1933, '34, '35. They were not necessarily members of the Communist Party but they were trained in organizing, and that was people that came out of the unemployed movement. . . .

The Communists were prominent in the organization of the unemployed in Detroit. And a very large number of them were blacks who had begun to get that training and experience as far back as 1930, '31, '32, '33. Then they naturally begin to shift over towards union organizing. I'm speaking not of union organizing from the outside but union organizing from the inside, because they get jobs. The unemployed struggles were a high point in Detroit, and blacks were a very prominent part of that experience. A black leadership and a black cadre emerged that were later on to play quite a prominent role in the organization of the UAW in various places, including the Rouge. . . .

The blacks played a special role in the organization of Ford itself in 1940 and '41. The Ford Motor Company had hoped to use blacks as a strike-breaking force. . . . They almost succeeded, but did not because some black religious leaders decided to identify with the up-and-coming trade union movement. Amongst these was the Reverend Charles A. Hill of the Hartford Avenue Baptist Church. He became the president of the Detroit chapter of the NAACP, which in 1941 became the largest chapter in the country, with twenty-five thousand dues-paying members.

■ SHELTON TAPPES

I was a member of the organizing committee, Ford Organizing Committee for many years. Later on we organized what was known as the
Negro Organizing Committee to give some special emphasis to the
overtures toward the black workers in the Rouge plant.

*When you were organizing in the beginning there, were you or-
ganizing white workers?*

Everybody. Most of the people who were prounion, it didn't make
any difference to them who approached them, they joined. Those who
weren't, or who were afraid, it didn't matter whether it was me or
someone else, they just didn't join the union, because they were afraid,
they were afraid for their jobs.

*But you didn't experience any of this stuff directly about being a
"Nigger" and trying to organize a union?*

No, I never had that experience. With any of the Ford workers. I
never did. I remember once a fellow came up to me and he wanted
to know if you had to be a citizen to join the union, and I said, no,
just work in the plant, and he asked me could I come to his house
because he wanted me to sign him up and his brother, a Polish fellow
lived in Hamtramck. But the best was a Mexican fellow who wanted
to know if they could join the union despite not being citizens, and I
said, "You don't have to be a citizen." He said, "Mexicans, too?" I said,
"Why, sure." And I'd say (he's looking at me) "Mexicans, too."

And so then he arranged for me to come to his house. When I got
to his house, you never saw so many people in your life in one little
house. These Mexican fellows who worked in Ford's (and he had about
forty of them there) had brought their wives and their kids, and you
can just imagine me in this, all this Spanish language. I didn't know
what they were saying about me, although I hear the word *Negro,*
which is the Spanish word for black. I knew that they were talking
about me, but I didn't know what they were saying. But I was well
received. . . .

Listen, the CIO program, in contrast to the AFL program, had a
strong statement in its provisions, its constitutional provisions, to organize all workers regardless of race, creed, or color. You know, this
was in the constitution of the CIO and it was preached very broadly. . . .
[Everyone was] more concerned about getting organized, and these
little prejudices were placed on a back burner in many respects. So,
extra efforts were made to show a brotherhood spirit. I can recall
something happening, that the newspaper reporters would want to

get a picture, and you'd see two or three people standing there waiting for the picture to be snapped, and then one would say, just a minute, just a minute. Then they would run and find a Negro brother and put him in the picture with them, just to show their unity. It was done many times, I saw that happen many times. It was typical of most CIO unions in that day, in that day.

■ DAVE MOORE

Most of the guys . . . in the forefront of the organization at Ford . . . highlighted and were determined that there would not be any division [by race or nationality] among the workers that they were trying to organize; and to a great degree, I would say they were successful. I won't say it was 100 percent. But I think the education that the Ford workers received from the organizers of the union at Ford carried over, and some semblance of it is still there today.

■ HENRY MCCUSKER

There was a big, big influx of southerners into those communities. . . . Generally speaking, most of them turned out to be pretty fair-minded and active members so far as the union was concerned.

■ DAVE MOORE

We had some southern guys who were working at Ford at that time, they were good union people. They helped organize it, and some of them came right in, and became real good union leaders at the Local 600.

■ JOHN ORR

Listen, when the [southerners] got in there and got that first big money, they weren't antiunion because they knew where it came from. They weren't that stupid. No, we never had any problem with antiunion sentiment from southern workers, never.

■ DAVE MOORE

Women played a hell of a role. Out at Local 600, we have what you call a women's auxiliary. They were wives and daughters or sisters of men who were actually involved. And women played a hell of a role in help organizing Local 600. After we organized they played a hell of a role in some of these . . . social activities—like organizing choral groups. We had what you call a Local 600 choral ensemble. We had . . . baseball teams. We had basketball teams. All integrated. We had golf teams. We had track teams. We had bowling contests and everything.

One of the first sit-down strikes that took place right here in the city of Detroit was staged by women. It wasn't staged by men. It was staged by women right down here on Woodward Avenue in a candy company [in 1927]. They shut the door and wouldn't let nobody in, and they wouldn't come out. They shut the boss out, and wouldn't let him in. For three days they stayed in that candy company down here on Woodward Avenue. . . . Walked out with a mouth full of cavities.

■   SHELTON TAPPES

Well, the early struggles really go, they precede the UAW. The original union that I knew of was the old Auto Workers Union. I wasn't working in an automobile plant when I joined that union but they were not particular, as long as you were a potential auto worker, why you could join the Auto Workers Union. It cost you a quarter to join, and you were given a card, and I'm so sorry I didn't save that, it would have been priceless nowadays. I think it was 15 cents a month were the dues, and if you were unemployed, why you automatically were granted paid-up dues, there would be no charge.

The Auto Workers Union for Detroit covered . . . I suppose the whole state of Michigan was Local 1. And New York, I recall New York was Local 2, and that included I think . . . Buffalo, New York, because that's where the Pierce Arrow plant was. (The Pierce Arrow automobile was probably the largest car ever made in this country. They had headlamps on the fenders which was very unusual for that time. I can still see those swooping like a swan's neck, you know, fenders). . . . The Studebaker plant moved from Detroit to South Bend and then Indiana became quite a producer [of cars]. This was an independent union at first. Now I don't know whether the AFL ever embraced the Auto Workers Union or not, but this is the one that Bill McKie headed up. He was the chief organizer for the Auto Workers Union. . . .

Your first experience of [unionism] was with the TUUL's Auto Workers Union?

Yes, with the Auto Workers.

Whatever made you think it was worth joining?

I was still quite a youngster when I came here, and I had never had a steady job. I attended all the demonstrations they used to have, the

Unemployed Council and all that sort of thing. And then you get worked up, and you understand what's happening. There were three groups, . . . the Communist Party, the Socialist Party, and then there was a Proletarian Party. (This was an independent Marxist group.) Of course, all those organizations are based on the teachings of Karl Marx, but they just had their own idea, you know, it's Methodist church, it's Baptist church. At various times, [they] would have demonstrations and big meetings. You probably heard of Hyde Park in London, but we had a Hyde Park here, that was the Grand Circus Park downtown.[39] Man, I'm telling you we used to have some real old, . . . speech-making on a soapbox. There were no TVs to distract you. There were radios, but you couldn't see anything just listening to the radio, and so the entertainment was one attraction. But then when you began to listen to the speakers, why you got involved, and I got involved.

■ SAUL WELLMAN

The Communists made a very profound contribution to the organization of the Ford workers and the subsequent development of that local union. Local 600 is the dominant local in the Ford empire. But in order to understand that you have to recognize that there is a long-range input that's involved here. . . . Now actually the Communist effort at Ford goes back to 1921–22. . . . It's a varied and a changing one. . . . In 1922, there were probably fifteen or twenty Communists working in the entire Rouge plant (and I don't remember how many people they employed in the year 1922). In 1934, I would guess between the Communist Party and the Young Communist League, maybe there were forty-five or fifty Communists.[40] In 1941, before the strike, maybe there was 110. And you have to think of them interchangeably, by the way, there's two organizations which are operating as one, the Communist Party and the Young Communist League. And they're both very important to understand. And then in 1941 it makes an enormous leap because the illegality of trade union organization has been broken. . . . See the party is not just a maneuvering organization trying to influence organizations and trying to influence leaders, it's trying to influence masses and it does that through instruments called leaflets, newspapers, publications, speaking, meetings, and things of that type. . . . People working within the Ford plant were working under extremely difficult and illegal conditions.

So what was developed over the years and that took twenty or thirty years is *outside support*. . . . When we had a leaflet distribution there we would have to cover eleven gates, and to cover eleven gates means that you have to get a minimum of thirty people to come out on a leaflet distribution. If you want to cover two shifts, you've got to get sixty people, and if you want to cover three shifts you have to get ninety people.

And we did that, and so that in a sense, the radical and the Communist community of Detroit and its environs was an outside support group. Another part of the story, which I didn't know how to get into, is that in a sense the Communist effort at Ford which goes back to 1921–22 is part of what we called a national concentration policy. . . .

Now the policy is not just concentration on basic mass-production industry, because you see the challenging task of a new emerging Communist movement in the 1920s, after the split in the Socialist Party, of how do you bring the trade union organization to the mass-production industries . . . had yet to be accomplished.

But then you had to concretize it, and not just deal with mass-production industries in general. . . . You had to deal with concrete industries, in particular, and in a sense auto and Ford lent itself better than in other places because of its concentrated character. . . . Detroit in 1930 up to 1950 was the fifth largest city in the United States. But its distinction was not its size, its distinction was and remains (and that's the crisis of Detroit) that it's a one-industry town. . . . There are thousands of one-industry towns in the United States. But none took on the size and the dimensions of this city. Well, that works two ways. It makes it easier to organize, that is, one-industry towns. And it also makes it more difficult, in the sense that you are dealing with employers, who can more directly deal with those that are trying to come in to organize. But it's a two-way street. It was this national concentration policy that essentially was (consistently or inconsistently, for better or worse) carried through [in Detroit, at Rouge] for many, many years by the [Communist] Party. . . .

But it has a spill-over effect, that's why you can also organize the GM plants there, the Packard, the Motor Products, the Hudson and Briggs. . . . But the main concentration was Ford, even though the difficulties were enormous. The only point I'm trying to make in all of this is that in order to do that you need outside help.

Because if you expect the people within the plant to be the agitators and the organizers they're not going to last very long, because what the companies had and what Ford had to enormous perfection was an internal spy system.

You couldn't overcome that, so therefore people that went into Ford had to exercise the greatest degree of discretion and caution. But the penalty of a great degree of discretion is to keep yourself isolated from people.

So the way you overcome that is by people from the outside making the contacts, doing the talking, issuing the leaflets, and things of that type. And so there was an extremely extensive system which lasted for many years.

How did they do that before they changed the leaflet laws in Dearborn?

Now, here's another little story. The transportation system in Detroit was so constructed that every streetcar line went into the Rouge plant. . . . There's a far east side and a west side and a north side, and these all had independent streetcar lines. But all of them would link up to find their way into the Rouge plant. . . . Well, there's a bridge there, if you can picture it, and one side of the bridge had a very large parking lot for the street cars. On the other side of the bridge was the old motor building. Up to 1939 or '40 instead of it being a gigantic parking lot, it was a gigantic car assembly point. That's where the workers would come in, that's where they would pour out of. . . . That's in Dearborn.

Now, before you come into Dearborn, in Detroit there's a main drag called Michigan Avenue. There's a street that cuts into Michigan Avenue called Junction, and it was at Junction where all the streetcars had to come, coming from different parts of the city before they went into Dearborn, and it was at Michigan and Junction that the main leaflet distributions took place. . . . And then, of course, many of us would go in at night and carry through illegal distributions of materials in the city. But if you got arrested or you got beaten up, you weren't going to get fired, because you didn't work for the Ford Motor Company.

■   WALTER DOROSH

How important was the ACTU in that early organizing period?

They played a role in there. I think they wanted the union. I don't challenge their—they supported the AF of L but after the AF of L got beat, then they became active in the CIO. But they played a role. Not all of them were in the AF of L. A number of Catholics were in the CIO organizing. Joe McCusker was an ACTU member, and he supported the CIO. This I know because I worked with Joe; we were organizing together. Yet he believed in the ACTU. I didn't. I wouldn't join it. I thought that the Church shouldn't put his nose into our affairs. I said, "Look, you guys didn't do anything about trying to organize until we got in and started organizing; and you guys want to get on the bandwagon. No dice. We are going to run this union for the good of the workers." Everybody tried to get involved in it. Everybody wanted to have their finger in it.

How many of the Catholics do you think went for the ACTU line?
They were split. . . . I believe that those that became active in ACTU were those who were very active in the church activities. They were members of the ushers clubs and things like that. They tried to do their duty, I guess, to church and God.

■ SAUL WELLMAN

Another subtle question (which many of our new left friends don't fully understand) is that . . . the strange phenomenon that one of the most important elements that brought about the organization of the mass-production industries were the skilled workers, who are generally the most conservative and backward of workers. It so happens that skilled workers have a greater loyalty to unionism than unskilled workers or workers who are transitory.

In the case of auto, it was the skilled workers who from the very beginning tussle with the company, not only because they're more militant, but because they're also more independent and they have better organization and they have a greater dedication to unionism—not for its abstraction but for its very concreteness. In that sense, the goddamn system that Henry Ford worked out was violated, because when you work in an automobile plant tied to an assembly line, you can't move.

Bill McKie was a skilled worker, he was a maintenance man, a sheet metal worker, a tinsmith, so he had to work around the different parts of the plant to do his job. That's how skilled workers became very important, they could pass the messages. It's little things like this, you see.

■ JOHN ORR

The tool-and-die building . . . were mostly red apples [antiunion], because of the working conditions mainly. It was the newest and largest tool-and-die room in the world. Bar none. And they were catered to. There weren't too many. There were some prounion guys, including Mack Cinzori, who was an apprentice there at the time. There weren't too many that emerged, as ourselves, from that original group—that emerged as union leaders.

■ WALTER DOROSH

Homer Martin was the president of the International Union, United Automobile Workers, and he was also at the same time on the payroll

of the Ford Motor Company. . . . Oh, he was a smooth operator. . . . (He
was a preacher. He was a Baptist minister, and, man, he could spell-
bind you, and he could talk a leg off you.) What was happening, every time we would organize, . . . many workers, they would be discharged—until John L. Lewis came in, [in] May 1940. I remember I
attended a meeting when he came into Detroit. At the local union, as
a matter of fact, when they scheduled him in they kept it on the QT,
because they didn't want Homer Martin in the meeting. Homer Martin still was the president of the international union.

John L. Lewis came in. He brought Mike Widman and some of his
other administrative aides. (It was on a Sunday about twelve o'clock.)
. . . We were volunteer organizers; we had about fifty in the room there.
. . . He said, before he [spoke] to us, he wanted to take a ride around
this Ford Rouge plant he'd heard so much about; he wanted to know
why it's so difficult to organize it. So he left; it took about an hour and
a half to make the rounds; and he came back; and the first thing he
said was, "I don't see any machine guns or national guardsmen around
that plant. When we organized the coal miners, and we had to fight
the Pinkertons, they had machine guns, bayonets, rifles." He made us
seem kind of fearful. He said, "You guys scared to organize?"

And then he put on a plan, a very subtle plan it was. At that time,
[there were] about sixteen plants, comprised of eighty thousand employees, in the Rouge plant. When we organized before, we used to
sign anybody up as long as he was [a] Ford worker. He says, "No, I'm
going to cut that out. Only turn in the names from your building and
from your own department, that's all." And what he did he started—

So that they could know who they were signing up?

Well, not only that. We would want to know their names. When I
signed up four or five people, I'd have to give those names to this individual; this individual had to give it to that individual. We wanted to
know where the spies were in the Ford set-up. You organized only in
your own building. Everything was set up as a unit. It was broken all
down. And after you organize in one department then you start to
organize at another department. And he only deals with you. Before
everybody used to just go to the local and give [the list of new names]
to the secretary-treasurer; and there was no controls.

Mike Widman, who was John L. Lewis's administrative assistant,
became the organizer. He took over. He says, "I don't want you to give
[the list of names] to nobody else. I don't care who it is. You just give
it to this guy. This guy will give it to the next guy. He will only know
who the next person is." That way, we finally organized the place.

■ VICTOR REUTHER

To a greater and lesser degree, some of the people who were still
working inside the plant were able to involve themselves in activities
outside the plant, attending meetings and so on; others had to remain
very much undercover for a while. But it is fair to say that people like
Percy Llewellyn and Walter Dorosh and others had sort of won their
credentials during that early period and had been sufficiently identified as initiators and early supporters that it gave credence to their
efforts to win election. . . . They were doing pretty much independent
work, because it wasn't until a full-time director of the Ford drive was
set up, and we had full-time organizers assigned to organizing Ford,
[that] it became a big open campaign. It wasn't until then that there
was a high degree of coordination and efforts within the plant and
without during the period that Local 174 had jurisdiction. And the
coordination with forces inside the plant had to be kept very QT, very
much undercover, because as fast as we signed them up they would
be fired. So, it was both a clandestine operation from within, and the
more open one through these recruiting offices on the outside.

*It was your brother's [Walter Reuther] idea to open up small
branch offices in neighborhoods that were remote from the Ford
plants in order to avoid the problem of Ford's domination around
the plant. Who would staff these branch offices?*

Well, I would say it was a combination of former Ford workers who
were fired or laid off, a combination of them plus ethnic workers. The
ethnic workers were very prominent in that drive, they had the support of some local language newspapers like *Glos Ludowy,* the Polish
newspaper. There were some modest radio programs that we used to
plug the Ford drive. Then, of course, there were some organizers that
were attached to the west side local like Stanley Nowak, Bob Cantor,
Bill Chemsly [?], myself, who would help provide a degree of supervision over these scattered local recruiting offices.

I think the women were very easily unionized. I have always felt
from the very first days of the UAW when I got involved in organizing
the Ternstedt plant, which had a very large number of women workers on the west side of Detroit, the women were the easiest to unionize and were the strongest supporters of the solidarity concept. I think
that's because while they may not have understood too much about
economics, they knew what justice and the denial of it meant and they
quickly saw in the union a force that was one, fighting to get jobs for
them and two, insisting that they be treated with the same consider-

ation as the men workers. I think the very fact that we moved quickly to get a staff that was sensitive to the women's needs made it very easy to unionize them. I think they brought a great strength to the union.

■ PAUL BOATIN

Okay, so in 1937, on my third trip back, I had lived on a farm, and I came with a tool box. I sensed the union was involved in organizing. After doing a little consulting, the union thought, "Hey, you're made to order. They'll hire you right away. You got a tool box, you work. You want to go into [being] a machine repairman. And you come from the farm. You know you're just a hick. No problem."

I signed up—I don't think I signed up any more than six or seven people, and I got fired. . . . The last individual that I was talking to was an Italian, and the "starmen," that was these, the people that represented the company. They weren't foremen. They just meandered all over. They were the eyes of the company. I went to this guy. And he comes to me later and says, "I didn't know. I didn't know, I'm sorry." I understood the poor guy. Eventually he became a real good union guy.

But from there on machine repair, they took me over to the foundry, okay? . . . Everything was black there. There were no ventilators and you couldn't tell a white person. There were very few white, but you couldn't tell them because most of the blacks were working there. And they [the company] thought I would quit, but I didn't, and they fired me.

So, in 1940, it must have been September of 1940, I knew the union drive was going to start all over again. I quit my other job, and through some connections that I had, I was able to get back [into Rouge] again under a fourth name. . . . I had become a volunteer organizer. By then, the company wasn't firing people any more because they had gotten their fingers burnt with the Labor Board, and all that. I learned some lessons that I try to remember to this day. The CIO had assigned a fellow by the name of Mike—all of a sudden his name escapes me. [Mike Widman.] Under him worked a fellow by the name of Norman Thomas, no, Norman Smith, Norman Smith. He was a disheveled, tobacco-chewing, overblown guy, but with tremendous understanding of the way the mind of workers functioned. He was an anti-Communist. He would give you a blood test. But they made a decision to take fifty credentials, fifty organizers' cards, and hold them to give to favorite people. So that when the day of distributing medals came, they would all be the topnotch. Walter Reuther was the number one organizer, and this guy [Emil] Mazey was number two organizer, and all of that. I had number 51, so I was actually the number one organizer. You see, number one, because the [other] fifty cards didn't count. They were in the drawer some place.

So one day Norman Smith sends for me, and I thought, "Geez, I'm going to get a bawling out." I had only had my voluntary organizer card about three or four days, and I hadn't signed anybody up, and I thought he's going to ball the hell out of me for that. So, he said, "Were you talking to a certain guy, so-and-so, in the" (he describes the place)? And so I said, "Oh yeah." I felt better already because he wasn't going to bawl me out. He said, "Did you tell that guy that when the union comes in, we're going to get him a quarter an hour back pay?" I had to admit it. I had a sheepish expression on my face. He said, "You did, didn't you?" He says, "And did he sign up?" I had to admit that he didn't sign up. He said, "If I ever hear something like this about you again, you'll never get a card as a voluntary organizer. I've got something else to tell you. I want you to go back, forget everybody else and get a hold of that worker, and tell him that when the union comes, the union is going to get him a nickel back pay, and I'll make you a bet that that guy will sign up." And it took me a couple of days, but that's exactly what happened, because the workers aren't, you must remember, now everybody else was organized, and we in 1937, '38, '39, '40, we hadn't built the union until the strike on April 1, 1941. . . .

It's just like, don't sit on the edge of the pond and dream about what a beautiful swimmer you're going to be. You've got to get in the water, and you feel your body sinking, and you develop a lot of abilities and understanding that you didn't know you had. . . .

The Ford workers knew about the intimidation tactics of the Ford Motor Company and they were aware of the fact that we hadn't organized the union, and we weren't such brave guys. And in the other shops, the union didn't get the workers 25 cents an hour back pay. They were glad to get the union contract signed up with certain minimal benefits, get the right of representation—that was the number one thing. So that anybody who came along and told them such a farcical thing, that you're going to get 25 cents an hour. That worker thought, "Uh-huh, better be careful. This guy is not a good union man. He's trying to trap me into something." You see? Because workers think in practical terms. That's the lesson I think I learned from Karl Marx. I had forgotten it then, that the workers . . . see the practical things. They see the practical things, and they've learned from bitter experience not

to fall for phony baloney. You see, 25 cents an hour back pay sounded
like phony baloney.

■ KENNETH ROCHE

When I was hired, in 1940, the union was just picking up steam to get
going. . . . So one of the guys in the shop who worked with me said,
"Are you in or are you out?" I said, "In what?" I didn't know anything
about unions because at that time my mother and dad never discussed
it at home. (I had just graduated from Fullerton High School. I was
eighteen years old.) But they knew about unions from Pennsylvania
because they worked in unions there. My mother got fired in a button mill in Pennsylvania for leading a walk-out. I came home that night
from work and I asked my dad and mother at supper. I said, "Well, some
guy asked me about a union today. What'll I do?" . . . My father and
mother told me to join the union.

■ JOHN SAARI

I recall some antiunion elements during the organizational days at Local
600. . . . Now, I know we're not born prounion. . . . I played on a softball team before the union was organized. They had recreation, and I
used to get a little flak. I was single then, and I lived in a hotel, and
some Ford workers in the hotel used to say, "How the hell? What do
you wear a UAW sweatshirt for?" I said, "Okay, I like to play ball. What
do you like? I like to play ball. What the hell I care whether it's UAW
or what? I like to play ball." And they shut up.

■ WILLIAM JOHNSON

Were you involved with the early organizing attempts?
    I was involved only at a very minor level. When I was in college at
Wayne (I got my degree from Wayne), I worked afternoons at Ford. I
went to school during the daytime, the morning session.
    Even in high school I had heard a lot about John L. Lewis. Of course,
John L. Lewis at that time was president of the CIO, and I had a lot of
admiration for Lewis, having watched the conditions in the plant and
the treatment that the average worker got at the Ford plant, in particular. That was the only plant I worked in. I felt there was a strong need
for a union. Even as a high school kid I had a strong leaning toward
the union, even though I never belonged to it. . . . At that time . . . I
heard about [the hunger march] from older people that had been involved in it, but I had no participation.

■ ARCHIE ACCIACCA

I went to work at Ford's in 1935. . . . but my union activity started in 1941, under the very first election. When we were on that strike, maybe this gave it birth, I don't know, but they were asking guys to participate in the flying squad.[41] And four of us were driving in my car; and we'd drive around, help guys at the picket lines, or if they needed something, then the flying squad would drive around and kind of keep things in order.

You were a member of the flying squad?

Yes. And I moved around quite a bit, and spent a lot of time, some away from home, when the strike was on. I was again not keeping too much time at home. So, we kept pretty active.

■ JOHN ORR

In 1937 I joined [the UAW] but I dropped out because I had subsequent layoffs, couldn't afford to pay and thought it was too much, and I had already given indication where my feelings were. I didn't rejoin until the early part of 1940.

Now, today when they are organizing a new plant you don't go in and make those people pay initiation fees and dues right off the bat. You hold that in abeyance until you get them a contract. But they didn't do it in those days. Well, they do today. I think Emil Mazey was responsible for that. As a matter of fact when a plant goes on strike now for the initial contract maybe one worker in three haven't paid a penny in initiation fees or dues, but if they go on strike in support of a new contract or a first contract, they get on the UAW strike fund. But not in those days. Those dues were only $1. And yet when they organized Ford they had some eighty thousand members in the Rouge plant alone. My God you were dealing with $80,000 a month. You got rich overnight.

You never knew how much the guy next to you was making. It was no set wage scale, and this and that, like there is now. So he could be making more, and he wasn't about to tell you, because if he was making more he didn't want you going to the boss and saying, "I'm as good as this guy." So there was jealousies all over the place. But when I took a wage survey in early 1940, or maybe earlier than that, and found out that, oh we were way underpaid.

They [the UAW] sent sheets in there to all the stewards on the job and in departments and took a survey that way. But you had to go to the individual worker and ask him what he was making in order to complete the survey. Some were reluctant to tell you, some were so ashamed. Oh my God. A guy, I was an apprentice by that time, may be making a \$1 or \$1.05 an hour. We had journeymen in there making 95 cents.

As I remember, that was the first big survey they ever took. And boy that's when a whole lot of us got in trouble because we were really going behind the NLRB then. Our right to organize, and do this and that, and our leaflets was going beyond interviewing Ford workers and asking questions like . . . just going up to a worker on company time and ask him to join. . . .

Most places you had a paid company lunch period. You weren't even free under the law to do it during that period because you were on the company payroll. And even when they had the half-hour lunch period unpaid, well they'd still grab you for doing it but a lot of the NLRB cases came from there or were from such incidents as that, where the law said we were free to do it.

I was negotiating wages and some working conditions before the union was recognized. We took, at a given signal one day, we all lit cigarettes; that was something new in the Ford Motor Company. Different things we used to do to demonstrate. Always under threat, but the movement had grown so much. Now these bosses they just wanted to get by. They were getting production or their work out, boy they tolerated more and more all the time.

Militancy

■ PAUL BOATIN

In a struggle with corporations, you've got to fight every day, every hour, every minute, every second, because their promises don't mean anything. They have no country, they have no god, they have no flag, they have no heart.

■ KENNETH ROCHE

The worker is a cagey individual. They're not dumb. They'll tell you, "You're right." Then, in a lot of instances, they'll do something else, because they always want to be on the winning side. There's some militant people that will batter down a wall with you, but they're few and far between. Now, most of the workers I knew, I got along with fine. They knew my ideas. They knew my ideology. They used to tell me, "Be careful now, they're gonna get you." And I'd say, "Well, I got you."

■ ART MCPHAUL

I became active, more or less, in the union movement, from the unemployed days back, and so forth, as a youngster. I was always anti-boss—you know what I mean?—because I saw what they were doing. And when the union came along, I was for the union; it's that simple. The first time I ever really joined a union—became an active member in a union myself where I worked—was when the union came in 1941 in Ford's, even though I worked to help to support the union long before that, to organize, that sort of thing.

■ PAUL BOATIN

One of the main things that everybody was concerned about, now that the union was coming, was doing something about the speed-up. I say this because this was part of the educational campaign that had preceded and been made an intrinsic part of the organizing drive, and after the union strike was successful, nobody had any delusions that just by holding a strike all problems could be solved.

■ WALTER DOROSH

Some of these young guys, when the union came in there, Lord, we were just pleased about their militancy. But everyday they had a shutdown, everyday. And we would go down on the floor and say, "What the hell is the problem?" . . . They says, "Wait a minute, we are not going to go for that." What was happening, it was competition—we didn't have any universal rates of pay, and we got what you can talk your boss out of. . . . They used to give wage increases in 5 cent increments. And if . . . a boss was a Mason, he'd say, "If you want to join the Masonic Lodge, I'll give you a nickel." That's the way it operated.

■ ARCHIE ACCIACCA

[When the union came in] we started getting security, and we started living like human beings. . . . If we thought something was wrong we'd have something to say about it—before you could never say it. . . . In the very first contract, we didn't get a heck of a lot, we just got recognition mainly, and a little bit of seniority protection, not too much. But as the contracts started coming out, we got more and more and more; and we got a lot of nice things today.

■ WALTER DOROSH

Right after [we got] organized, they [the supervisors] were afraid. They were hiding. We had real power. They would come to the committees, and say, "Look, get this guy off my back." The guys were just—they felt free. Boy what a wonderful feeling. "Get this guy off my back. He's eating me up alive." They were afraid there for a long time, even the superintendents. Whenever we had any problems we couldn't solve on the floor, we would come down, "Okay, let's go to the superintendent's office." At that time we had about four thousand people in our building. We'd have about two thousand people around the office; and the supervisor would . . . say, "What's going on? What's going on?" . . . He would be actually shaking like this. Our superintendent at that time was Joe Derby, and he was just bouncing off the pavement. He said, "Okay, we will take care of it. We'll make a decision. Everybody go back to work." Okay, then everybody'd go back down the aisle. And another thing. We demanded a coffee machine in the place, and got everybody standing about the coffee machines. They [the supervisors] were just in a hell of a position. They couldn't get no production going for life or death. Everybody was thinking, "Oh, what power!"

■ DAVE MOORE

Did you see a big change in the attitude of the workers in the plant before and after it was unionized?

Yes, it was a big change in attitude. It was almost a 99 percent turnaround—100 percent turnaround. They were more defiant to the supervisors. They had their say so. [If a guy] was involved in an argument [with] the foreman, disagreed with the supervisor, everybody in that department could stop work and come to [his] defense. . . . It was there, the militancy. It was there, the desire and cooperation among each other, the concern for each other, especially at Local 600.

■ PAUL BOATIN

The basic difference between [progressives and] the average run-of-the-mill committeeman who didn't believe in militancy was very clear. The progressives felt that the best way to settle the grievance victoriously is to debate it out there where the workers could see the committeemen arguing with the supervisor in front of the workers, so they'd get a feeling that their own sentiments would be strengthened, their own education would be enhanced.

What about the opposition? The best example I can give you is of a union committeeman who had totally misunderstood, and had no respect for, the power of the workers. A worker had had an argument with his supervisor about his production. The committeeman was sent for. The committeeman went up to the worker and he said, "Now look, buddy, I am your mouthpiece. You want to have anything said, you say it through me." Putting that poor worker in such a low-down position that even the supervisor felt sorry for that worker. I witnessed this myself—believe it or not—and this reduced the militancy of the workers. Trading away any of the rights of the workers, putting grievances on paper instead of negotiating them out in the open had a tendency to . . . make the workers feel that they have no role to play in the union. . . .

Generally speaking, the umpire system, in the process of putting grievances on paper, creates such a prolonged process that sometimes it takes a whole year before the grievance is actually settled. That worker can be dead or can have been fired. Instead of the committeeman arguing vigorously in the presence of the worker, strengthening the worker so that the next time a dispute arises that worker will have a stronger backbone, that worker becomes disgusted. He remembers filing a grievance six or eight months before, and he's been told for months and months and months that the grievance will go to the umpire. Usually the umpire takes a middle-of-the-road course. His salary is paid half by the company and half by the union, and he plays the role of a mediator. The umpire system is really an attempt to siphon off the resentment of the worker and deaden the militancy of the union.

■   ARCHIE ACCIACCA

The leadership, most of the time, does not get involved with [wildcats].[42] They know better. You're subject to severe discipline in a wildcat strike. But sometimes some workers would get into something; it could be an argument with the foreman; it could be something about working too hard, some disciplinary action, or something. One word leads to another, and workers start siding in with the one guy; and then before you know it, you have a little scrimmage. In our building though—I don't want to pat myself on the back, but I was in good shape. I had good control over my people.

One time on a shipping dock, I remember real well, the committeeman (a good friend of mine; we were two peas in a pod) had a wildcat down there that day. They were making the workers load [sheet metal] into the boxcars. When you're using sheet metal, it could be very dangerous; a lot of it is sharp, and it cuts, and it's hard to handle. Anyhow, there was a safety problem: they figured that they were getting hurt. The foreman was pushing to get those cars out; they were in demand; they needed the parts. The guys got mad, and they stopped working. I happened to have been in the building down at the other end. All the guys got down in the lunchroom, and I went down there, and the labor relations guy was down there already. He started talking to me, and I says, "Look, don't bother me." In front of these guys— they knew I was with them—I told him, "Don't bother me, I'm talking to my guys, and I'll see what the problem is first, I'm not going to get it from you." So, I went over, and I talked to the guys. I told them, "We're going to take care of that. Don't you worry about it." So, I went and told the [labor relations] guy "Look, you're going to do it this way, the way that they want it, or you are not going to get these guys back to work." In a little while, I had them back to work—in no time.

We were a militant, but controlled, unit, I think. We were in good shape.
So, they got the safety measures?
Yes, we worked it out. Yes, we did; yes, we did.

■ SAUL WELLMAN

There is a difference between wildcat strikes between 1941 and '45 and wildcat strikes between 1945 and '50. The political exigencies of the war no longer exist. So, we had no problem supporting wildcat strikes. I'm not generally approving of every strike that takes place; and I'm not approving of every wildcat strike that takes place—not because it hurts the boss, but because it throws up other signals. . . .

The very term *wildcat* means a spontaneous struggle. A spontaneous struggle is something that takes place at the spur of the moment, and [can] take place over the craziest issues that nobody could really anticipate. It will explode over anything. I've tried to promote strikes on profound issues amongst workers, and couldn't get to first base; and then I would wake up one morning and find out that a bunch of guys went out on strike because there wasn't toilet paper in the toilet. I mean it's crazy because the fact is that you pay a penalty when you go out on strike. You lose a day's pay; and workers go to work mainly to get a paycheck. They don't go because they love to go to work; they want the money. . . .

As an old experienced trade unionist who views class struggle in a very serious way, [I know] that every fight that you get into is not necessarily a fight that you're going to win—or you should [even] fight under the conditions that the boss is in a better position than you are in. In other words, the weapon of strike is a Sunday punch and you don't use your Sunday punch every day of the week. There are a thousand different forms of resistance to the employers that you can employ under different circumstances. But many workers are not sophisticated enough to understand that.

Progressive leadership should be sensitive to the restlessness and moods of workers. . . . I think that part of claiming to be [a] progressive [leader] is to understand the moods of the people down below, and be sensitive to them, if not be able to anticipate [a] wildcat strike. You see, once you get out on strike, you got to get back into the plant; and that has to be negotiated; and to negotiate requires leadership. . . . So, everything about a wildcat is not positive, except that it says that workers are militant and they're not going to take the shit that is dished out to them. But after you say that, then what are you going to do about it? How do you do it in a way in which there are a minimum of victims?—because there's no great accomplishment. You get angry, and you cut your nose off to spite your face. Now, I'm not arguing against militant action. I'm saying that those of us who are more sophisticated about these things have to be aware of the consequences—not to head them off, but to read the signals. If you look at wildcat strikes, 80 percent of them have nothing but victims attached to them. So, that's not very smart.

I'm an old warrior. I know the difference between guerrilla warfare and positional warfare. One of the reasons we wage guerrilla warfare is because we're not strong enough to conduct positional warfare. So, when we conduct guerrilla warfare, it's hit and run, with the objective of causing as few casualties as possible to yourself.

Heroism manifests itself in many ways. One of the ways is not always that you destroy yourself. That's not heroism, that's suicide; and we've had enough revolutionary suicides for the last thirty years to last us for the next three hundred. So, that's why I say that when I hear or see or observe a wildcat strike, I look at it very, very carefully. On the one hand, it says militancy of the workers; and, on the other hand, it says there is something wrong here that workers have to express themselves in that way. . . .

You see, there's grievances there all the time. But the main thing is how . . . people are involved in the resolution of their grievances. That's really the most important thing. (The labor movement has become institutionalized. So, there are procedures, and so on and so forth, which are really intended not to settle grievances but to wear you out. But how do you get around that?)

Every time we got into a fight in the shop that I was in, the first thing I would do is count noses; if it was me and the guy that was aggrieved getting into a fight with the boss, I would say, "Let's wait five minutes and talk it over. Let's go find out why the guys are not supporting us." Because the name of the game is to win, not lose. . . . Not that you go into every struggle with the assurance that you're going to win it, sometimes you have no choice. What I'm saying is that if you do have the choice. . . . The question is, what do you do about it? How do you do it? . . . This struggle that we're in with the employers is one that will go on for many, many years, with time and time and time. (Even under the stage of socialism, we're going to have strikes and struggles.)

■   KENNETH ROCHE

[During World War II] there was no stoppages allowed. They had them, but the leadership came in and made them go back to work. At one time, . . . in the rolling mill, . . . several of the crane operators were overcome by fumes, and at that time the workers on the job walked off. . . . And the [other] workers walked off in sympathy, because these fumes were going up and making these people dizzy and giving them all kinds of fainting spells. They had a big meeting on it with the Ford Motor Company. Percy [Llewellyn] was in on it. He said, "Look," he says, "what's the big idea? You people are insisting that these people work in these cranes, when these fumes are bothering them." They said, "Well, they're supposed to work up there, and we don't see anything wrong with it." He said, "Well, it's dangerous for them to go up there." Anyway, the problem was solved by negotiation, and they were able to get the people back to work by promising that the condition would be taken care of . . . but I don't remember exactly how.

So, in cases where people were objecting to the conditions—?

If it's your health and safety involved, you were perfectly legitimate in going off the job. . . . A lot of times the company would put you in a position where your health was in danger, even during the war, we had a lot of cases like that. That's the one I remember most.

■ JOHN ORR

What do you think about the incentive pay issue during World War II?[43]

Well, some guys wanted it because it was the only way to beat the wage freeze. The guys that didn't want it, or ran on a campaign like Walter Reuther—he was going to eliminate incentive pay systems throughout the industry, and whatnot. Yet it was under his regime that [an] incentive system was put into the steel division in the Ford Motor Company. Of course, he didn't call it incentive pay, he called it "tonnage." They produced so much steel over and above a certain tonnage, they got a bonus. If you can tell me the difference between that— "tonnage"—and incentive pay, . . . then you got the answer. But the workers wanted it, and they still want it. Now they're faced with losing it, and they don't want to give it up.

Were you in favor or opposed to it during the war?

I was opposed to it. Well, I'll tell you, a lot of progressive stuff that would speed up the war work, and all this and that, I could never see it as a practical matter.

What did you think about the argument that that was the only way to increase the wages?

Well, that goes back as far as the incentive system is old. A norm would be set and you break that norm and you would get a part of the increase in wages. Of course, the boss got the bigger share of it be-

cause the more you make off the same machinery, the cheaper the
individual cost is. The per capita cost. But the next thing you knew
they combined and made a new time study and the norm . . . went up.
So it was a rat race. You could never win.

■ KENNETH ROCHE

This "sixty and out," they [the Reuther caucus] were opposed to that.
They want to get out at sixty years of age. Thirty and out. That came
from Flint. That was a very interesting fight because at that time Reuther wanted a profit-sharing plan, and the workers wanted a thirty-and-
out retirement. In other words, you work thirty years and you're out.
Finally, 98 percent of the people . . . at the UAW convention paraded
for twenty to twenty-five minutes with all these jackets, placards, and
everything else and Reuther said, "Well if that's what you want, I guess
you can have it, thirty-and-out." Since then, we have built on it. Now
they're proposing $1,500 for pension in the next contract, so I see they
started a movement for it. But all these were groundswell movements
that never had any impetus from the leadership. They were discouraged until the groundswell got so big that they had to move and to cede
to these people.

■ WILLIAM JOHNSON

In the Ford contract, we could always strike over rates on new jobs,
health and safety, and production standards. Those were three
strikeable issues during the life of a contract. We didn't have to wait
until the contract expired. We could strike on those issues as separate issues.

■ JOHN SAARI

We've been having five-year contracts for about thirty-eight years plus.
Now, they've dropped down to three-year contracts. Whereas, we felt
that a contract every year has two purposes. One, is the economy.
Whichever way it goes, [a one-year contract] gives you a chance to
recoup and renegotiate things. You get what I mean? Two, the fact
that . . . contract time is a good educational process. You get people
thinking. . . . We was always distributing literature. We used to write
up a piece of literature, and we'd be looking for a mimeograph machine at three o'clock in the morning, and we had to be at the gate at
five to pass them out. But we were there.

■ DAVE MOORE

In 1950, UAW signed an agreement with Ford that only authorized
strikes would be conducted, and that anyone who participates or in-
stigates an unauthorized strike can be discharged.

Well, the guys found ways of getting around that also. Union guys,
it didn't affect them. They walked out.

Or they fought in other ways. There were all kinds of ways a machine can be taken advantage of. Anybody can short-circuit a machine.
Anybody can cause a machine not to cut the stock properly. Say . . . that
lathe is your sole responsibility. Operator don't have a damn thing to
do but operate it. You the one that keep it in operation. You are getting paid for that. You can go read your books; as long as that machine
is running, you get your pay. . . . As long as that machine is running,
you are producing that stock properly. Now, the operator will be running it. And if the foreman . . . is giving guys a hard time, the job-set-
ter and the operators—Okay, tell you what, . . . that machine is supposed to cut that stock 45 percent depth. Now, it may go deeper than
that; that means that stock is scrapped; it's putting out scrap.

There are many things they could do. They have all kinds of ways
of getting back. These were some of the things that the guys used.

■ WALTER DOROSH

We shut down. Everybody said we had them by the throat, because
he [Ford] had the Lincoln plant, and that's all he had, besides . . . a few
satellite plants around the country. So, they made a decision that they
were going to decentralize that plant.[44] They were going to build plants
all around the country. And we went to court on that, in 1952. We went
before [federal] Judge Freeman in the city of Detroit. We had Ernie
Goodman, who used to be the UAW attorney before [Walter] Reuther. When Reuther took over, he threw him out, he was part of R. J.
Thomas's administration. We worked about three or four days, and we
presented the case. Our argument was that by the company decentral-
izing [this] makes our jobs insecure, of eighty thousand workers. . . .
The judge, in handing down his decision, said that the case is a good
case, that it was meritorious, and then he said that if he was to make
a ruling—he didn't say so much that he would rule in favor, but the
Ford Motor Company couldn't decentralize unless [Ford] talks to the
union.

But he said, "I cannot handle this case, I cannot make a decision,
because the . . . contract is not with Local 600, but with the interna-

tional union." He said, "I will give you so many days . . . to bring the international union in to join the local on this case." And then he will render his decision. I was on the staff then at the Local 600 with [Carl] Stellato. Stellato was president then, and he went down to see Walter Reuther, and he wouldn't see us. . . .

And he wouldn't join us in that case, and Judge Freeman then dismissed it. That case had serious ramifications. . . . If [we'd won] . . . that decision, industry would not just be able to close up a plant, move, down South, run away, because they want to make big profits in other locations. . . . It caused grave consequences for the community, for the city, and everybody.

I hope I never mellow. That's why I'm retired. I was administrative assistant with Leonard Woodcock, and then I worked for Doug Fraser. But I didn't work with him as his assistant. I worked with the skilled trades department. And when they started making all these concessions, I started arguing with him, all the guys, the last contract negotiations. I says, "This [is] contrary to all the basic things I learned in this trade union movement." And I projected, when I ran for election, I projected a proposition. "Okay," I said. "Okay, instead of making these concessions to the company, let's put them in a bank, let the company put them in a bank for us. They owe us this money; we take 40 cents cut, put 40 cents in there. When the company profits it can give the money back. I'm not interested in breaking a company." He [Fraser] said, "Oh, we are going to break this company." [I says,] "Don't worry about these capitalists, they take care of themselves. They don't need you to do their bidding for them."

■ DAVE MOORE

In spite of my differences with Walter Reuther, I'll say that . . . in his grave or wherever his ashes may be, he's fighting like hell today. I had many differences with Walter. I don't think Walter would have did some things, as far as a leader is concerned. . . . The things that we have won, I don't think we would have given up. And I know the guys who came along before, who were president before Walter, R. J. Thomas, Dick Leonard, and those guys, no, they wouldn't have ever given up anything. They would have never made any concessions. But now you have a different breed in the UAW. A different breed in many ways. You have a different breed in leadership. You have a different breed of personnel, and a different breed of the workers.

I know my experience has always been that if the leadership gives militant leadership, you will have a militant membership. If you have a conservative leadership, you will have a conservative membership. That doesn't mean that the membership is agreeing with everything the leadership's giving. But they had no one to go to bat for them when they faced the onslaught and the awesome power from the Ford Motor Company. "Let's now be nice to the company. Let's get a team [with the] company, with a program going where we share the responsibility." Well, the hell with the damn responsibility. That's their responsibility. "This is your plant," we are saying, "we got a union in here. Our people are going to have dignity and pride on the job. They are going to be respected by your foreman and supervisors. We got a contract with you, we expect you to live up to it." You are saying, . . . "The company has a right to do this. The company has a right to do that." Okay [we say], "You got that right. But you are going to exercise that right with some kind of responsibility. The contract says you got to do this."

But now, today there are concessions. The order of the day is pitting one plant against another plant. The order of the day is presenting one department against another department. It's finally got down to one worker against the other worker—which we fought so damn hard to eliminate. People died to prevent this kind of thing from continuing to happen. People got murdered. People got beaten. People went to jail. People suffered. People lost their jobs. People were ostracized to prevent the very thing that's happening today.

Black and White, Unite

■ STANLEY NOWAK

I was born in Poland, and you probably could guess that. I came to this country at the age of ten. My people and my entire family located in Chicago, in the packinghouse district. The famous Chicago packinghouse. I went there to parochial school, and my brothers worked at the packinghouse. That was during the First World War. At the conclusion of that war, there was a huge strike. First there was an attempt to . . . organize the packinghouse workers, and then the strike took place. . . . My brothers were participating in it. . . . The company brought in black people from the South to work as scabs. And I saw the white workers who were on the picket line—they could not put a picket line within the packinghouse because that was all company property; it [was] on the outside. They would drag—these pickets—would drag these black workers from the streetcars and beat them up. And I saw that. The only explanation my brothers could give me was, "Look, they are scabs and they are trying to break our union." The union was broken up, of course, and there were some very bloody fights.

■ SHELTON TAPPES

To blacks you—the union—did have an extra appeal, . . . equality and a chance to advance, where to whites, it was more economic . . . I think we had one black foreman in the whole plant, but we had about eighty straw bosses, black straw bosses.[45]

■ DAVE MOORE

I was born in the Deep South—born in the state of South Carolina, 1912. My father was a fireman on the railroad—white man's fireman on the railroad. . . . [Being a fireman] at that time, for a white man, was below his dignity. They only had blacks. Blacks could never become an engineer. My folks left South Carolina back in 1923, and we moved to Columbus, Ohio, and I attended some of the schools in Ohio.

My father had a cousin working in Detroit. The Ford Motor Company was paying 5 bucks a day. I went up there to get some of that big money. Left Ohio. I wasn't out of school. . . . My mother and father and younger brother stayed.

Later on they moved to Detroit, back in 1927–28. And I've been here since. . . .

At the time was your father employed at Ford?

My father was working at that time for a contractor here in Detroit. He didn't go to work for Ford because he could make more money from the contractor. Later he went to work at the Revere Copper and Brass. But he was laid off. . . .

I didn't like Detroit. I left here three times—ran away, went back to Ohio. Third time I left there [because] I couldn't make it. All my family was here, and I stayed here. As you know, the depression hit this country in 1929, and I came from a large family. There were eleven of us—seven boys, two girls, plus my mother and father. And naturally, being black we got hit the hardest. Many whites were hit also. The depression didn't spare anybody. . . . But the blacks was always the last hired and the first fired. And with a growing family of seven boys and two girls, it was real difficult for us to get along. But we struggled.

I came back here in 1935, back to Detroit, and I got a job out at Briggs Manufacturing Company at Chrysler—got used to making bodies for Chrysler, and for the whole GM setup. I got hired in there, 32 cents an hour. They had all the black guys sanding the bodies with their hands. And you could sand, . . . and you just got so tired. 32 cents an hour, they was paying the blacks—32 cents an hour to sand. . . . The bodies were sanded out, and then went to where the white guys were, who put what you call the primer on; and they were getting 36 cents an hour, 4 cents more an hour than we were. But we had to do all the hard work. And [the bodies] went to another section in the lot where they sprayed paint on, and they were getting 4 cents an hour more than the other white guys were.

■ HORACE SHEFFIELD

I didn't really grow up in a union family. But I grew up in a family that encouraged thought. . . . But, in fact, [during the organizing], my dad opposed the union [at Rouge]. . . . [He] was in the production foundry. He became a foreman. Later, however, [he] changed, and he became active in the foremen's union out there. . . .

Early on in my life, very early on, I got involved in a range of activities. I joined the NAACP when I was about sixteen or seventeen. . . . That was around the time of the depression. . . . I began to get a little active, agitating around the depression and that sort of thing. I was never an ideologue. I guess I became very conscious of the discrimination that evolved on black folks. And that affected me very much.

Did you get any of that from your father?

Well, of course, my parents, they would talk about it at home, and then I began to read, I was aware of it—hangings and that sort of thing, and the various things that blacks felt. So, that had a very strong impact on me . . . [and] gave me some of the elements of militancy very early on in my life. . . . I had been exposed to some socialist groups, young groups. I had gotten involved with the . . . national youth group to fight against the war. Of course, there were other blacks in Detroit who really got caught in these kind of movements too. So, I was certainly ready for leadership in this kind of effort to organize Ford's.

■ SHELTON TAPPES

Most of my friends and companions as I grew up here [in Detroit] were from Georgia, Alabama, Louisiana, Mississippi, and . . . Arkansas. Most people didn't believe me when I told them I was from Nebraska, because it was very unusual to find a black person who was born in the North.

[At school in Omaha] in the eighth grade, I was the only black boy in the class; and there was only one black girl in the class.

Was that all your schooling—eighth grade?

No, I graduated from high school, and went four and a half months to the University of Nebraska.

My father was from Mississippi. When he was fourteen, he left home. His parents sent him away because they were afraid he was a little bit too outspoken and they were afraid he wouldn't live to be twenty-one. So they sent him away, sent him to Memphis. This was when World War I was brewing, and the nation was getting prepared, and one of the industries that was preparing was the meat industry, so, first he went to Chicago to get a job in the packing plants, and couldn't make it there. So he went to Omaha, and Omaha at that time was the third-largest meat-packing city in the country behind St. Louis. It was Chicago, St. Louis, and then Omaha and St. Joseph, Missouri, these were the four meat packing [cities]. So, he went to Omaha and he got a job there, and that's where he met my mother. My mother is from Kansas. . . . Her father had passed, and she and her sisters were so happy to get away from the farm that they rushed to Omaha, where their brother, their only brother, lived. He left the farm as soon as he was old enough. Their old man must have been quite a tyrant. So the girls came to Omaha, and she met my dad. I was born there.

You said something about your father having been too outspoken?

Yeah, they were afraid that he would be lynched or something in Mississippi. My father hated the word *Negro*. He said, "You are 'black.'" That's sixty years ago or more now.

Was there a large black community there when you were growing up?

Not a large one, but a pretty, well, I guess a pretty well-established black community. . . . There wasn't any really established black neighborhood. There were pockets where people sort of migrated together. But generally speaking you'd go, I never knew what discrimination was, like movies and things like that, until I came here.

When I came to Detroit, I never will forget, I went to the Michigan Theater, the Adams Theater. I went to see Al Jolson in the first talking picture, and he was black-faced, "Sonny Boy," that's when he sang "Sonny Boy." They tried to get me to go upstairs. I said, "No, I don't like to go upstairs, I like to sit downstairs." And then we had a word or two, but I still went downstairs and sat where I wanted.

Was your father involved with the union also?

No, he wasn't. My father disliked unions, because his only experience was with the AF of L. My uncle was a bricklayer, this was my mother's brother. He was a journeyman, and a journeyman is qualified at any time to supervise a job. You know, the Bricklayers Union is kind of peculiar—everybody belonged, foremen and all, and superintendents. . . . So, my uncle at various times was the foreman. But he couldn't join the union.

■ JOHN SAARI

My first wife was a southerner from Tennessee. My present wife is from Kentucky. So, I must love the southerner. But when I married the first one (she passed away, died of tuberculosis), well, the people she knew up here, they wrote letters to their hometown and said that "Blanche married a black foreigner." So I told Blanche, "Well, gee, it's about time we take a run down to your hometown." She was afraid because I was foreign, foreign name. . . . So, we went down, and when . . . they introduced me, they saw me, and they expected to see, with them they attach blackness with being foreign. So, they got an education there. They say, "Well, a foreigner can be white too."

■ DELORIS AND KENNETH ROCHE

Kenneth Roche: The southerners were definitely anti-Negro and anti-
Catholic and anti-Jew, the same as they are now. The maintenance unit
was what you call a real, real racist unit in the Ford Motor Company.
Largely southerners. Millwrights, riggers, hookers, people like that, and
always rednecks. Rednecks from the South was in the leadership of
that unit.

Why was that? They had gotten the skills in the South?

I don't know whether they got the skills in the South. I don't think
they did, but they got them when they come up here because it doesn't
take much skill to be a millwright. You carry a wrench around, a pair
of pliers and things like that. Doesn't take skill. You move stuff on
production lines and you move machinery. . . . There wasn't anybody
black in their unit, one or two at the most in the maintenance unit.
You would never find any blacks in the maintenance unit. They were
very, very racist. They go like this, such and such and so and so is running for office.

What does this mean?

Deloris Roche: We didn't know either.

Kenneth Roche: I didn't know at first. They go like this. Like you're
coloring your face. . . . That's the way they believe.

Deloris Roche: Or the expressions they used. We weren't familiar,
we never used to talk like this—"jungle bunnies."

■ SHELTON TAPPES

I didn't get a job in the automobile plant until 1937. But there are a
lot of us who went down to Detroit's Fort Shelby [Hotel, for the first
UAW convention in 1935], out of curiosity. The peculiar thing about
that convention was that there was one black delegate in that group,
just one, and I stumbled upon that very fellow. About two hundred delegates came, and they were from Michigan, Wisconsin, Ohio, Indiana
and Illinois, principally. There might have been some from Pennsylvania, some few, but if there were, they were with the Ohio delegation.
And this black fellow was in the Ohio delegation.

Later on, I found out from someone that this black delegate—he
couldn't remember his name—had been at the first convention of the
UAW, where the UAW was founded, in the Fort Shelby Hotel. . . . He
was telling us how Dillon [the AFL organizer] had berated him for
bringing this "Nigger" to "our convention," as he put it. . . . "Oh, he
just reamed me," he said, "for bringing this fellow." But, he said, he

was a nice fellow. "We worked with him, he's a member of the union." Dillon couldn't understand it. But that was the sense of the times I guess.

■ DAVE MOORE

It was there, the desire and cooperation among each other, the concern for each other, especially at Local 600. I don't think there was any, in fact I know by experience in the labor movement, there was never a local in the whole UAW that I have known where the solidarity and the togetherness and the brotherhood was more exhibited by the blacks and the whites as in the Local 600.

Why do you think that was the case in Local 600?

Well, I think it was because number one, because of the people who were involved in organizing Local 600.

Guys like a [Walter] Dorosh, guys like a Bill McKie, guys like a Johnny Gallo, and who had not only said it, but demonstrated by action, "The only way we are going to ever get beat by the Ford Motor Company. . . . All of us got to be together. We should not be divided based on race. What happens . . . to Dave Moore as a black man [happens to] Sally Jones as a white woman." And this was instilled in the Ford workers. They had a close-knit brotherhood there. There is still some semblance of it still existing today, but not like it did at that time, 1941 on up until just a few years ago, in fact. . . because of the leadership and the particular type of the individuals who were involved in organizing the Ford plant at that time—because they, the byword in this system was, . . . "The only way we are going to accomplish our objective is, we got to be [together]—regardless of what your religion or your political thing, your ethnic background or your racial identity may be." They wouldn't tolerate it. . . . I never seen anything like it before. I haven't seen it happen since. . . .

I always said that whatever the leadership of any organization does, it reflects on the membership. And it most certainly happened at Ford during the organizing drive in the UAW. Those in charge of . . . organizing the UAW in the Ford plant exhibited and carried out in their own way and handed it on down to the membership; and nowhere in the UAW have I witnessed any examples of brotherhood more than I have seen in the Local 600. And that goes all the way after we organized it, to conventions, and where discrimination is still rampant in our society. . . . Take back in the 1940s and '50s, there were some hotels where black delegates to a UAW convention couldn't get in there. But . . . if a black guy was being refused admittance to a hotel or motel, . . . that hotel

was almost torn apart and would have been torn apart, if they didn't
give them a room. White guys was doing it for us. And we even had run-
ins with other locals in the UAW. The white guys did, from Local 600,
defending black guys. Some of the white guys from other locals around
the country [would say], "Just what in the hell are you doing, . . . he's a
Negro, he can't do it, he can't eat in this room with the rest of us." . . .
[But] these [Local 600] white guys, "God damn it, if he don't eat in here,
nobody is going to eat. . . ." And we put up a picket line, sometimes we
did. The white guys themselves would organize.

But at some point time catches up with them. Most of them gone
on now, some of them dead and gone a lot of them retired and not
active anymore. But these are things that happened. And after it [Lo-
cal 600] was organized, then war came and a lot of blacks and whites
came from the South here. Housing become an issue. Certain places
in the city didn't want blacks. Projects were being built. We in Local
600 were insisting that these projects being built by the federal government, using [our] money, is open to everybody. Even some of the
damn government officials say, "Well, you can't do that. You can't let
blacks in here. You can't let whites in here either." And they tried to
pit some of our own white guys against the blacks, moving in different projects. But we—the whites and the blacks—would picket and
demonstrate together.

We fought for integrated housing, at that time during the war. "We
got a damn war going, our future is at stake, and you say Hitler is the
enemy. Damn it to hell. . . . The guy's on the verge of going to the army
to give up his life of defense of you, and you're telling us that he can't
live here. Here, he got his draft papers in his pocket, and looking for
a place for his family to live to go to defend this place, and you tell
me that he can't live. Well, to hell with that crap." And as I say, I go
back again, these were things that were did by guys from Local 600.
We had some from other—I won't say that other locals were just antiblack. You had individuals in those locals, but it was not as overwhelming and together in the other locals in Detroit . . . as it was in . . . Local
600.

*Were you successful in any of those attempts to get the government
to integrate housing?*

Oh yes, oh yes. I'll give an example. You take the Sojourner Project
out here in northeast Detroit, that was one. You take the Herman Gar-
dens over here on the west side, that was one. And you take the neighborhoods themselves, where individual housing, where blacks had
never lived before in some neighborhoods here in the city of Detroit.
The only time they were there, they were serving as domestics, or

chauffeurs or something like that. But you would always find—we had what you call a flying squad at Local 600. Wherever there was a trouble spot you had this flying squad. These were guys we called the head crackers, black and white. (I got my uniform home yet. . . .) And wherever there would be a trouble spot, whether it was involving the union or whatever it was, if it was involving a worker, whatever the problem was, black or white worker, the flying squad from Local 600 is going over to give this guy some help. "We want 50 guys here at 6 tomorrow morning. We are going to go to Samanski's house, Samanski's having some trouble with the police department." Or he is having some trouble with this, whatever it was we were there.

It sounds like you sort of modeled after the teams that went out with the unemployed councils.

Yeah, well that's where we took our [idea], in fact we were the first local, and the whole UAW organized what you called a flying squad. . . . All their locals followed our lead later on. . . .

The true history, I say just the *true* history . . . [of] the labor movement and the union organization of plants here in Detroit has never been written . . . from the standpoint of the rank and file . . . especially the participation and the contribution that the blacks made in organizing the union here in this town. It has never been written. And it has been deliberately concealed. When I say deliberately, I can prove it was deliberate. And this has been one of my sore spots with the leadership of the UAW, including Walter Reuther, he's dead and gone, God bless his soul, and he and I had many run-ins on this. I was kicked out of the UAW for twelve years along with Johnny Gallo, along with Paul Boatin, and along with others. . . . And even after we made all this fight with the companies . . . the same damn discrimination began to involve itself in the UAW as a whole . . . around the country and at conventions.

I was among those who took Walter on many times about discrimination in the UAW and the record shows that from the time we organized the UAW, no blacks, man or woman, sat on the board in any major position up until 1961. It took us that long to get it, 1961, yeah 1961, and yet they were going all around the damn country hollering about democracy and what the UAW stands for. And this was one of my sore spots with Walter and others around him and others before him and others to come on. And if you look back in the scenes of the UAW convention, Buffalo convention, the 1943 convention, the 1946 convention, the 1947 convention, the 1948 convention, the 1949 convention, the 1950 convention, you will see that this issue was one of the main issues of the convention. And I'm proud to say that I was involved in it. . . . Local 600 was carrying the torch—black and white.

The local was giving dances, blacks and whites dancing together. They would give picnics, the kids were there playing together, they would give, they would have choral ensembles, all of them singing in the choir together, they had bands, they played together, in the Labor Day marches all of them competed for prizes, and this kind of thing. Even though they weren't living in the same neighborhood together, they would visit each other, and these are the kind of social activities, I think, that went on that helped elevate this brotherhood and togetherness more openly and more viable and more determined.

Did you have a big showing at those social events? A lot of people came out?

Oh, yes. Again I go back to Local 600. We had what we call one of the biggest halls there. During the winter months, we have all of our activities inside. During the summer months, we have events at Belle Isle. We would have them at some of the big parks outside the city, city-owned parks, like Rouge Park during the parades. After the parades were all over, guys would get together with their families, the kids down by the river down here, go to Belle Isle, say, "Local 600 is going to have a picnic, a Labor Day picnic after the parade." The parade was the highest big point in labor in the city of Detroit at one time. Everybody participated in the Labor Day parade in the streets. It was just something like the Mardi Gras in New Orleans and every local had their own band. They would compete who had the best flying squad, who had the best band, and who performed in the parade better, you know what I mean. The precision march or just slow march or whatever it was.

And we all assembled down here in a place called Cadillac Square after the parade is over. That's where most of the presidents would come, Truman, Eisenhower, everybody would come to Local 600 on election year to make a speech. We would have 120,000, almost 150,000, people in this square, and everybody stayed; nobody left. They put all their instruments down and sat and waited for the speaker to start. And this was the highlight of labor in this town. Everybody looked forward, when the Labor Day parade was over they started to building for the next year. Floats, beauty queens.

We had black beauty queens, winning black contests here in the city of Detroit. . . . Labor coming from labor, black women. Nowhere in the country would you find an organization [that] predominantly whites were sponsoring, that would select a black woman for a beauty queen. . . . It was unheard of. But we had it here. Some of the leading performers of the stage and theater came here. Paul Robeson, Humphrey Bogart, Dalton Trumbo, Kirk, what's the guy's name? Douglas, Kirk Douglas, he's the guy, they would come to the Local 600.[46]

Rioter injured in Ford Hunger March, March 7, 1932. (Archives of Labor and Urban Affairs, Wayne State University)

The funeral for five workers killed during the Ford Hunger March, Communist Party Headquarters. (Archives of Labor and Urban Affairs, Wayne State University)

Scores of thousands of workers line the sidewalks along Woodward Avenue as the funeral march passes. Banners call upon the workers to join the Auto Workers Union. (Archives of Labor and Urban Affairs, Wayne State University)

The Rouge Complex in Dearborn, Michigan, was the single largest industrial unit in the world. (Archives of Labor and Urban Affairs, Wayne State University)

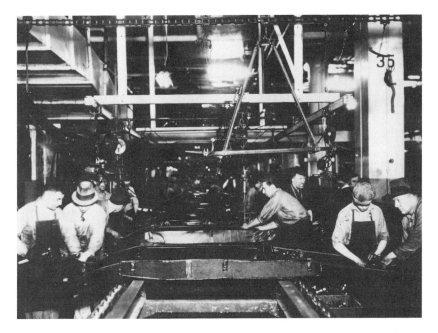

Ford Motor Company assembly lines, 1932. (Archives of Labor and Urban Affairs, Wayne State University)

A Ford worker during the 1930s. (Archives of Labor and Urban Affairs, Wayne State University)

Union organizers hand out leaflets at the Rouge gates during the 1940s. (Archives of Labor and Urban Affairs, Wayne State University)

Strikers outside the Rouge plant, 1941. (Archives of Labor and Urban Affairs, Wayne State University)

Strikers outside the Rouge plant, 1941. (Archives of Labor and Urban Affairs, Wayne State University)

Ford NLRB election, May 1941. Michael Widman and R. J. Thomas holding sign. (Archives of Labor and Urban Affairs, Wayne State University)

The Ford Motor Company, represented by Harry Bennett (in bow tie), and the United Auto Workers sign first contract. Seated at left is CIO President Philip Murray. At Bennett's right is UAW President R. J. Thomas and Secretary-Treasurer George Addes. Standing, extreme left, is Michael Widman; at the extreme right, UAW General Counsel Maurice Sugar and CIO General Counsel Lee Pressman. (Archives of Labor and Urban Affairs, Wayne State University)

Voting at UAW Local 600. (Archives of Labor and Urban Affairs, Wayne State University)

Left to right: Nelson Davis, Percy Llewellyn, Shelton Tappes, and W. G. "Bill" Grant. (Archives of Labor and Urban Affairs, Wayne State University)

Ford Motor Company assembly line, 1949. (Archives of Labor and Urban Affairs, Wayne State University)

John L. Lewis visits UAW Local 600 [1951]. Left to right: William Hood, Carl Stellato, Lewis, Pat Rice, and Michael Widman. (Archives of Labor and Urban Affairs, Wayne State University)

Some of the Local 600 representatives at the 1947 UAW convention. (Paul Boatin)

Ken Bannon (Archives of Labor and Urban Affairs, Wayne State University)

Paul and Anne Boatin

Walter Dorosh

John Mando, 1953

Bill McKie (photo by Mike
Zarro, Archives of Labor and
Urban Affairs, Wayne State
University)

Art McPhaul, 1973

Dave Moore

John Orr

Margaret and Stanley Nowak

Victor Reuther (Archives of
Labor and Urban Affairs,
Wayne State University)

Walter Reuther (Archives of
Labor and Urban Affairs,
Wayne State University)

Kenneth L. Roche

John "Whitey" Saari, 1952

Horace Sheffield (Archives of Labor and Urban Affairs, Wayne State University)

Shelton Tappes (Archives of Labor and Urban Affairs, Wayne State University)

Saul Wellman (Archives of Labor and Urban Affairs, Wayne State University)

■ WALTER DOROSH

[In the] 1946 [UAW] convention, I think it was, the left wing introduced a resolution at the convention suggesting that a UAW black vice
president be created. The Reuther forces objected to this, and said that
it was "reverse discrimination, putting the blacks in a box, [they] could
only run for that job." . . . If you get the proceedings of the '46 convention, it was at Buffalo, I think, the left wing said, . . . "The reason
we are suggesting this is because there are a lot of black workers in
the UAW. They have no representation, and they ought to have at least
one black representative that they could point to." But the board consisted of twenty-six representatives, and . . . if I remember, one-quarter of the membership of the UAW [was black] and they have no representation. And surprisingly one of the chief spokesmen against it was
Horace Sheffield. He was one of the black community leaders. . . . And
he spoke against it. He is the guy that coined the phrase that it's "reverse discrimination." He admitted since then it was a very sad mistake, that he was deluded by Walter Reuther. . . . Walter used him ex-
tensively whenever there was a black and white issue, Horace Sheffield
would be there always taking [the] side of the administration. . . .
    That was one issue that divided us considerably. . . . Walter Reuth-
er was good on the black issue, he was very good on it, he supported, let's say after the Buffalo convention, he saw the mistake, but he
couldn't reverse it, because the people that comprised his right-wing
leadership were antiblack at that time. Strongly antiblack, and they
didn't care, they were indifferent about it. (In other words, they had
in some respects the same attitude that the AF of L had . . . towards
production workers. "You should be organized into a skill." And we
couldn't convince them to organize the production workers, the basic steel industry workers.) But the civil rights issues divided the two
groups considerably. The question of opening new opportunities for
blacks. The progressives were always projecting ideas, programs for
promoting blacks into jobs. In other words, giving them their day in
court. They [the Reuther caucus] couldn't see it, and it was that kind
of philosophy, I believe, that time will take care of everything. It
doesn't always hold true, because so many things can happen.

■ SAUL WELLMAN

The Communists were advocating black-white unity. And they were
trying to practice it. But that wasn't easy.
    So, for example, in 1941, when the Communists were in a promi-

nent position to contribute to the determination of who the leadership was going to be in the new Local 600, they proposed that one of the four top officers should be a black. It was agreed that the office of recording secretary would go to a black. That's when Shelton Tappes was elected; and from 1941 until 1986, the position of recording secretary of Local 600 has always gone to a black, even though the levels of black leadership now go far beyond that.

But in 1942 at the Buffalo [UAW] convention, a half a dozen Communists who were delegates proposed, at the point of the election of national leaders, that one of the three top leaders be a black. They didn't propose a name, they just said that, "We have to select one of the people to be a black." And they were demolished, absolutely demolished.

■ SHELTON TAPPES

[An] antiblack committeeman, he may not take up a grievance just because the person is black. I can recall one . . . very glaring case. . . . A woman was charged with ringing the time card of a man who they purported was her boyfriend. They said they saw her make two passes at the time clock; and each time she made a pass she had a card in her hand. They said that they never saw this fellow ring the card out, but later they saw she and he walk out of the plant "almost arm in arm." They let the grievance go up.

I just happened to be in the unit visiting, and they told me about the case. They said, "Of course, we didn't take it up." They said, "We're not going to appeal it." I said, "How much time do you have on the case yet?" They said, "Oh, a couple more days." I said, "Appeal it. Let me turn it down." Well, it was Ford Department C [?], and I handled that unit's grievances at the umpire level.

So, anyway, I checked this grievance out. The foreman claimed he had seen this lady make two passes at the time clock. And I found out that the place where he said that he stood and watched her was so far from that clock, there's no way for him to have been able to say what cards—if she did have two cards—which ones she rang out. Therefore, as far as I was concerned, the man was innocent. Now, we've got to prove that [the foreman] didn't see her make two passes. Or if she did make two passes, she had the same card, which was pretty easy to do. . . . The old clock, you'd hit it with one hand and hold the card with the other, but these new clocks you put the card in and [it's supposed to punch automatically]. So, if it doesn't do it, then you'd do it again, okay.

So, then, on this "arm and arm stuff," here is the story. I find out that these people ate lunch together every day, and she brought the lunch, a beautiful lunch, and she'd spread it out, and they would eat. Then he'd go back to his job, and she'd go to hers. Of course, she had a husband, and he had a wife. This went on every day, and they did leave the shop rather intimately, okay. The one thing, though, that hadn't been brought out was that this fellow, when he got her out of the plant, he deposited her in a car with her husband. Now wait a minute. He was black, and she was white. Now, here, this is the problem.

The man whom she had lunch with—

Was black. She was white. Well, what they didn't know was, these two people had been kids in kindergarten together, and had been raised all their life—their mothers were friends, their fathers were friends, and they had been raised up together. And the husband was just as much a friend of this guy as she was, because the two families had fun, they even took their vacations together and all this, okay.

So, anyhow I unraveled all of it; and we won the case, by the way. He was restored to work with all back pay and everything; and she was restored her job with all back pay and everything. But she didn't come back, because of the nasty stuff that was going on around about her among the other women.

Here was a case where the company insinuated that there was something off-color going on; and the union picked it up. . . . And if I hadn't been there, they would never have made [an appeal].

■ ARCHIE ACCIACCA

We were making this supercharger job, we were making parts for tanks, we were making various parts for defense and all the seniority was interchangeable.[47] Anyhow, the supercharger job was going out, and in our building there were two departments of the aircraft building where . . . they were assembling certain parts for the Pratt & Whitney engine. When this supercharger job was starting to take people off, phasing out, high seniority guys would come along, and I had a job to see to it that they were placed, replacing junior people. Well, two black guys [with seniority] happened to come along, nice guys, that were inspectors. The youngest [two workers] happened to have been in the Pratt & Whitney engine department . . . so the representation came out of Pratt & Whitney—that was a plant on its own. . . . But since they were geographically located in the pressed steel they applied seniority with us, understand? . . .

So, anyhow, when these two black guys come through, being inspectors, and the two youngest were over there, I gave them a slip to go down there; and they replaced the two youngest ones. Holy Toledo, not only was it bad that they went over there, but two blacks coming down there, there wasn't a black person in there. Two blacks went down there, and holy, all hell broke loose and they had a wildcat over it. Man, I told them, "No way," then I stood my guns all the more. I told them, "Those people are going to go in there." And I went to labor relations and said, "You better not take them out of there." They wouldn't go back to work. They got people from the local union to come over and talk to them. I talked to them. After a while they went back to work.

■ SHELTON TAPPES

One outstanding thing that happened in the motor building was the trials of O'Brien and Fitzcasey, who were midnight shift committeemen who had gone to one of the white girls, and asked her why she was always having lunch at this table where the black girls sat and ate. And when she told them that they were her friends, why they started some kind of a movement with the supervision, some kind of plot with supervision and they got her fired. Of course, she was pretty astute, and she informed the day shift and explained to them everything that happened. So it winds up at a big meeting at MacKenzie High School on Sunday, and they asked me to come out there.

Gee, that place was jammed with people standing along the walls, and Paul Boatin was at his best that day. He made a speech I'll never forget. Oh, he roasted those two guys, so he recommended that they set up a trial committee and these fellows be kicked out of the union pending trial and everything he proposed went over, and of course the local had to put them back to work because they hadn't been found guilty. So we said until they're found guilty, but we took their committee posts away from them and they had to go to work. So anyway they had the trial and these fellows were found guilty and I forget what the sentence was, but they were suspended from the union for some length of time, couldn't hold office but they were allowed to work because, [it was] a little patriotic thing, being wartime and stuff.

Then later on one of the fellows, O'Brien, sued the union for a quarter of a million dollars and he named Bill Grant, Paul Boatin, Bill Cooper and myself and the local union. We had a trial that lasted about five weeks, and I was on the stand for three days myself. It was so funny, the lawyer he had was Davidow. . . . He was the original counsel for the UAW before [Maurice] Sugar. . . . And he was fired by R. J. Thomas for his right-wing tendencies. . . . The first question Davidow asked me, "Are you a subscriber to the *Daily Worker?*"[48] Well, anyway, the case, we won the case, directed verdict, so we never even had to put our case in.

Davidow exercised his right under the statute to call the defense witnesses, and the judge explained to him that he has a right to do that, however he has to accept their testimony. So he called, grandstanding, Walter Reuther, R. J. Thomas, George Addes, all international officers and then Local Union 600 officers.

What they [the supporters of O'Brien and Fitzcasey] were hanging their hat on was, when the matter left the unit after the unit made its decision, it went to the General Council; and the General Council debated that thing for an hour or two, and they finally upheld the decision of the unit. My secretary, through a typo, failed to put down that the motion had passed. All she put down was "motion made" and then under the motion she said "supported," but she never put "carried." It was an oversight, because everybody in that meeting knew that the motion had carried. . . . I think we had a division of the house and all kind of howling going on, points of information and all that jazz. . . . Anyway, that was what he [Davidow] was trying to hang his hat on. The left and right got together on that one. Even though the right-wingers were the ones who had voted against the adoption of the unit's report, when they got down there in the court they all testified that the motion had passed, and that there had been a fair decision, and all that sort of thing. So, when it comes to defending the union, why they all move together.

■ JOHN ORR

[The blacks became prounion] for several reasons. It's hard to explain. There were new avenues opened to them, positions of leadership, even if it was a job steward in his own department, it was something he had never attained in his life before, or on the bargaining committee, bargaining for several thousand of his subordinates, chairman of the building, and what not.

■ SHELTON TAPPES

They were what we call hill-billies, but usually from Appalachia, Virginia, West Virginia, Southern Pennsylvania, Maryland. . . . They were antiunion, and antiblack too. I'll recite an experience. This was after I had been defeated as recording secretary before I became education director, in 1944.

[I was elected to the bargaining committee]. . . . So, one of the first
duties I got was a call from the Labor Relations Office. They said, "Shelton, you know, we have a new method now whenever a fellow quits,
we don't allow him to quit unless there is a union representative
present, and we'd like for you to come down and talk to this fellow."
So, I came down and I walked in, and he introduced me to the guy,
and told the fellow who I was. He said, "Now, fellow, before you say
anything to me, I just want you to know I just can't help it, I can't help
it. I tried but I just can't help it."

"Tried what?"

"I tried to work with them."

Well, as it turns out he had been given a job with a black foreman.
And, of course, there were some black fellow workers there. And he
said he tried, I believe he did, he tried very earnestly. But he said, "My
upbringing. I have never been around them." I said, "You haven't been
around who?" He said, "The Ni—colored people."

He just insisted that he had to quit. "I don't want to hold anything
against those people or anything like that. But I just can't help it, that's
the way I was raised."

So he quit.

■ DAVE MOORE

There were forces in the UAW never did want to see blacks get the
recognition that they deserved, for the contribution they made during the organization part of the UAW. Not just talking about Ford, but
I'm talking about General Motors, Chrysler, all of them. You should
know this. Racism is a part of our society, I don't give a damn what
nobody say. . . . I had to face it [racism] ever since I was born. My
mother and father faced it. My grandfather and grandmother faced it.
My great-great faced it, ever since that ship sailed along the shores of
Africa.

And for any major white organization or institution to come along
and advocate equality of all of its members at that time and even today to a certain extent, was not a popular stand for a white person to
take. For [Local 600's] membership consisted of the majority white,
almost 80 percent or 90 percent white. But there were some whites
who were willing to do that. . . . To be part of the UAW's history, and
to be part of the UAW's way of advocating democracy itself. And some
elements in the UAW didn't want that. And they not only didn't want
it, they would damn sure be willing to go to hell and back to prevent
it. And they did. (And when the issue of "Communism" came along,

well, it was grabbed and seized upon by those in the labor movement as well. Many people were eliminated, not only in the UAW, not only by Walter Reuther, but throughout the whole labor movement, the UAW, the longshoremen, the textile workers, the farm workers.)

Take a look at the proceedings in 1949 UAW convention in Milwaukee. A guy named Bill Johnson, a black guy, made one of the most profound speeches on why a Negro should be advanced to the UAW executive board. And the answer to that was that, "You are following the Communist Party line. The only people who want to have a black on the UAW executive board is a Communist or Communist sympathizer. And this is nothing but Communist propaganda." That's the answer they gave us. We had supporters. This wasn't all just coming from [Local] 600. We had supporters from other locals throughout the whole country at these conventions on this issue.

Walter [Dorosh] played a hell of a role, and he was ostracized. He was called a Nigger lover. He was called a Communist. But he stuck to his guns. And I think he made, along with others, he made a major contribution to the cause of civil rights, and equal rights, and promotions of blacks to positions of leadership in Local 600. He got a hell of a history behind him. I admire the guy. He's been a friend of mine over the years. And I have seen him when it was impossible for a white person do so some things that he did.

I will give you an example. In 1973, as late as 1973, when Coleman Young ran for mayor of the city of Detroit, the UAW was pushed against the wall as to who it was going to support. You know, the UAW didn't support Young when he ran. Walter was president of Local 600 at the time; and he defied the whole international union, and had Local 600 go on record as supporting Coleman Young. . . . But he had the support of the membership of Local 600—black and white. You had some whites in Local 600 who didn't support Coleman. But they were in the minority.

■   HORACE SHEFFIELD

Which caucus do you think overall was more concerned with fighting racism?

Well, let me tell you. Let me be perfectly candid now when you say, "more concerned." If you wanted to say who was more vocal, I would say the left wing. That was, meetings, and every place else. That does not say that Walter Reuther was less concerned. Some of the forces in the right wing were not less concerned. Now, I would say one of the

differences, there may have been a larger number of members in the
right wing who were not as concerned as some of the leadership like
Walter Reuther and the rest of them. But now when it gets down, really being vocal, though, being extremely vocal, during those days was
important. For whatever reason they did it, that's what got the left wing
a lot of credit. Okay? But I would say that there were forces in the right
wing, or else I wouldn't have stayed, who . . . were deeply concerned.

■ VICTOR REUTHER

While sometimes the caucuses of the UAW on both sides, both caucuses, wanted to use the racial situation to prove that they were the
ones who were the strongest in supporting the blacks, the truth of the
matter is that neither caucus could move faster than the educational
work in the union permitted it; and, secondly, we were damn fortu-
nate in the UAW that both caucuses always advocated representation
for blacks and for women—both caucuses always did. They may have
differed on making it a part of the constitution before the educational
work was done.

When you realize that we came out of an atmosphere in Detroit of
race riots, no group contributed more to an easing of the relationship
between races than the UAW, and I credit both caucuses for that.[49] You
know, I am delighted that the black issue was never made a real factional issue.

■ SHELTON TAPPES

[Carl] Stellato and a group of his staff members, including myself, had
gone down to Reuther's office and requested that he place at least one
black representative on the national Ford staff. The national Ford staff
at that time had seven people besides the director, and they were all
white. Reuther agreed. Reuther says, "Whoever you want," he says,
"we'll put on." We said, "We can't name your staff for you." So, we sent
him a list of eligible people, but didn't put my name on there; and we
didn't put Jimmy Watts's name, who was also out there at the time.[50]
Seven people.

They called all these fellows down one by one, and interviewed
them, and went over their background, and, to our dismay, they didn't
hire any of them, and said, "None of them are acceptable enough,
because we feel that the first one should be somebody that is beyond
reproach. Nobody can say he can't cut the mustard. He's got to know
the contract. He's got to be somebody that we can set up as an exam-

ple, and not be somebody that would set us back. There are some Ford plants where a black representative better know what he's doing when he goes." . . .

So, about a week later, here comes Jack Conway, and he said he wanted to spend some time with me.[51] "I won't interfere with your work. I'll just sit with you. We'll go to lunch together." For two days he really pressed me. So, finally, he got the three of us together—Carl, myself, and Jack; and we got in that office; and Jack laid it out to us. He said, "Walter insists that Shelton be the man. He's got the experience. He's well known; and there can be nobody who would be able to say that he couldn't do the job. He would be received by the other Ford locals no matter where they are, because they all know him, and they know his reputation. That's the reason Walter wants him." . . .

So, well, Carl—Carl is the one that really hammered the nail in place, because he said, "Look, I was down there running my mouth. I requested they put a black on, and now they're willing to do it." He said, "How will it look? I'm the advocate. How will it look if my own staff member refuses to take the job?" Okay, there I am.

■ SAUL WELLMAN

Detroit was the final destination of the Abolitionist Underground railway of pre-Civil War days. Blacks were an integral part of the early work force of the newly developing automobile industry at the turn of the century. They were in the plants during the early union organizing days. A community of resistance and struggle already existed, be it in the neighborhoods or plants which produced the first black mayor—the present mayor—Coleman Young. He and others worked closely with the Communists in the 1940s and '50s.

To this day he cannot be red-baited for that relationship. And when he is questioned, Young says, "Yes, I worked with Communists. I respected them highly. My main concern has been the interests of my people. In the 1930s, the 1940s, and the 1950s, the only whites in this community who ever gave support to the black struggle were the Communists. I certainly found it easy to gravitate towards them, and I certainly am not going to turn my back on them today." Now, that's quite a statement. This isn't just that Coleman Young is a principled person. He reflects the attitude of a substantial part of the black community. Another person is George Crockett, the congressman, who went to jail after serving as defense counsel of national Communist leaders in 1949. The 13th Congressional District elects him. And re-elects him, and reelects him. He can say things some people consider outrageous about advanced political questions and nobody looks askance.[52]

All I'm saying is that this is the product of a long-range experience, and so the blacks reflect that. Now it doesn't mean that there aren't other social and political tendencies at work, social democratic tendencies and nationalist tendencies and things of that type. There are many tendencies at work in the black community, but whenever the black community in Detroit has maximized its unity, left and Communist blacks have always been a recognized and accepted part of it. . . .

What I'm saying is that through the years Communists were making a conscious effort to promote the idea of black and white unity. Blacks were aware of it. The record is replete with examples. For, as I said, in 1943 and '44 they made a fight—which was unfortunately lost—to try to break Jim Crow in Dearborn.

In 1943, there was one of the most violent and bloody riots that took place in the city of Detroit in which forty-three . . . black workers were killed. They were killed by white workers. You have to understand that the character of the automobile work force changes drastically between 1940 and 1942–43.[53]

It changed drastically in the sense that first the basic form of production in the automobile plants changes, they're not building any automobiles in 1942 or '43, they're building tanks and so on and so forth.

Auto becomes responsible for 25 percent of defense production in the United States and America was the arsenal of democracy, we were building the stuff. (And it was a war, by the way, which the Communists fully supported. . . .)

Secondly, the work force is changing, . . . because the Rouge, they're not building automobiles, they're building tanks and whatever else they're building. . . . In other words, the so-called stable work force that had been developed between the two wars drastically changed, and there was an enormous infusion of new workers. I don't know what the statistics were but a very large part of workers were brought from the South into the automobile plants.

The majority of them were white, reflecting the ideology of Jim Crow, the racism of that period. White workers didn't like the idea of working alongside of black workers.

We mustn't put the Rouge workers on a pedestal. They're workers like anybody else. With all this progressivism and Communist and radical influence. . . . in 1944 the left progressive leadership was defeated in Local 600. W. G. Grant was the president of the local. He was defeated because the left and Communists in 1943 and '44 had been trying to deal with the problem of Jim Crow in Dearborn. Fifty years later and I don't have a good enough explanation for it, Dearborn is still a Jim Crow town.

In 1960, the population of Dearborn was around 100,000–125,000, and there were 67 blacks living in the city. I don't think it's much more now. You know, it's an irony, it's an anachronism.

How can one square the fact that Local 600 is the most progressive local in the world, that is, in the capitalist world, and its headquarters are in a city that still remains Jim Crow, where blacks can't live? In 1944, under the pressure of Communists active in the local and active in the city of Dearborn (I think they were trying to push through a housing ordinance or something that would make it possible for blacks to move in there), 3,500 people, citizens of Dearborn, assembled in Dearborn High; and they hoot and they boo the [local's] leadership out of the hall. And then they go on to defeat them in the next local election.

Are the people who live in Dearborn, are a lot of those workers from the Ford plant?

Most of them. So go figure that out. All I'm saying is, it's not so simple.

Reds

■ HENRY MCCUSKER

Some of the people that you're now probably interviewing, sit down in their building behind a lot of boxes on Joe Stalin's birthday and sing "Happy Birthday" to Joe Stalin.

■ PAUL BOATIN

I was a member of the IWW [Industrial Workers of the World]. . . . It died because it didn't understand the class struggle.[54]

■ DELORIS AND KENNETH ROCHE

Were there very many Wobblies around in Detroit near the Ford plant?
   Kenneth Roche: Some of them worked on the railroad. I didn't have any personal contact with them, but I knew that they were in the plant, some of the old-timers. Like that Roy Davis. He was an old Wobbly.
   Deloris Roche: Floyd Incompata was a Wobbly. We used to go to Wobbly parties when I was a kid. I didn't know why, I didn't know what a Wobbly was until I grew up. It would be maybe ten families and their kids, wasn't huge amounts.

■ PAUL BOATIN

I had seen people killed in Italy by the fascists, and my father himself had been in hiding. My father was hiding for about eight months in the swamps outside of Ravenna. . . .
   [He] was an Italian anarchist, and he received Italian newspapers which reproduced attacks that were made against Henry Ford I. . . . Ford was called an anarchist who was going to destroy and destabilize the capitalist system. . . . So the fact that he was called an anarchist gained him access to the super-leftists. (The anarchists are supposed to be the

super-revolutionaries, to the left of everybody.) So when I came to Detroit, I came here to work for Mr. Ford, in my childish appreciation of the fact that he was being given that kind of publicity, and that he was being attacked by the capitalists. That made him a respectable man, an honorable man in my eyes.[55] . . . After eight months, I began to awaken and no longer called Ford "Mr. Ford." I called all the bosses sons of bitches, and I got beat up and shoved against machines. I remember it knocked my breath out. That was the first time I got discharged.

■ SAUL WELLMAN

I sucked socialism at my mother's breast. I was brought up in a socialist family and was raised originally in New York, and became involved in Communist politics there. . . . In 1931 and '32, I became active in union organizing activities, and organized a union of young truck drivers in 1933 in New York. I was a member of a union from 16 years [old] on, [and] that actually began my active trade union experience. I was the head [president] of a union of Teamsters in New York until 1936, when I went to Spain. (That Teamsters local—Local 806—is quite a large local, and is a very strong local today. But it's been completely taken over by gangsters.) I spent two years in Spain.

Instead of returning to the labor movement, I became a staff member of the Young Communist League . . . and from there went into the Communist Party. In 1943, I went into the American Army and fought in Europe in the 101st Airborne Division. I was wounded at Bastogne, Belgium in the winter of 1944.[56] I came back . . . in June of 1945, and joined [the party's national] staff . . . in New York.

■ MARGARET AND STANLEY NOWAK

Stanley Nowak: I spent hours at the library, a private library in Chicago . . . and it has classics and among the classics . . . they had Marx's first volume of *Capital*. And I remember how I was introduced to it. I asked the librarian there for books on economics and he gave me a few here and there. And I was not making any headway, so I told him I don't get much out of it. So, he looked at me and said, "Are you serious about it?" I said, "Yes, I want to learn all I can at a time." "Well," he says, "if you are serious, I'll advise you, but you cannot take this book out of the building, you'll have to work here." I said, "Fine." So, . . . he showed me a first volume of Marx's *Capital*. And I would come there every day and spend a few hours working at it, and then back. Oh, I don't know, I spent months on it. It was very hard work for me, because Marx used in his quotations—

Margaret Nowak: Mathematical equations and all that stuff.

Stanley Nowak: And I did not know the mathematics. Not only that, but in that first translation that was published by Charles H. Kerr Company, Marx used a lot of quotations in other languages, and they would not translate those quotations. The Greek language and all those. [Laughs.] . . . But I struggled with it, and as I did, . . . I started traveling, and started speaking on economics, and people would throw questions at me. So, that's how I acquired my education. And I finally landed in Detroit in [one of] my tours.

Margaret Nowak: In one of his unemployed councils. That's when we met.

Stanley Nowak: That's how we met, yeah. And I remained here. . . .

Margaret Nowak: He would travel from city to city with just enough money . . . .

■ SAUL WELLMAN

People don't join the Communist Party because they just got through reading the three volumes of Marx's *Capital* and the twenty-seven volumes of Lenin. They join because of a particular issue that attracted them to the party, or a particular person who influenced them to join the party; and that particular issue can be anything, including the struggle for a traffic light on the street corner, helping to build a union, joining in the effort to win the war, etc., etc. . . . So, the challenge of the party . . . is how we change and transform people when they come into the party. The process of socialist consciousness and awareness is not something you have already completed when you go through the doors of the Communist Party, but it's only the process that begins there. And if the party can't fill it out, if it can't add to it, if it can't keep people growing, then it really doesn't succeed in holding them.

■ ARCHIE ACCIACCA

I had a feeling that the reason I belonged to the left wing is that they had more vigor, more drive, more fight for the workers, but I've seen some right-wingers, too, have some drive.

■ VICTOR REUTHER

In the days of unionization at the Rouge plant, [being a Communist] was not a handicap, because the Communists at that stage, when we were organizing the union, had a damn good reputation of being a militant group—a group that would be up in the morning early to distribute leaflets, and would not shirk their responsibilities, would take any task.

They were not alone in that; there were many others who did the same; and for them to imply that they were the only ones who did that is utter nonsense. I give them full credit for what they did. But I know they were but one small part of a much bigger group. The young Socialists, and the young Proletarian party members, and some Trotskyites, and some old-time ex-Wobblies—they worked just as hard and just as dedicated and made just as great a contribution.[57]

■ HORACE SHEFFIELD

The Communist Party was quite a factor—well, I won't say *quite*—but it was a factor. They had a strong presence, especially in the foundry, among blacks. They really tried to organize there. . . .

Now keep in mind, you had just a handful of people who were really Communists. In terms of numbers at the Ford local, don't think they had members by the thousands. They didn't. They were an organized, well-disciplined group, and they could make it appear that they had thousands by the way they galvanized people. . . . They were right out in front, in the organization of Ford's. They certainly championed black liberation, . . . In the early days of Ford's, some of their stances made some sense to folks, especially on some domestic policies. They were all clearly also actively involved in the organization of Ford's. So that gave them some leadership base, beyond being Communist.

But, by and large, if you wanted to think yourself, do any independent critical thinking about things, you had no place in the party. I never joined. . . . The Communist Party over here was nothing but an appendage of the party in the Soviet Union. . . .

The blacks that they put into leadership, to me it lacked so much of what we needed. . . . Clearly there were exceptions; but for the most part they were lackeys, and men who were opportunists, because with the large force that they [the Communists] had, they were a pretty powerful group.

And there were those who belonged to the party because they adhered to all the things. There were those who joined it and adhered to it because they saw it as a power base. They were opportunists. . . . I saw how abruptly, overnight, they changed from a party that opposed the war to one who went all out. . . . Before the Soviet Union entered the war, why they believed you ought to keep the right to strike. But overnight they changed, once Hitler invaded the Soviet Union. That was just one extremely graphic example. But it went on all of the time. . . .

Whatever the line was, they followed. . . . Now, sometimes there were those who walked away from it, and just got out. But they became marked persons.

[When] the right wing, the Walter Reuther forces, grew stronger, that clearly allowed the opportunists to drop out. The power base was shifting. And, of course, the witch hunts and all that sort of thing, the un-American Activities [Committee].

■ SAUL WELLMAN

Shelton Tappes was not a Communist, never was.

But he was a sympathizer?

It would take too long to detail the pernicious influence of anti-Communism in the United States. But one thing stands out. If you want to introduce an issue that confuses and divides people, then raise the Communist issue.

The task of challenging the authoritarian and dictatorial power of the employers was overwhelming. There were many workers and leaders who were determined to confront this power, who themselves were never remotely Communists. They did not find it difficult to work with Communists or Communist sympathizers. The outstanding example is the Republican UMW leader John L. Lewis. He recruited hundreds of Communist organizers; and he described them as committed, reliable, dependable, and daring.

That's a long introduction to saying that Shelton Tappes was neither a Communist nor a Communist sympathizer, even though he worked closely and easily with Communists like Bill McKie, Nelson Davis, Johnny Gallo or Art McPhaul. Neither were R. J. Thomas, George Addes, Richard Frankensteen, or Walter, Victor, and Roy Reuther—when they were closely allied with Communists in the early organizing battles in auto—and hundreds of others.

What's "left" at the time? Take Hodges Mason, for instance. He was in Bohn Aluminum Local 208. He was even to the left of the Communists, and never would have any part of Reuther. . . . The divisions [in the UAW] really were very sharp. But these divisions . . . just can't be fixed in simple left-right terms. You can put them into many different categories.

I would guess that by 1945 and '46 maybe a third of the membership of the [Communist] Party at the Rouge were black. Most of the blacks were concentrated in the foundry and in maintenance. They were not the skilled trades [in the maintenance unit] . . . but floor-sweepers and stuff.

The overwhelming majority of blacks who joined the [Communist] Party, joined because they met a unique group of white people who were fighting alongside them and also socializing with them. That had nothing to do with the principles of Marxism, Leninism or socialism or state power or anything else. . . . We began, for example, to understand why we were having a big turnover amongst blacks in the McCarthy period. One person in particular said to me, and it sort of epitomized what I thought was the problem, he says, "Look, it's hard enough to be black, and now to be Red and black is almost impossible to deal with." I think he was saying a whole lot.

■ KEN BANNON

Well, the Commies would meet periodically but they were a little bit different breed. . . . But . . . we would meet amongst ourselves, people . . . who were . . . close to Walter [Reuther]. . . .

So, did people who considered themselves socialist or members of the Socialist Party pretty much act as individuals when they were working?

Yeah, individuals, we had an anti—what we called were anti-Commies and anti-Ford. Well, philosophically, we were "anti" then. But when you were trying to organize the plant, what the hell, you're not going to kick a person in the teeth, for god's sake, who is helping you to accomplish what we want to accomplish.

■ SAUL WELLMAN

In 1946 I came out to Detroit, soon after the UAW convention in which the catastrophe had begun to develop with the election of [Walter] Reuther. I was given the assignment of coordinating activities of Communist automobile workers in the United States. We had roughly about three thousand [members] then in almost all the automobile plants in the industrial Midwest that ranged from northern New York, Ohio, Michigan, Indiana, Illinois, Wisconsin, as well as plants in Missouri and California.

In 1945 and '46 and '47 . . . there wasn't an important automobile plant . . . that didn't have a group of Communists in it. That must have been in forty or fifty plants at least, and it ran anywhere from five people to 450, the largest group, of course, being in the River Rouge plant. (We had . . . about 1,500 in the state of Michigan.)

The election of Reuther was a devastating event, and the question, therefore, was how were we going to maximize the response of the organized Communists and, we hoped, influence the left wing. That's how I came on the scene. We organized what we called the National Auto Commission, which was part of the national trade union department of the Communist Party. I was the secretary of the Auto Commission. Its job was to coordinate the activities of these Communist auto workers. I was actually more like a traveling salesman.

The only place [at the Rouge plant] we did not have some kind of a party group was in transportation and in maintenance.

What other strong party clubs were there among Detroit auto workers besides the Rouge Local 600?

Local 155, an amalgamated local of skilled tool-and-die workers. . . . Nat Ganley was the business agent and John Anderson was the president. Local 208, which was Bohn Aluminum, led by Fred Williams who was a Communist, Local 205, Packard 190, Plymouth, Local 51, Chrysler 7. There was a small group in 212, which was led by the socialist Emil Mazey, Local 735. . . . We had a CP club in Walter Reuther's Local 174, . . . West Side Skilled Trades Local 157.

The Communist organization in the shop area had nothing to do with the leadership of the local union. . . . Its existence didn't depend on a friendly or unfriendly leadership. It's just that a group of Communists worked in the particular plant, and it was their instrument for participating in the affairs of the local union.

What kind of relationship did they have with the Mazey regime?

Hostile, antagonistic, the same with Reuther in Local 174. I'm talking of people like in the Abe Lincoln Club.[58] I don't remember who they were. So I would call up the section organizer of the Foster section and say, "Hey look, we're going to have a leaflet distribution on Friday night, and we need fifty people." It's a big plant . . . eleven gates, three shifts. If you're going to cover all the eleven gates, you have to have two or three people at a gate to hand out the leaflets, which means you have to have thirty-three people for one shift. If you're going to have three shifts, you're going to have to get ninety people. It's a lot of people. . . .

So we had to figure out how to distribute them. I'd call up the Foster section and say, "Look, we're going to have a leaflet distribution this week, can you take Gates 5, 7, 9 and 11, the day shift, it's going to require fifteen people?" So what does the section do, the section calls up the branch organizer or the club organizer of the Abraham Lincoln Club and says, "Look, we need four people." And then they get in touch with the Ben Davis Club, and say, "Look we need four people."

Let me tell you what a [Communist] club is like. The club would meet regularly about twice a month. . . . It had an executive committee made up of a club organizer, an organizational secretary, an educational secretary, a literature director, a financial secretary, a membership director, a *Daily Worker* agent. Now, not all clubs had that many because it depended on its size. But most clubs had it. In other words, if there were only eight or ten members, then they would sort of divide these chores among themselves. A larger club would have an executive committee that would meet in between club meetings. In its hierarchal structure, there was a section committee at Ford which united the activities and energies of all the fifteen or sixteen clubs. The section committee had a similar table of organization. There was the section organizer, organizational secretary, education secretary and so on. . . .

An organizational secretary . . . is somebody who has to make sure that the decisions that are made are carried out. . . . An education secretary is responsible for the organization of educationals. The literature director is responsible for the distribution of literature. These are internal things. . . . Now, internal education means that you will have a current events session, and you'll discuss the news of the week or the month or the year. Say the party has a national convention, and a very important document comes out, to be discussed by the entire membership, that will set forth, we'll say, the line and policy of the party on a particular issue. That has to be discussed. So, educationals are organized around that. . . . Internal education would also go into the ideology of the party, Marxism and Leninism and stuff like that.

External education [differs]. In the Rouge foundry we had the Nelson Davis Forum. . . . There existed a respect and credibility for the Communists based on past performance of standing up to the company and helping to organize the UAW. Nelson Davis was a unique public figure in that he was identified with the Communist Party and with building the union. . . . He was respected. He was very popular. He was active and energetic, and he was very able to get people to do things. . . . Not all the clubs were equal. Not all the clubs functioned in the same way. Not all the clubs had the same successes or failures. The experiences of the clubs were as varied as their numbers. It was not easy. There was a struggle to maintain that type of organization.

Of the 450 people in the [Communist] Party at Rouge, no more than 20 percent were activists. In other words, when the party began to grow, not only at Ford but throughout the country (we grew from eight thousand members in 1929 to almost one hundred thousand members by 1939), we attracted a lot of new people into the organization, but, like most organizations, not everybody was an equal activist.

■ HENRY MCCUSKER

I don't think any officer[s] at this international union, even under the Thomas administration, were card-carrying Communists. I don't think so. Not to my knowledge, they weren't. But they wielded outside influence, wielded a lot of power amongst some of the officers of the international union and the regional directors in the international union.

What did it mean to be influenced by the Communists?

Well, when the party line changed, the Communists, they never knew what they were going to do. The party line changed for them in Moscow, and it changed three or four times a day. So, you would have them running around here spouting off about one thing in the morning; and then the party line would change in Moscow, and they were spouting off something else in the afternoon.

What about these officers who were influenced by them?

Well, they were, that was doing something, so far as the structure of the international union was concerned.

What do you mean by that?

What do I mean by that? I mean by that, that it was a bad influence.

Can you tell by the way that they acted, their trade union policies?

Yes, many of them, many of them, you could tell at that time. . . .

But can you give me an example of how it might have affected their policies back in the 1940s and '50s?

No, I couldn't give you any particular examples. But I know what they used to spout off here. "You whites get out of the way or we're going to walk right over you." They were non-Communists that said that. They were in the left wing so far as the local union was concerned. You had the right-wingers and the left-wingers.

How did the right wing conduct its union affairs—the right-wing union leaders?

They were honest with the membership; generally speaking, that happened. And they had as much to offer, and sometimes more to offer than the others. I don't say that a Commie couldn't have something good to offer.

■ SHELTON TAPPES

You could distinguish the Communists from the fellow travelers, because when the Communists got into a strict party-line issue, then the fellow travelers would waver, and wouldn't go all the way out with them.

Would all the Communists stick closely to the line?

They'd adhere to the line, yes. They adhered very strictly to the line. I think that had a lot to do with dissipating the strength of that wing— the rigidity with which they adhered to the line at times.

How about the people who dropped out or were kicked out of the Communist Party? Did they normally turn to the right or stay with the left?

No, they stayed left.

■ DELORIS AND KENNETH ROCHE

Did left-wing people talk to the workers about issues like socialism?

Kenneth Roche: Some of us did; and some of us didn't. Some of them went on because they were politically oriented. I always talked socialism to the people, and told them, "Look, this is what it is." They accepted me. It was something I had to explain to them, and could explain, by my own experience in the labor movement, and my own experience in life. They never resented it. I always got elected. I never been defeated after I got elected.

Deloris Roche: He never had anybody supporting him either. You always ran independently.

Kenneth Roche: Not only that. I don't care whether the right wing was opposing me, or sometimes my own people were opposing me, because they didn't agree. They said—even my own people like [Walter] Dorosh and Mack Cinzori—"You talk about socialism. What are you talking about socialism to the workers for?" I said, "Who else are you supposed to talk socialism with?"

■ SAUL WELLMAN

Did Communists talk socialism in the plants?

Some might. Some might not. It depends on the individual. Some are more skilled at it than others. Some know how to do it, and others don't. I'll let you in on a secret. Many people that are members of the Socialist movement don't know the difference between socialism and rheumatism. . . .

I would think that the old Communist movement, and the old Socialist movement, . . . or even the old Wobbly movement was more skilled in its anticapitalist energies than the modern Socialist and Communist Parties. There were many forms of educating for socialism. The old Socialist Party published the Little Blue Books . . . put out by a publisher called E. Haldeman, in Girard, Kansas. There were about four hundred titles of Little Blue Books (oh, about three by five inches) that dealt with every conceivable topic of public interest, and easily circulated. They were helpful for shop-floor discussions or lunch-hour discussions. They sold for 2 cents or something like that. Then in the late 1930s, there was a four-page publication [put out by George Seldes] called *In Fact*. It came out every week. I think it had a circulation of about two hundred thousand. Many of us would get five copies, ten copies, twenty copies, thirty copies. We'd take *In Fact* into the plant; and there would be discussions about all kinds of questions. I remember the most popular one they had in 1939 was why people should quit smoking. Mass people's issues. We don't have enough of those tools today.

The Communist Party did a lot of educational activity of that type. I remember in 1946 we produced a paperback book that we sold for a nickel called *Why Work for Nothing?* It dealt with *Capital* and so on and so forth, without mentioning Marx's name once. In 1937 or '38 or '39 the Roosevelt government had set up an economic investigation commission called TNEC, the Temporary National Economic Committee. They made an examination of where capitalism was. It came up with some very important information and statistics. So, we took that information and we turned it into the pamphlet *Why Work for Nothing?* which helped organize hundreds of shop-floor discussions on economics. Many workers grasped the complexity of such questions as wages, prices, profits, surplus value, etc., better than most people coming out of the Harvard Business School. There were many such activities; and that's part of, I guess, agitating for socialism, because socialism isn't just how to describe an abstract socialist society. Socialism is the alternative to capitalism. So, you have to understand capitalism, and its built-in inequities, if you want to be for something else.

■ KEN BANNON

I was never, never in support of [the Communist Party's] aims. I happen to be a Catholic, and a practicing Catholic. I could recognize the good they were doing to help organize Ford. But when you'd go to the meetings, you'd hear their philosophy on different issues, for goodness sake, that "there is no God," and "blah, blah, blah," you name it, and "the system is no good," and so on. Well, the system still isn't as good as it could be, but it's the best system in the world; and the other gosh darn thing is, it's a system that you can work in and change somewhat.

The best organizers were members of the Communist Party. . . . I had occasion to attend . . . Communist Party meetings; we all did. What the hell could you do back in the late 1930s? So, what the heck, we were all grabbing at straws, so to speak. But, as I mentioned, I think, I never joined the party, although . . . [I] almost signed a card.

Now, what would happen at these Communist Party meetings? Would they mainly discuss union organizing efforts, or what?

Well, it all depends upon what year you're talking about. If you're talking about during the organizing days of Ford, it was primarily getting the Ford workers into the UAW. If you talk about 1942–43, it was the Second Front.[59]

World War II was on. "Let's get America moving into Europe, for God's sake, and help Russia." That was the party philosophy at that point in time so it all depends upon the time of year. They followed the line dictated by the Soviet Union. . . . If you read the minutes of the 1943 convention up in Buffalo, and study the influence of the Communist Party in the UAW at that point in time, a good portion of that record of that convention was devoted to the Second Front. They wanted the UAW to come out in favor of a Second Front, and we who were supporting Dick Leonard and Walter Reuther and that group, we finally defeated that [Communist-led] group. This, in my opinion, was really the breaking point within UAW—of the back of the Communist Party.

Was their pushing of the Second Front?

That's right.

■ JOHN ORR

You said the Communists were good organizers. What about other ways that they conducted their union-management relations? Do you think that they were more tough on grievances or more likely to strike?

No, that's a lot of malarkey.

As a matter of fact, we had a real left-wing president, Paul Boatin, in the motor building, and Ed Lock was president of the tire plant.

Walter Reuther got us involved in a five-year contract, . . . following World War II. It was just a pact of peace with the Ford Motor Company for a very nominal sum of 5 cents or 10 cents an hour. We were saddled with that thing. We wanted to break it. We didn't know how; the contract had a no-strike [clause]. . . . We used some damn excuse that the companies weren't living up to the cost of living formula, or they were computing the cost of living based on the consumer's index wrong; I forget the specifics. We insisted they reopen the contract, and they refused.

Now, the international union couldn't advocate strikes; they signed the no-strike. But they encouraged them. Walter Reuther at that time said, "It's a living document; and, sure, we've got to sign agreements; but conditions change. . . ." Oh, he could speak.

We started to pull a series of shutdowns in the Rouge plant, building by building. These two well-known Communist chairmen of two buildings, theirs never went down.

■   ART MCPHAUL

Where did the idea for a pension come from?
Well, it was the left wing that raised the question of the pensions to start with, and fought for them. It was the left wing. Most of these things that were in the best interests, originated in the left wing, not the right wing. I can't remember one single thing that the right raised that, in effect, was in the [workers'] best interest.

The first people usually to raise these things were the Communists mostly, in the *Daily Worker* and so forth. They campaigned for this sort of thing all along. Of course, many of the workers, including myself, of course, picked [these ideas] up, and brought them into the union, and fought for them; and they became issues that the workers supported. Certainly—no matter who the originators of the idea—they were good ideas. The right wing, and nobody else, could actually oppose them, because the average worker could see, could look, yes.

■   PAUL BOATIN

I was a better and more alert union leader because I had the [Communist] Party to advise me. . . . The party wanted more! The party was not being built; Lock, Gallo, Robertson, and myself were the only constant party members; not enough papers sold; not enough subs coming in; not enough planning and speaking to get Second Front resolutions passed at meetings; and, besides, [party officials said] we were acting too much like traditional unionists—a real bad malady that would ruin the party and take all the spark out of the union. There should be more attention to political questions and less to union questions.[60]

There was a division of opinion [among Communists] about the position that [Earl] Browder took. I was with Browder. . . . Browder was stubborn. [William Z.] Foster was stubborn. They were both right; and they were both wrong. But they were wrong primarily in the fact that rank-and-file Communists like me—I'm talking about the 1946 period, '46, '47—when the *Daily Worker* devoted half of its front page to the danger of Browderism. In the meantime what was going on in America, what was going on in Michigan, the Reutherites were taking advantage of that internal fight to throw guys that they didn't like out of the union. And the Communist Party was so weakened as a result of that, that they weren't able—the Communist people weren't able— to pay attention to the problems of the workers. And, consequently, the corporation was then able to start their process of destroying the unions.

■ SAUL WELLMAN

In the middle 1950s, as we were coming under more and more attack, and we were being driven into isolation and away from the mainstream, we became more sectarian. We did a lot of stupid things. We began to try and impose a certain discipline on trade unionists, in particular, or the rigidness of a political line, that they could not deal with. So, we lost hundreds and hundreds of trade unionists, from top and bottom.
      In distinction to the much more loose relationship they had during the 1940s?
      Right, right. I think it's to their credit that they didn't hang on because—
      You're talking about the struggles within the UE, and so forth?
      Right, right. Those struggles [to impose the party line on UE leadership] were wrong struggles.

■ SHELTON TAPPES

What led to your own differences with the Communist Party?
      Threats, and an effort to force me to join. They called a meeting at one of the meeting places on Michigan Avenue. Billy Allan was presiding. What angered me was, they asked me to come to this meeting, and they didn't tell me why, what it was about or anything. Then when I got there, they had me in the outer hall there cooling my heels for about an hour, a good hour, it was the summertime, a summer evening. I got there about shortly, oh about 7:30; and I didn't get into the meeting until nine o'clock. When I got in there, I see all these fellows from the local, different units; and I'm very curious, and every chair is occupied except one. There they are, they are fanned out like this. . . . I come in the door, and up here is a round table. Allan is behind it, and there are two people flanking him, and then the chair's in front. It's

like an inquisition. So, I'm shown the chair, and I sit on it. The coolness from guys that I'd always received with a lot of congeniality bothered me. I was concerned.

Allan, very austerely, says, "Shelton," he says, "you see your fellow workers here; and we've invited you because we have some questions we want to ask." And then he named three people who had been assigned, as he put it, to work with me, to see that I signed an application for membership in the party. He said, "Each one of these people failed." I remembered the different times when these three people had almost adhered to me for days on end; and while they talked about the party and all that, I didn't remember any of them specifically insisting or asking me to join the party. Okay, so I took that in and he said, "You have consistently refused. We have supported you all these years; and you've been elected; and while you haven't been 100 percent, we have appreciated the kind of support we got." He went along this line for quite a while, and then he said, "Now, don't get the idea that we're picking on you only. This goes for other people that we have supported," he said, "George Addes, W. G. Grant and others."

Well, I was pretty sure that they didn't call them in for an inquisition like they called me, but, anyway, this is the way it went. So, he finally wound up and then several people got up and spoke their piece. I guess this was all pretty well staged, and then they asked me for my answer. I told him, the only reason that I never joined the party is because I didn't want to. . . . I said, "If there ever is a Communist Party that's strictly an American party and we're talking about things that are wrong in America, and we're not necessarily attached to what happens to somebody in Russia, then maybe I'd think about it a little closer. But other than that, no." Then I went on to tell him, "I've never had any grief for people who joined any party they wanted to, to each his own. Some of these fellows here are my good friends. The fact that they belonged to the party has never phased me one way or the other, and I was never bothered about it; and I'm sure that they weren't bothered by me, because nobody insisted on me joining the party. I'd been asked, you know. Bill McKie asked me once, and I think Byron Edwards asked me. Maybe Boatin did; I don't know whether he did or not. Oh yeah, and there was another fellow, he was a barber over on the east side, I think. But Bill McKie, right after I was elected recording secretary of the local, with that Scottish brogue of his, he said, "You better be thinking about coming among us, boy, you better be thinking about coming among us, boy."

I was subpoenaed [by HUAC in mid-1951] and I could have used the Fifth Amendment, and probably would have if I wasn't [still] so angry.

(I described this meeting at the hearings). I was just angry at those people [in the Communist Party].

That meeting with party people had happened recently?

Yes, well, not too—you know Bill Johnson was in his first term I think. [That was in 1946.] It was so close to the [local] election, it was almost ridiculous that we hadn't put together a slate. But the committee that was bringing in the names for the various positions on the slate continued to bring my name in, and every time they brought my name in they would find some reason to delay action on the committee. All of this was being caucused within the party itself, and brought into the left-wing caucus; and so, well, I knew what it was, especially after the committee had even changed my position from recording secretary to vice president, and they still rejected it. And the committee had also accepted a name that they had advanced from the floor and put it on the ticket; but my name was still on there. So, they had just enough power to keep rejecting the report of the committee.

They thought they'd convince you to join that way?

Well, no, this was just retaliation for my attitude and my refusal.

Did you ever figure out why they went after you like that in the first place?

I never have, I never have. So, anyway, I told Bill Grant and some of the other fellows, I said, "Now, listen," I said, "we'll never get a slate together as long as I keep going to those meetings." I said, "I'm going to stay away." "Go ahead." He said, "But if they leave you off?" I said, "If they leave me off, I'll be the campaign manager. Let's get the thing on." So, I stayed away. They held that meeting up here at Northern High School. . . . I wasn't there; and the committee came in with my name on the slate again. So, they nominated Bill Johnson from the floor. And Bill Grant stood in for me. He nominated me, and he stood in for me. They took two votes, by sound and by raise of hands, and it was unclear. So, then they had a division of the house, "Everybody in favor of Bill Johnson on this side; and everybody in favor of Shelton Tappes on this side." The chairman didn't vote, so that—wait a minute, how was it? There were 602 people. The chairman didn't vote; and it turns out 301 for Bill Johnson and 300 for me.

In later years, they [the party] sent a committee to me to apologize, and this fellow James Jackson, who at that time was the Michigan party head for a short time. It was during his regime that this all happened. Now, in arranging for this committee to apologize to me, Jim Jackson confessed that he made a mistake. He said, "Unfortunately, the mistake resulted in cutting off the career of Shelton Tappes." It did; it aborted a career.

Now, I don't have the problem of what happened to me. It's not that it bothers me, because I never took any position I ever had as mine. I thought it belonged to my people, and my achievements, I thought, was the elevation of black leadership. Black people were moving up and assuming their place. When my career was aborted the way it was, those who followed, they weren't as forward as I thought they should have been, although this guy Bill [Johnson] who had, did. . . . They may not have known who the other officers of Local 600 were at a given time, but they sure knew who was recording secretary [when I was]. . . .

The committee came to apologize to me. I said, "Well, I can accept the apology. I don't think that I've been hurt nearly as much as the rest of those people out there in that plant who now don't have anybody who has enough thrust behind their convictions to really do the job that should be done. That's all I wanted to do."

When did they apologize?

It was around about the fall of 1951. I went on staff in 1950. It was, I would say, about three to four months after the HUAC hearings. . . . Oh, everybody didn't feel like apologizing. They call you—what is it?—a stool pigeon. But I told them, "A stool pigeon is somebody who stools on his fellows. You people were not my fellows. I wasn't a member of the party."

■ VICTOR REUTHER

It wasn't until the Soviet troops marched into Hungary that Dave Miller had grave questions about his [Communist Party] membership.[61] I remember talking with him at great length about it during—you see, there were some Communists and Dave Miller is typical of them, and [Bill] McKie also, who were philosophical communists, as well as disciplined party members. It was possible to have an intellectual discussion with them. It was possible to retain a personal friendship with them despite violent differences on party policies. I and Walter also still felt a great personal friendship for McKie and Dave Miller because of the early contribution they made, even though we had to break very sharply with them during the war.

■ SAUL WELLMAN

I'm not an opponent of the Communist Party, but I feel that it became irrelevant. (That's why I left the party in 1958.) The main problem that it faces is that it is tied too much to the Central Committee in the Communist Party of the Soviet Union.

Did you think that became a problem only in the late 1950s and afterward?

No, as I look back at it, I think it was a problem that began with our birth, so to speak, that is with the Russian Revolution and so on. I don't necessarily view it as a mistake. . . . I view it as one of those unfortunate developments. It was an inevitable deformation. . . .

I feel [that the Communist Party] made a profound and important contribution to American democratic development and thought. It was the most important socialist working-class organization in the United States, especially during the 1930s. In the seventy-year experience of the Communist Party, the 1930s decade is its most profound period. This is when the party made its greatest contribution.

Right-wingers

■ DAVE MOORE

On the right you had the ACTU, the Association of Catholic Trade
Unions, I believe it was. And you had the Masons and you had the
Knights of Columbus.[62]

■ KENNETH ROCHE

I never went to church after I was eighteen years old. Before the union
came in, the preacher at St. Clemens, Father Oakly, he'd preach against
the union.

Father Coughlin was on the radio every Sunday. My parents listened to him faithfully. He was talking about "social justice"—a demagogue, like Huey Long and the rest of them. They listened faithfully; and I used to tell them, after I was in the Local 600, about what
he was doing. They wouldn't believe me. They thought he was wonderful, him and his "social justice," yakking about "the Jews," and
"the Communist conspiracy."

■ KEN BANNON

The ACTU? The American Catholic Trade Union group? Ah, they weren't
that active [in the Ford organizing drive]. I'm a Catholic, and I never
joined the ACTU until well after we had organized [Ford]. As a matter
of fact, I think I was over at Local 400 when I joined ACTU. . . .
What would a typical ACTU meeting consist of?
Well, it would open with a prayer, what have you, and the encycli-
cals on labor. They would support Catholics [in the UAW]. Walter Reuther was an agnostic. Well, all you do is pick up . . . old copies of the
Wage Earner, particularly . . . around the 1940s, the middle 1940s.[63]
They, Paul Weber and Doherty, did a hatchet job on Walter Reuther.
Who were they supporting then?

Well, they weren't supporting anyone really; and, furthermore, they didn't have a hell of a lot of support amongst themselves, as it was.

How big do you think the group was at the Rouge plant? How many Ford workers, do you think?

Oh, hell, if they had five hundred, they had a lot at that point in time.

■ PAUL BOATIN

The majority of the people that worked on production lines, the foundry, on the hard jobs, were of foreign extraction. Italians, Polish, lots of Polish. The bosses were either English or German or Appalachian whites, okay. So, you had that antagonism. Amongst the Poles, you would have a lot of ACTU. They responded to the anti-Communist attacks.

■ ART MCPHAUL

Oh, yes, there was a difference between right and left. The more conservative, red-baiting element, company collaborators, and that kind of people, concessionists and that sort of thing, were the kind of people that made up the right wing. . . . Look, there were some in the right-wing group, some committeemen, who really worked, so don't get the idea that everybody in the right wing just didn't fight for their workers, because that's not correct. Certain of them did. But the general policy is what I'm talking about—because you also had in the left wing, certain committeemen who were lazy too, that didn't do their jobs.

■ ARCHIE ACCIACCA

Do you think that the ACTU had much influence over the average Catholic worker in the plant?

I'm not too sure they did. I'm a Catholic myself, and I knew a lot of Catholics that were left-wingers, a lot of them. The ACTU had some influence, I would say a minor influence, not much.

So, they didn't bring their politics into the church or when you went to church on Sunday you didn't hear the ACTU line?

No, no, no.

■ KENNETH ROCHE

Were there a lot of Catholics in the leadership that weren't with the ACTU?

Yes, there was. The ACTU eventually died out because it was too
much of an extreme organization. They couldn't get elected adhering
to its policies. If they took the ACTU line, they would have been dead
ducks every one of them. You bet they would have wound up like
Henry McCusker. But a lot of them changed. They became what you
call middle-of-the-road people and business-as-usual. "Don't do this.
Don't upset the apple cart. Don't try to do anything that will upset
Reuther. Don't try to do anything that will upset any of the business-
as-usual routine." This is the way they operate.

■ HORACE SHEFFIELD

They [the right wing] were definitely a minority at the Rouge. I can
tell you that. But largely, they were kind of a citywide group, and you
attended caucus. Walter Reuther called caucuses and you attended
those. . . .
   *How close was the right-wing caucus at the Rouge associated with
Reuther?*
   They were very, very closely associated. Joe McCusker, for instance,
who became president of the local union and went on to become a
regional director. . . . There were others around the plant that—
   Joe McCusker was close to Reuther?
   Oh yes, Joe McCusker was, yeah.
   So, would Reuther attend the caucus meetings and make suggestions?
   Well, not out there, not out there. . . . We might invite Reuther to
speak to the caucus on some occasion, but we all considered ourselves
a part of a broader caucus that went beyond the plant. Yeah. And there
would be large occasions, not that frequently, during the year, when
some major thing [came up], and we attended in a huge citywide caucus. You know, we had a citywide caucus that met from time to time.

■ JOHN MANDO

The rolling mill unit was always considered a right-wing unit. It was
always pretty well identified as a Reuther slate, aligned with the international. That's been the history of the rolling mill. And it is still the
history of the rolling mill. But during that period when I ran for unit
chairman, I ran against a gentleman by the name of Frank Kenny, who
has since passed away, who was considered the right-wing candidate.
I did not run as a left-winger or as a progressive or as part of the Progressive slate. I ran as an independent.

■ WILLIAM JOHNSON

We had what we call a right-wing group, [consisting of] . . . the Reuther group and the Catholic Trade Unionist group. ACTU, or the Association of Catholic Trade Unionists, were . . . very ardent supporters of Reuther. (In fact the only [pro-Reuther] guy that ever was elected president of the local, Joe McCusker, in 1945, was very active in the ACTU.) . . . The Catholic group were opposed to the so-called Communist elements that they thought were part of the Progressive slate—which, in fact, was really the old Addes-Leonard-Thomas group. . . . The Catholic trade unionists, by and large, were the more developed trade unionists, because they had a programmatic approach that the rest of the people didn't really have.

Where did that come from?

Well, it was training and indoctrination in the trade union movement from the Catholic church's point of view. That group supported Reuther, although Reuther had a pretty checkered career in his earlier days.

Were they successful on the shop floor?

Not too often. The local was almost entirely dominated by an anti-Reuther group until 1953, when we decided we would lay down the hatchet and try to work with the international union. But prior to that time, if your label was a Reutherite, you were sure to be defeated. You wouldn't win. . . . Most in the [ACTU] group came out of the maintenance and construction [unit]. A sizable element were in the tool-and-die unit, but they were always a minority. You had a smattering of them anywhere you had a concentration of Polish workers. "Polish" and "Catholic" were synonymous. Virtually all Polish were Catholic.

What about the Italians?

The Italians were about mixed; they ran about half and half. Half would go along with the Catholic Trade Unionist's point of view, which was to point them in Reuther's direction; and the other half just stood back. A lot of the Italian workers had worked in the mines before they came to Detroit; and they had a John L. Lewis perspective, rather than Reuther. So, they were fairly well split.

Ninety-nine percent of all blacks were in the anti-Reuther caucus.

Poles, to a great extent, never achieved local union officer's status. They were committeemen and bargaining committee people. I don't think I can recall a Pole ever being elected to any office higher than a local trustee. Never one of the four top offices.

Did you say that the ACTU was pretty influential among the Poles?

Well, yeah, they had a predominant influence on any Catholic group. Even if you were black and you were a Catholic, you went with that group. . . .

Were there a lot of Catholics in the Rouge plant?

Oh, we had a substantial number of Catholics; and we had a sizable Masonic group, too.

■ PAUL BOATIN

The only right-winger out of the blacks was [Horace] Sheffield. Every other black was either a middle-of-the-roader or a progressive.

■ KEN BANNON

I had my own caucus at Rouge. Sure, I was at [Local] 400, but I had my own caucus. I had Gene Prato and Bill McIntosh, what the hell, I had a big caucus at the Rouge.

So, those were the people that were basically considered to be the right-wing caucus at Rouge?

Okay, well they can call it right wing, but it was a hell of a lot further left than the Commies; and the Commies were only concerned with the war at that point in time. Come on, what the devil. How could we [the local] help Russia? Russia was in the doldrums then.

■ SHELTON TAPPES

I wouldn't indict the right wing for the way in which they handled grievances, because, I think, for the most part union representatives in the Ford setup were pretty diligent in handling the problems. For me it's easy to say because, remember the days that I was in and around the shop, the union was still very new, and there was a lot of enthusiasm and, therefore, there was an anxiety to make the union work. That depreciated as the years went on, until today, I think, most of it is personal aggrandizement that motivates people more than anything else. But the right wing and the left wing I think generally they applied themselves quite well. Now, there were times (and I can't say this of the left wing)—there were times when a left-winger getting in trouble might have some problems with right-wing opposition taking up his grievance for him, but this was more in [the] leadership. The rank-and-filers were not as easy to distinguish as far as their loyalty within the union was concerned. So, . . . their problems were attended. But a leader having problems, he'd have to face some difficulties, especially

if he was a left-wing leader depending on right-wing representation. . . .
For example, suppose you had a left-wing committeeman who had
some problems with the foreman, and [he'd] be . . . disciplined himself. His right-wing top committee, he may or may not take up the case.
The unfortunate part of it is that step-by-step, higher up the ladder, they
took the same attitude that the committeeman did on the floor; and
they let the company lead their thought on the grievance, which is
always fatal, you see.

■ HORACE SHEFFIELD

The Association of Catholic Trade Unionists did exert, in some instances, a very positive influence. . . . [Paul Weber] was a leader who really
also understood the needs to weld black and white together. [He]
didn't work at Ford's. . . . But we got to know him. He was visible
around the trade union movement, and quite a resourceful person.
   *What kind of a relationship did the right wing have with the
ACTU? For example, would Weber come and talk at the caucuses, or
would they just have their own meetings?*
   They had their own meetings. There was not that kind of—at least
visible—alliance. I'm sure Joe McCusker belonged to the ACTU. You
know, he was quite a staunch Catholic. His brother Henry and others
out there. But it wasn't anything that they wore on their arm . . . so
you could tell that they were members of the ACTU. . . . The left wing
beat them down, and called them fascist, or whatever.
   But your impression of them is much different than that?
   Oh yeah. . . . I can see through the CP propaganda; and hell, I can
see through it on the other side. Yeah, yeah. There's no question about
it, that they [the ACTU] made some positive contributions.

   I guess the thing about the right-wing movement, and the leadership is that . . . they were more thoughtful. There was much more rea-
soning went on. Really, there just wasn't this coercing almost, so to
speak, to a point of view or to the line. You know, you had more flex-
ibility about that.

■ WALTER DOROSH

The progressives were always initiating new ideas, and the right wing
generally wanted to just leave things alone, and things will take care
of themselves. Progressives were generally initiators of new dimensions
for negotiations, and this is the way I had always seen it. . . . [But] I

think they were the same, once the policy was set. I think they both went out and tried to do the job. They were obligated to. All the years I have seen them operate, I don't think that they didn't attempt to do the right kind of job. I think that they wouldn't pursue it as diligently maybe, but I don't think they tried to sabotage the union. . . .

But people that made up the left wing, as I said before, generally stood for a position. They were always projecting something. They were always moving in. They were always introducing resolutions; and the other group always opposed it. As I said, the right-wingers in the plant I think they fought for grievances just like anybody else did. I can't deny it. (Joe McCusker was on a bargaining committee with me in the tool-and-die, and he ran as a right-wing president for the Local 600, and was elected. He didn't deny he was pro-Reuther. . . . Man, he did a good job. He wrote the grievances, processed the grievances, to go in there and battle.) But they never projected, never. Let me give you an illustration. There is something wrong with the seniority agreement, and we know it's wrong; it benefits the company, and doesn't benefit the worker. You don't know these things sometimes until—you negotiate them, and then in practice, you say, "Holy God, we left a big hole there." They [right-wingers] won't take steps to correct it. You know, they won't project.

Democracy

■ MARGARET AND STANLEY NOWAK

Stanley Nowak: I went to work at the age of fourteen. . . . I worked for Hart, Schaffner & Marx. There was already a union there. We didn't need to organize for a union there.

Margaret Nowak: In fact, you had to join the union after you were there a certain length of time.

This was in Chicago also? It was a union shop?

Stanley Nowak: That's right. It was a progressive union. They founded the union—were old-time socialists from Europe: Polish, Jewish socialists. And they had many very progressive aspects of it. They would not deduct dues from the paycheck. You had to come and collect dues from them. They were against the check-off system.[64] And they also had a provision that no worker would be laid off for lack of work. The work would have to be divided. I haven't seen that done anywhere since then. There were a number of very progressive things. And in the shop that I worked, there were quite a number of Jewish socialists from Poland, who migrated from Poland, and they took sort of an interest in me. [They] delighted me with books and taught me a lot of things. Later on, they elected me as the youngest steward. They called it "chairman."

Margaret Nowak: That was in 1922.

Stanley Nowak: Yeah. The youngest steward in the [union's] history, and they called it chairman. And the reason for it was—one of the reasons I would say was—that the entire leadership of the union and the local there was Jewish. And, of course, they founded the union, that was logical. But there were other groups, ethnic groups, and among them were quite a few Poles, Russians, and Rumanians with them. So, . . . they had a very democratic election. Every year the chairman of the local would be reelected, and every official. And at the election, anti-Semitism developed there. And by my countryman, a Polish fellow, the underground said, "Well, Jews control everything." I real-

ized that, as little as I knew, and I knew something, I realized that it
was bad because the union was good, the edicts were good, and just
because they were Jewish origins, so what? So I did not agree with it.
And the leadership came to the conclusion that the way to block this
thing was to have a non-Jewish person to run for that office. So they
put me in. They trusted me, and insisted, and I finally agreed to it; and
it's true that once I appeared as a candidate, this other man withdrew,
and all anti-Semitic campaign stopped, because they couldn't Jew-bait
me.

■ DAVE MOORE

The dedication, the understanding, the honor, and the determination
of these representatives to do a good job, . . . to be honest with their
constituents, [was there]. And they were, most of them. I don't care
what group you get, you are going to find some rotten apples. But in
most cases the representatives out at Local 600 were basically honest
with their constituents because they had to be, [or,] in the old days,
you didn't last but one term. And, in fact, you were subject to recall.
They caught a guy, and they had the goods on him. They would recall
you by signing a petition. A person had to be a good representative.
Now, some guys got elected, and they weren't; and they didn't last but
one term, and they were gone and forgotten.

■ JOHN SAARI

Did you ever think of running for office other than committeeman?
    I gave it a thought. But, you know, I think one of the weaknesses
of my character was that I always felt the other guy could do a better
job. But I have come to learn that that isn't so, that isn't so.

■ JOHN MANDO

The first time [I got nominated for office], believe it or not, I had to
be talked into accepting the nomination. Honestly, I was not all that
enthralled with the notion of being an officer or a committeeman.

■ DAVE MOORE

For a worker to see you smiling, as a representative, and a foreman got
his arms around you, that was the kiss of death. You couldn't, when
you confronted a foreman, you couldn't show any smile on your face.

The best thing you could do, if he started to explain to you or something like that, you could just stand there and look at him, and say, "Well, look I want this did, understand, Fred? I don't want any more of this you harassing her or him. Now, if I have to come back in this department, goddamnit, your production stops." That would happen. The whole department would stop.

Management wanted to know at that time why that foreman wasn't getting that production out, and especially at the time when production was needed so bad; and they would tell him, "If you can't get along with the guys down there, goddamnit we are going to get a guy who can." This was management saying this.

■ WILLIAM JOHNSON

In order to get elected, you had to be pretty militant. Otherwise you didn't have much chance, particularly in the earlier days. You had to be fairly militant. You had to take an anticompany stance. If they thought you were close to the company at all, you wouldn't get elected.

■ PAUL BOATIN

After the strike in 1941, which was 100 percent successful, and even prior to the union contract being negotiated, there was much discussion as to what the constitution of the union should have.

[One issue was] what the contract should contain. For instance, that's no longer discussed now, but already there were those who were against the introduction of the umpire system into the grievance procedure. Not that they had any particular dislike for the umpire as an individual, but they felt that the fight should not be put on paper, that the fight should take place where the workers could see it.

■ VICTOR REUTHER

As far as I recall, there was only one short period in the history of the UAW where the opposing forces could clearly be described and accurately described as "the struggle between the left and the right"; and that was the period during the initial struggle against the irresponsible leadership of one Homer Martin. Homer Martin clearly was a leader of the right. He had private dealings with the Ford Motor Company. He pursued a policy of trying to take the fledgling UAW, a CIO union, back into the conservative AF of L. He pursued policies inside the union that were worked out in harmony with one Harry Bennett, who was a hired gangster of the Ford Motor Company, whose main thrust at that period was to break the incipient UAW; so, Martin was truly the symbol of the right. Opposing Martin was a very broad collection whom I would more accurately describe as militant unionists rather than left, for the great bulk of them had no political leanings of any kind. They were typical of the work force of the auto industry, people out of the hills of Kentucky and Tennessee, and they were not political sophisticates. However, among the leadership of the Unity Caucus, which opposed Martin, were Young Socialists, Young Communists, young members of the Proletarian Party, some Catholic Action trade unionists, some older ex-Wobblies, quite a collection of political activists of the so-called left. . . .

There has always been a faction in organized labor that wants to compromise with the boss, and I consider them "right-wingists" or conservative trade unionists. I call those who seek progressive change, militant unionists. I don't like "left" and "right," because it's lost its meaning; it's so easily misunderstood. When you have militant Catholic trade unionists working in the same caucus with Socialists and ex-Wobblies, you can't call it a left-wing coalition, because the Catholics are not left-wingers. They may be militant unionists; they may be against the boss; but usually the term *left* means, almost, *Marxist.*

And that has absolutely no meaning in the trade union movement, because 90 percent of the members of each of these caucuses were what we used to call (well, not originally, but almost) "scissorbills." That's an old trade union expression, of a Jimmy Higgins who doesn't know up from down, but he knows who the boss is, and fights him. So, Marxist terminologies, believe me, they're very misleading, extremely misleading.

■ DAVE MOORE

The left wing had the Communist Party; and you had so-called liberals, who wasn't members of the Communist Party; and you had progressives, who wasn't members of the Communist Party; and all of those made up the left.
Were there Socialists?
Oh yeah. You had Trotskyites.
Which side did they fall on?
The Socialists? They would swing back and forth. They would be with the left for awhile on a certain issue and they would go to the right for awhile. And you never could tell where the hell they were going to be. They wasn't a big force there. Small force they had, but it

was in-between on the different issues. It all depends on what the issues were.

■ JOHN ORR

How did the Communists act in the plants during the war?

They were among the best organized, but there were very few Communists who identified themselves. . . . I was chairman of the left-wing caucus in Rouge for years. . . . The rumor was always, we were just a front for the Communist Party. Somebody told me they used to have caucus meetings in the hall down on Sylina Street before they would come and invade us en masse in our caucus, and present their program to us. Well, I never asked them who they were, who they identified with. We took the subject matters they presented as such, and debated them, and went with them or against them.

■ SAUL WELLMAN

Many of our people were organizers for the Progressive Caucus. They were activists and leaders of the Progressive Caucus in some of the largest buildings. On a number of occasions, some Communists in some buildings did not go along with the Progressive Caucus. . . . If you have any ideas that the Communists represented a monolithic group or a monolithic point of view then you're wrong. The real world one lives in is not monolithic. To be a progressive doesn't mean that everybody thinks the same way, or everybody responds in the same way, or everybody's ambitions run along the same lines. There's always variety.

So, the local got more sophisticated, and more mature. As it got older, as more people got ambitious, new problems began to arise (I'm speaking now after the war), . . . differences developed even amongst the Progressives. They were not always ideological. Sometimes there was personal ambition. So, strange alliances began to be formed.

Tommy Thompson was a guy who . . . had ideas that were very close to Reuther's. But he could never ally himself to Reuther and survive in a place like the Rouge. . . . In 1943–44, he allied with the Progressive Caucus. And there were people within the Progressive Caucus who tried to figure out how to dump him. On the other hand, there were people who were progressive and sophisticated, who also, for their own selfish purposes, decided to identify with Thompson. . . .

You know, the quest for power is a very attractive and a very corrupting thing; it does strange things to people. Some guy wants to get elected, and he's a member of the party, and he doesn't want to subject himself to the discipline of the party, or the discipline of his group, or the discipline of a caucus. So, he decides to go off by himself. How he balances that becomes an interesting and complicated matter.

What influence did the Communists at the Rouge have on the workers' political views and voting practices?

I'd have to have some very concrete stuff in front of me, because I'm inclined to say that I don't think we basically changed the pattern of mass response in politics. . . . The reality is—and that's what confounds us—that the automobile workers union, which we had something to do with shaping, is considered one of the better unions, in the sense that it practices a better brand of social unionism as against business unionism. But the auto workers in the main—well, in the last election the majority of the white auto workers voted for Reagan. I think that the input radicals have on particular situations is one that has to be examined very carefully. The challenge for radicals is not to exaggerate what their input is, as important as it is. And as I look back at it, I think that we had a tendency to exaggerate what our input was, not that it was minimal. For example, the Communist Party today will say that it is responsible for the organization of the CIO, or it is responsible for Social Security and unemployment compensation, and all the other social legislation. That's nonsense, and that's not to say that their contribution was not important. But the Communist Party certainly wasn't "responsible" for these achievements. In the 1930s, a major upheaval was taking place in the country, and without that upheaval we would not have been able to play the particular role that we played. Therefore, it's more important to figure out what it was, instead of claiming the credit for it. . . . We were not even decisive, but we were very important.

If the nation was moving in a progressive direction, it's because the objective conditions had matured to make it possible. (It's just like somebody is trying to figure out why was Reagan so popular, and they say, "Well, it's the weakness of the left." I think that's nonsense.)

You have to understand the objective situation in order to deal with it, before a change will take place. You can turn yourself inside out, and come up with the correct "policy" and line, but you're not going to change it.

■ ART MCPHAUL

How did you go about eliciting worker support?

Fought for those things that were correct, fought the company, and fought for their interests, *period.* I made no special approach to them. . . . I treated them right, fought for them, fought the company when they were wrong (which was almost always). That's the way I won their support. I took one position all the time, that was against the company. Now, if the worker was wrong, I would tell him he was wrong, "I will support you this time, but don't do it again, because if you do it again, I won't support you. It's wrong; you should not do it." I took a straightforward position and they respected that. . . . Not only did I consider myself [militant], but everybody else did, too—including the company. That was one of the reasons I was fired.[65]

■ JOHN SAARI

We had quite a few mine workers. But what happened, because of the popularity of John L. Lewis for what he'd done, naturally a lot of the so-called people who wanted to run for office they spoke of John L., and in fact they even portrayed themselves as mine workers.

■ WALTER DOROSH

I ran for president with [Art McPhaul] in [the stamping plant] building. I was laid off then as a tool-and-die maker. In that building, McPhaul got elected [vice president] on my ticket. . . . He got elected and never served a day. He got fired.

See, what was happening, this was the militant days of our union, this was 1948. I got laid off, and I could have gone off and gotten a job as a tool maker or stay in the plant. I agreed to stay in the plant. I went to work in the stamping plant. I was working for a Polish boss, a personal friend of mine, I knew. . . . What we [my ticket] were doing, we were carrying on a campaign during our lunch period. We used to get up in the lunch room and speak. I was running against Archie Acciacca, and I charged Archie [with] agreeing to speed up in the plant. He agreed with the company to put counters on machines. Before they never had no counters. Archie said, "Well, everybody is going to do their share of work"; and he became concerned about the company's effort. Anyway, there was a number of other things he had agreed to, and we contested him on it. . . . So, this Polish guy [the foreman] comes up to me, and said, "Come on, I'll give you a tip." I said, "What's happening?" He said, "I was just called down to Labor Relations. I understand you're speaking in the lunchrooms." "Yeah," I said, "I'm up for president." "I know you are," he says. "There is going to be Ford Service and Labor Relations in there; and, under the contract, I understand you guys can't speak in the lunchrooms"—which is true, you can't speak in the lunchrooms. "They are going to have your speech on a recorder. With the speech, they'll nail you. You'll be discharged." So I said, "Wow, I better get down to McPhaul." McPhaul was a full-time committeeman. "Will you excuse me a minute? I want to go talk to somebody to make sure he don't get hurt either."

So, I go down and get all of them, Max Chait, [Andy] Anderson, Dorosh, we had nine men on the slate; but there was only about four speakers; the other five were just good guys; you couldn't get them to talk in front of a crowd. I was a rabble rouser. McPhaul was a rab-ble-rouser. Max Chait was a rabble rouser. So was Anderson. The four of us were making a lot of noise. They had three main lunchrooms; and they used to get about five hundred people in the lunchrooms. And we would stand up on the tables and speak. The first day I got up, and spoke, and Archie wasn't there. He said, "Boy if you say a word against me again, I'll be there." I said, "Okay, you be there. I'm going to be there the next day." So, I was in the next lunchroom, which was the bigger one. They had two on one end, and the biggest one in the cen-ter. Archie was there, and he got up, and he said: "He's not a produc-tion man. He's a tool-and-die. He don't care about you guys." He didn't hit the issues though, and, well, he beat me bad there. . . .

I got a hold of McPhaul at the committee desk and I says, "Hey, I'm not speaking today in the cafeteria. You shouldn't. Let Archie speak." He says, "Are you taking the word of a foreman?" I said, "What have we got to lose? If nothing happens to Archie today, you can go speak tomorrow. What's the problem?" "Look I'm not going to be a quitter. We got these guys on—" I said, "Okay. I'm not speaking. I'm going to take that word that was given to me."

And so they got Archie and everybody. They fired them all. Well, I went to the hearings. I had to go to the hearings downtown before the umpire; and I defended Archie and all of them. They wanted a witness for and against; and nobody would go up there for Archie, because they didn't care too much; and I said, "I'll go." And my story up there was that, "They've always done it. What's all the concern about?" So, anyway the long and short of it, the umpire reinstated Archie, but he kept the others fired, McPhaul, Anderson, and Chait. Archie was reinstated to full employment. And we could never under-stand that. Well, Archie gave a story up there. "I know this is illegal, but I don't want people to consider me as a coward to get up to speak. If they speak, I'm forced to do this thing, on whichever stand. They started this, and it is important for a guy to get up."

■ SHELTON TAPPES

One of the reasons the CIO was so far ahead of the American Federation of Labor is because the CIO members had better political understanding than the American Federation of Labor did. The American
Federation of Labor people were very staid and conservative and to
them the only important time to be interested in politics was every
four years' presidential elections. So, you go and you vote Republican;
and then you go on back to your job. But in the CIO there were education classes at all times, there was political action. Local 600 is a good
example. We had more than just a grievance machinery out there. We
had a library with about, I'd say, about 1,500 volumes at one time.

■ DAVE MOORE

Were issues—of politics, solidarity, class consciousness, and this kind
of thing—talked about on the shop floor?
   Oh yeah, oh yeah. On the shop floor, around the machines, during
the lunch-hour breaks, guys used to come down. I'll give an example.
The guy [Art] McPhaul got fired for talking in the lunchroom, during
lunch break, about the rights of workers, and what you had to do, and
those things, about solidarity, sticking together, what your rights are.
"These are the things we got agreement on. Don't you let nobody take
them away from you. If you have any doubt about it, you think you're
wrong, you ask that foreman to get you a representative. He is obligated to do it"—which they were. "If I'm not in that department—if
your field rep is not in that department—you tell that foreman you
want a union representative, and have him call the office; and somebody will come down and explain to you what you are entitled to. But
never let nobody give you anything that you have any doubt about."
   They would talk about the contract during lunch hour. They would
talk about the different issues up in the lunchrooms. They would have
debates in the lunchroom about Taft-Hartley. They would have debates
in the lunchroom about Joe McCarthy. They'd have debates in the
lunchroom about the Korean War, . . . whether we had a right to be
there, whether our forces should be pulled out, what caused it.
   At that time in the late 1940s and early '50s, the mid-'50s, and in
the late '50s, you had the workers in the shop who were there at the
time the union came in. Most of the guys in the shop were veterans
of the strike, and veterans of organization there. During the late 1950s
and early '60s, that's when the work force began to change. They be-

gan to get younger people in who had never been exposed to struggle. The mistake that the union made (I say it was a mistake maybe it
was deliberate, I don't know), they didn't educate their workers about
the struggle.

■ JOHN MANDO

There were secretaries in there that were considered the right-wing
secretaries, because they were more friendly to the so-called right-wing
buildings. [My wife] was identified as a left-winger. She was considered
one of the progressives. Her favorite buildings were tool-and-die and
the motor building. And it was funny (it wasn't funny) but there used
to be friction between secretaries as a result. This thing carried right
down to the secretaries.

■ JOHN ORR

Yeah, those attacks [on the left], boy oh boy, . . . you don't know how
personal they could get. Have women call your wife at home and tell
her you were in a bar with some woman, "He's in the bar with me."
Or go to a convention and come back. . . . And bust up your home,
anything. Force you to resign to maintain peace at home. Anything. [We
never] . . . resorted to those tactics. I sure as hell never could interject
into anybody's home life or anything else. Drinking habits, womaniz-
ing, anything else. I used to say, "I'm not a moralist. I won't prejudge
you."

■ WALTER DOROSH

John Fitzpatrick (who was later head of Stellato's campaign committee, when he ran in 1950 as a right-winger) was chairman of the ACTU
at the plant. He was Irish-Catholic. He was the old fatherly type. (He
was kind of elderly when we brought the union in there. I guess he
must have been around fifty-five and I was only about twenty-one then
[in 1941]. . . .) He would come and talk to me, "Look, let me give you
some advice. I'm an old man. I have gone through experiences. You
have to follow your church teachings." I would tell him, "John, I don't
care." I said, "If I want to go to pray, I know where the church is." But,
I said, "We're not going to mix the church with our trade union movement, because it just isn't going to work. I don't want to get involved
in these fights."

When we used to have elections, if the [ACTU] were supporting one slate of candidates, the Masons were supporting the other, automatically. . . . Every plant used to have its own set of officers, president running down; and if the guy on the top wasn't a Catholic, John wouldn't support him. He would put another guy in there, it would be a third slate.

■ JOHN MANDO

I don't know if you know this, [but Stellato] left the international staff as a regional assistant director to run for Local [600] president.

■ KEN BANNON

[Carl Stellato] worked for Percy Llewellyn as a staff member.
But then you said he went back to the plant.
Yeah, after Percy was defeated.
I thought Stellato came from the international, that he was on the staff in 1949, and he came back to Rouge just to run.
No, he was back [in the plant.]
But he had the backing of the Reuther slate, right?
That's right. . . . We met in Walter's basement on Longfellow and we agreed to support Carl Stellato as president.
How did you come to support him, if he had been previously associated with the left?
Tommy Thompson [the president of UAW Local 600 at the time] was very, very close to George Addes and that group.
So he was just the lesser of the two evils?
That's right.
Okay, so when he gets elected on the Reuther slate, it's not as if he was a real solid Reutherite.
No, that turned out to be unbelievable. But anyhow.
Do you know if the right wing in the Rouge supported him wholeheartedly during that 1950 election?
Oh sure, that I know. Well, [in 1951] he barely won. That was when Joe Hogan [the Local 600 Progressive Caucus's candidate for president] almost knocked the living hell out of him.[66] And there's a question as to whether or not Joe Hogan won or not. As the result of that close election, Carl Stellato began to play games with the left wing. . . .
He knew he wouldn't get too much opposition from the right, because we kind of destroyed ourselves over him. At the point that we take Carl Stellato and make him our candidate, and he begins to build

up his forces, he uses the right-wing group; and then he leaves us, and goes to the left-wing group, how are we going to get all of our people back? It took us a while to do that.

After he was elected, Stellato put five officers on trial for Communist sympathies. Do you know where he got the idea?

The international union—because of the Taft-Hartley affidavits, what have you.

So, they wanted to have the local take care of it themselves?

They put the administration over the local.

After the HUAC hearings, right?[67]

Yeah.

So, what was Reuther's reaction when Stellato started affiliating with the Progressive Caucus in the Rouge?

The same as yours would be, double-cross.

■ HORACE SHEFFIELD

When he was first elected president of Local 600 in 1950, Carl Stellato set up that trial of the five who were accused of being Communist Party members.[68] *How did you feel about that?*

Well, of course, to me that was just opportunism. Yeah, really, I mean. That was part of the politics that he saw that would enhance his own image and enhance his power base.

So, you don't think that had anything to do with the international? There was no—

Well, let me say, I don't think it had anything [to do] with principles, as far as Carl Stellato was concerned.

Now, what was the reaction of the right wing when Stellato, who was elected as a right-winger, turned more to the left?

Well, of course, consternation and opposition. . . . They felt betrayed, because he saw this as an opportunity to enhance his power. It was just that clear.

■ JOHN MANDO

[After] Carl Stellato broke with the international union . . . [the rolling mill unit, which was always considered a right-wing unit] formed a coalition [with him]. . . . It may be a little difficult for me to explain this, because we were not really opposed to the international union, but we were closely aligned with Carl Stellato. In the early 1950s. I particularly had a great deal of problems because in our caucus we had people who were pro-international [and] . . . [who were] anti-international, and people that were pro-Stellato and anti-Stellato. We had constant turmoil; so much so, that for several years we used to have a great deal of difficulty trying to put a slate together because people were tugging in both directions. Back then, we used to have our conventions every year (and then they used to have one every two years, and then they went to every three years). So, we were having elections quite often at that time.

What caused people to side with Reuther versus Stellato?

Well, as I say, the rolling mill unit was a right-wing unit way back when. Actually, it would have remained a right-wing unit all the way through, except for that flap, the loss of premium time. That's really what created the division. They were anti-international because they lost the premium time. More so anti-international than pro-Stellato, because of what happened in the 1949 negotiations.

It was so difficult to put [a slate together]. We would be allowed four delegates for a convention. The unit chairman, normally, would be a candidate heading the slate. We used to have such a rhubarb that I refused to run as a delegate for several elections because . . . I just couldn't reach a meeting of the minds. So, we'd wind up where we tried to compromise the two groups within our caucus by saying, "Okay, we've got four delegates. We'll say we are going to elect two delegates that are pro-international and two delegates that are pro-Stellato." And we tried to [make] do on that basis.

Well, I was just trying to keep the thing together. I was taking the position: "Look, we can get along with the international; we could have a coalition with Carl Stellato; and still get along with the international union." This was the best way to provide service to our members. So, rather than get into this dogfight, the political dogfight, concentrating most of your time on politics, that worked. We got good cooperation from the international union. We had good cooperation, excellent cooperation, from the local leadership, Carl Stellato, in particular.

Carl Stellato, in my view, was the most dynamic, most competent, local president that we have had—not only in Local No. 600, but throughout the UAW.

■ DELORIS AND KENNETH ROCHE

How do you think Stellato got the backing of the Rouge workers in 1950, after he had been on the international and then ran on Reuther's slate?

Kenneth Roche: He had a good following, a good political group, and the opposition was practically nil.

Deloris Roche: He was a good Catholic, and that was the year for the Catholics.

Kenneth Roche: He was able to charm. He'd take an angry worker into his office; and in five minutes the guy'd come out patting him on the back. He was that type of guy. He had much personal charm.

■ ANNE BOATIN

Well, in the motor building, this is rather interesting, all of the officers, the top officers, were all white. Every one of them. There was never a black until Paul ran in 1950, and his vice president was black. He chose a black. Well, that just spread throughout the local. "What are you doing, Paul? Once you let this happen, the blacks are going to take over." Of course, they did a terrific job on him. "Nigger-lover"— and everything else.

■ PAUL BOATIN

There were Polish workers who had helped organize the union, Ukrainian workers. But foreign-speaking workers did not get elected to office. . . . The more mature understood the union. Others became disenchanted.

None of them tried to shorten their names and do it that way?

They were too proud. They had contributed to building this giant organization, and they couldn't see why their prestige, and the contribution that they made, wasn't recognized. To be appointed to a voluntary committee that didn't even pay expenses to drive your car. All the nonpaying jobs, all the things that nobody else wanted, [they] got.

■ HORACE SHEFFIELD

I went back in the plant in 1944, when a political shift [occurred]. The Reuther forces suffered some kind of defeat [in 1944]. Was that the fight between Leonard and Addes? I don't recall. Back in those days, when your side lost, you went into the plant. This matter of surviving the political shifts did not come about until about 1946 or '47. The union drew the policy that really whoever was new president, new international administration, did not mean any wholesale dismissals of staff and bringing on new ones; they ended that.

■ WALTER DOROSH

Walter signed the five-year contract, and we were furious about that.

We disrupted at the conventions, and all over, and we raised hell with him. We said he had no right, without convention decision, to sign a five-year contract—[we'd] just walk in and say, "Who the hell made you God?" [We] carried on a campaign in *Ford Facts,* which was our [Local 600's] official publication. I was the head of the paper then, and I really blasted him.

■ SHELTON TAPPES

I worked in the Ford foundry in the Rouge plant. I was a machine molder.... Until I retired, I was still under the jurisdiction of the foundry. When I retired from Ford Motor Company I had thirty-nine years of service. I only worked for Ford Motor Company about two years; all the rest of the time I was on the union leave of absence. But my time, my seniority went on, accumulated. So when I retired from the UAW I also retired from Ford Motor Company.

When you were an officer in Local 600 you weren't also working in the foundry?

I wasn't working, no. I was on union salary. The four top officers, president, vice president, recording secretary, and the secretary-treasurer, were all full-time salaried positions; and the four of us had leaves of absence. [These] were renewed every year on the anniversary of your first leave; and mine continued right on through my whole career.

I had three successful elections in Local 600. I ran for recording secretary of the local, and won hands down—very easily. My campaign manager was a fellow named J. B. Jones.

Once I became a staff member at the international union, I also renewed my leave of absence every year.

After I was defeated, I was granted a month's vacation by the [local] union, a month off with full pay. So, I took the family, and we went away for a month. And when I came back, and checked into the plant, I find out that they had had a special election. There were two vacancies for the bargaining committee [in the foundry]. Somebody put my name in, and I was elected to the bargaining committee. So, here I am, instead of going to work on the job, I go to work in the union office.

I functioned [there] less than a year, because the regular local union elections came up. I got with a group of guys, and we decided that we would support Carl Stellato for president. They depended on me and my knowledge of different people who were candidates. I told them that I thought Carl was a pretty solid and steady fellow. (He had worked for me one time at the local, when I was recording secretary.

I had charge of the top bargaining committee who handled the grievances before they went into the umpire stage.) We supported Carl, and
successfully. Then I went right on back in the shop, but I chose the
night shift. I always preferred the midnight shift. You know, fewer
bosses around, and then you got, they gave a midnight incentive, 10
cents extra an hour. One morning about, I guess it must have been
about four or five o'clock, Carl Stellato walks in the plant; and he said,
"Well I've been elected." He says, "I'll be installed next Sunday, at the
General Council meeting. I've got to name my cabinet. I want you to
work with us." I told him, "No, these people wouldn't let me work
for you. You'd have no peace." He said, "Well, why did you support
me? Why did you work so hard?" I said, "I wanted a good president. I
just wanted my local to have a good president." But he would have
no part of it; so, that's how I started back. First, he put me in charge
of the plant committee; and then he transferred me over to education
director.

You didn't hold elective office again after that?

Never did, in the local, no. From there, I went to the international.
Walter had—believe it or not, Walter Reuther sent for me.

He wanted you out of the local?

Yeah, sure

*Weren't you afraid that by going to the international that you
would get cut off at the knees if Reuther decided to—?*

That was the reason I hesitated; that's the reason I refused it. I know
there was a sinister reason, too. They wanted me split away from [Carl]
Stellato. . . .

The only thing I could say is, "Well, Walter knows what my politics
are; and, unfortunately, all the years that I've been a delegate, I've never
voted for him. Does he expect me to change?" Well, he knew that I
was going to raise that question, and he says, "Walter's prepared to
accept you as you are, with one condition; and that is, you do no pol-
iticking as an international rep. Whatever your opinions are, you don't
get on a soapbox, so to speak." Well, that's understandable, after all,
he signed your checks.

He effectively silenced you as a voice of the opposition?

Yeah.

■ WALTER DOROSH

Full-time, you got a committee desk, and you are full time on the job
[as committeeman]. And it's the greatest strength in the world. It's the
best job in the world. It was just a great feeling. I hated to give that

up. When I was on the bargaining committee, I was in charge of the whole plant, and you don't have that direct first stage, you have the second stage. . . . And then you sit in the chair and you're busy with the brass, and you don't have that daily contact that is great. So, when I went back, Carl [Stellato] says—you know, after he won the election—"Come on back." "No," I says, "I don't want to go back there. I love being right here."

■ VICTOR REUTHER

It was a very firm principle that Walter held to over the years, that you must draw a clear line between an enemy and an opponent. An enemy is one who is seeking to destroy you, and it's all right to destroy him. An opponent is one who you seek to win over. And I think [this is] one of the reasons why the UAW finally established teamwork in the leadership and solidarity in the ranks. One reason why the years of internal struggle and factionalism was ended is that Walter made a concerted effort to reach people who were salvageable, who were not bitter-enders who wanted to continue a factional fight just for the sake of opposition. He tried to reach them, and reason with them, and win them over. Doug Fraser, who was prominent in the Progressive Caucus, became a lieutenant for Walter, and successor to him as president. Dave Miller, who was the opposition spokesman of the west side local to Walter, was honored by the international union in having a building named after him. Dick Leonard, who was a member of the executive board and prominent in the Addes Caucus, was hired by Walter, when Walter became president of the CIO, as one of his lieutenants in Washington.

I could give you chapter and verse of a long, long list of people throughout the whole union. So, if that happened in River Rouge, don't look for some mysterious reasons, some devious reasons. That was going on in the whole union. People were finding their way to make a continuing useful contribution, and to get out of the business of just bitching.

■ WALTER DOROSH

We, Local 600, were too big for Walter Reuther. We used to go to a convention, we used to have three hundred delegates. And the convention at that time . . . used to have 1,500 delegates. We had quite a sizable crowd. And at the 1955 convention (or was it 1953 or '55? I forgot which one now), Stellato ran for vice president. We just nominated [him,] and ran without any campaigning, and he finished in the runoff. No candidate had sufficient votes. There was three that ran for vice president. After that election Walter Reuther also changes the constitution. At that time, if you remember, when Walter Reuther got elected in 1947, you could run for the presidency one office at a time. If you lost, then you could also run for your own job again, vice president. And if you lost that, you could run for secretary-treasurer. You could run for some job. . . . Walter Reuther got elected president, and R. J. Thomas ran for vice president and got elected. After the convention, after the Stellato convention where we almost upset Reuther, he said, "Oh, no, from now on you are going to have to elect everybody at one time, one vote." It changed the whole concept of the convention.

■ DAVE MOORE

They don't file grievances like they did then. They don't follow through on the grievance procedure like they used to do [in the 1940s and '50s]. . . . If they can't resolve it with the supervisor verbally, write in a grievance. That's what the company don't like for you to do, write grievances. They do not like that, because once that grievance is processed and it goes through the procedure, and it goes before the arbitrator, you don't know who in the hell is going to win.

So are you saying that both right wing and left wing had to be militant?

Oh, yeah, they had to be. . . . I think they represented them, they had to, at the time that I was in the shop, if they wanted to stay in office. They had to make a hell of a showing, or they just didn't stay in office. . . .

It [pushing a grievance] could be [done] in many ways. A right-winger at that time could represent a person on the floor; . . . he would raise hell on the floor. Now, once that grievance was filed, when that grievance gets to the bargaining committee, the next stage up, that right-winger had to come in and say what happened, and give all the details on it. The guy is going to ask him . . . "Is this all the information you got in [this person's] defense?" and he say, "Yeah." Well, they say, "I want you to go out and get some more. I want you to get some people who are standing around. I want you to get the names of the people who are standing around. Get their version of what happened. I want you . . . to bring someone in here who is going to be on [this worker's] side, who is going to be a witness." . . . Now, once he's told that; if he didn't do it and that grievance had to go out; and the word got back that there was a witness . . . and the committeeman didn't pursue that, didn't make any effort to get that in a grievance so it could be looked at when it gets to the arbitrator, that guy just didn't get elected.

I would say [that] in the 1940s and the '50s, I think both a right-wing committeeman versus a left-wing committeeman tried to do what was right. I think the left wing pursued it more aggressively, and more diligently and with more extent, than the right-wing guy did. He [the left-wing committeeman] would not take any kind of answer from the supervisor that was not in favor of the person they were representing. . . . That was a difference in the political set-up at Local 600. But a right-wing committeeman in 1940 and 1950 and the early 1960s would be considered a left-wing committeeman today. He would.

■ KENNETH ROCHE

I was in a committee for about fourteen years, twice elected unopposed, in the tool-and-die, which is very difficult to do. No matter who was in the leadership, I still got elected. But at the end they started to gerrymander the districts around, and they got me on all these high-class tool-and-die makers that didn't want to be fighting the company too hard. I was being gerrymandered out of a job . . . because we had right-wing leadership at that time; and I was about the only one left in the left wing in the tool-and-die. I could see the handwriting on the wall; so, I put my name on a bid list to go to the rolling mill. ([Everyone] wanted to get there, because when you got there, you got an incentive. In other words, you got a regular pay plus.) An opening came, one of the fellows retired in my classification. So [in 1974] I resigned my job on the tool-and-die committee, and I went in and started working there. They appointed somebody else to take it over, and they had an election.

■ VICTOR REUTHER

I don't think there's any place for union factionalism. I think there is a place and an urgent need for a democratic opposition. I think it is a sad day for labor, when the administration of any union tries to stifle democratic debate and discussion.

Are you including caucuses in that?

I am including caucuses, I am indeed.

So you think that the caucus system is a good structure?

I think it's okay, if it deals with issues, and not just supporting people to give them jobs. When caucuses no longer are identified with issues but are only identified with keeping people on our side in office, then they no longer serve their purpose, then they become destructive. I think at a time when trade union leadership throughout the whole U.S., including the leadership of the AFL-CIO, thinks it's okay to publicly criticize Ronald Reagan (and I agree with them, he deserves it), but cannot tolerate criticism of themselves and their own trade union action by members, then that's a sad day; and it's a sign that internal union democracy is being trampled on; and that's happening today inside the UAW. That's why I've spoken out so often in recent months. I'm not going out to organize a progressive caucus though.

Do you hope somebody else does?

I hope there will be a lot of voices calling attention to these shortcomings, whether it's done in the form of a caucus or not I don't know. But one way or the other those voices should be heard.

The Henry Wallace Campaign

■ PAUL BOATIN

In 1948, Local 600 played a key role in the formation of the Progressive Party, and most of the officers at the local attended the founding convention in Lansing, Michigan, for the formation of the State Progressive Party.

■ SAUL WELLMAN

We threw everything into the efforts to support Wallace, but the outcome was a dismal failure. He got a little bit more than a million votes, and in Michigan it was just as bad. It might have looked better than it did in Oklahoma or Illinois or something like it, but it was bad looking against bad.

Blacks were a very important part of the Progressive Party movement. Nationally, Paul Robeson played a pioneering role with Henry Wallace, who was the presidential candidate [of the Progressive Party, in 1948]. For example, Wallace was the first serious white liberal candidate to go into the South to campaign. He campaigned in the context of non-Jim Crow meetings. Don't forget, in 1946 and '47 and '48, Jim Crow is still rampant in the South. . . . The black issue had just begun to render the Democratic Party, out of which came the Dixiecrat movement. Strom Thurmond, the Democratic governor of South Carolina in 1947, became a Republican shortly after. But before he became a Republican, he organized the Dixiecrat Party, which was anti-Truman, [and] anti-civil rights. . . . Henry Wallace moved into the South, and he had to deal with the question of Jim Crow and segregation. The person who was alongside of him throughout the entire southern campaign, which was enormous, was Paul Robeson. Paul Robeson attracted black masses, and the black masses in 1947 and '48 responded to these issues a little bit differently than they did later, in 1958 and '68. It's a very, very early stage. . . . A very important person in the Wallace movement was a black woman publisher by the name of Carlotta (or Charlotte) Bass. . . . There was a lot of support, but the mainstream of black life did not enter into the Progressive Party. . . . In Michigan, up to 1948 and immediately after, the most important full-time public figure in the Michigan Progressive Party was the black, Coleman Young—who was later to become mayor of the city. Blacks were in the Progressive Party's leadership. . . . But it doesn't mean that it's adequate for the situation. Their participation was not enough to make the Progressive Party a credible alternative to Truman and the Democratic Party.

■ DAVE MOORE

When [Henry] Wallace ran for president, I was accused of going against the UAW policy. I supported Wallace, and so did Coleman Young, the present mayor. There was a lot of people in the Local 600 who supported Wallace. Some people got punished for that also. The local as a whole did not support it. . . .

[Wallace] came to speak here in Detroit. He had quite a few people show up. But some were frightened away. It wasn't as much, I would say, that, I guess, Wallace wanted, or some of those who were supportive of Wallace wanted.

But there were quite a few people in the labor movement in Detroit who supported Wallace. Some of them didn't openly do it. Some said, "Look, I'm with you, but I would rather not be publicly identified." At the time that Wallace ran, the hysteria was on. Truman had dumped him. The Red scare was on. People would be called before un-American Committee. In general, overwhelmingly, the labor movement was against Wallace.

■ WALTER DOROSH

It kind of split the local. . . . I think most of the people, while there was a lot of activity for [Henry] Wallace, . . . felt that this is an adventurous thing—that Wallace didn't have an opportunity to win, and consequently you're helping to elect [Thomas] Dewey. These kind of discussions. Some guys were just hurt by it; they said that Harry Truman was Roosevelt's [man]. I'm talking about the older progressives who grew up in the Roosevelt era. And that created quite a division. While the Wallace forces were numerous, I think it would be about a three-way split. Well, maybe not three ways, because there was no Republican support. The right wing was 100 percent behind Truman, of course. They just thought it [supporting Wallace] was the wrong thing. A lot of progressives changed their positions, and went with Truman. The people in the plant (I was in tool-and-die then) kidded us. They said, "You guys are foolish; you'll just get Dewey elected."

Do you think that you got out a good-size vote from the Ford workers for Wallace?

I don't know. I couldn't say. I can't remember that period now. But there was a lot of activity. I lived in South Dearborn at that time; and Wallace finished first in my precinct. There is no question about it. Yes, Wallace finished first in South Dearborn. You'll find that to be a fact. I think it was Precinct 5, I was in, at that time. Everybody on my street [voted for Wallace]. I was precinct captain; and we were very active. I would pick the people up, and took them to vote, and everything. They said "That's the guy you should go for."

■ JOHN ORR

Oh, my building [tool-and-die] went all out [for Henry Wallace]. Of course, we were in violation of UAW policy. But at that time we had a president named Virgil Lacey, who was quite a gutsy individual.

■ DELORIS AND KENNETH ROCHE

Kenneth Roche: We took placards down to the Labor Day parade. Lee Romano was sitting on top of a sound truck.[69] I was holding a "Wallace For President" sign. He said, "Get that guy out of the parade!" I took the sign, and I started running towards the sound truck, and I said, "You son-of-a-bitch, you! Don't you tell me what to do with my signs!" They left me alone. I walked all the way down Woodward with that sign, but boy was he mad; he was boiling. But he was afraid, because I was young then, and I wasn't about to take any crap. I think I was about the only one in the Local 600 delegation who marched in the parade with a sign. All the rest of them they made them throw away.

Deloris Roche: There was a good movement here, a good Progressive Party movement.

Kenneth Roche: Oh yeah, it was a good Progressive movement in Local 600. Big meetings downtown, and we had a Progressive group going. We had meetings, several of them.

Did you think that the campaigning for Wallace got the vote out for him in this city?

It got as much as it could out, believe me. It was effective. I think
Wallace got more votes around this section, not in Dearborn, in Detroit, than they ever expected him to get. We ran a good
campaign . . . for Wallace.

Deloris Roche: A lot of hard work.

Kenneth Roche: A lot of hard work, energy expended, distribution
at plant gates, and everything.

*Did the Progressive Caucus within the union pretty much go for
Wallace and the right wing for Truman?*

Yeah.

Or did the right wing sometimes go for Wallace also?

They didn't go for Wallace at all.

■ JOHN SAARI

I took it upon myself [to form] the "Dearborn for Wallace Committee."
. . . We worked at it, and we had a good thing going. But there was one
thing that was missing. You see, Reuther and all these forces, they
agitated that [Truman was] the lesser of two evils and that "Wallace is
going to split the Democratic vote, and the Republican will get elected." All this, and the workers ate it up. We didn't have too many labor
people from the top involved but we did have some . . . secondary
leadership from the union.

From the UAW, from Local 600?

Local 600. But we lacked the board, the top officers. . . . Of course,
at that time, I think, the right wing was pretty well on its way to total
control.

Did you get many Ford workers to vote for Henry Wallace?

I don't think so. Oh, the flak I used to get. We used to pass literature
out at the motor building. At that time [it] was right on Miller Road, and
there was a gate going right in there, a lot of the progressive forces laid
away from the Wallace for president [campaign] because of, perhaps,
their own position within the trade union movement, in the building.
They were an officer, and maybe didn't want to get defeated.

And to me things like that don't make no difference. I didn't care.
In fact, I really didn't care to be a committeeman, I really didn't. I resigned one time because—with the way things were, the top controlled everything—you had to compromise yourself. I thought that
maybe it'd be better if you took the issue and fought it out, really,
whether you got elected or not. The issue wasn't you getting elected,
but people. . . . Freedom is precarious. . . . That individual, although he
may have believed in Wallace, he didn't have the freedom to move.

What influence was he under? He was under the tyranny of the majority. Right? He was under the tyranny of the majority. He was afraid to move.

They didn't defeat me; and I used to put up a fight for Wallace. I used to pack a lot of literature in that place. And I used to also be watched over; I went in with literature. A lot of other left-wingers went in with literature, and [if] they caught them, boom, boom, . . . they got a couple of days off, a couple of weeks off, something like that, depending upon how many times they got caught.

Red-hunt

■ MARGARET AND STANLEY NOWAK

Stanley Nowak: [I was a kid when I saw] the Palmer Raids in my own neighborhood. . . . Russian, Polish, Lithuanian . . . social clubs raided by the police.[70] They used these tactics that on Sunday, Saturday night, Christmas Eve—

Margaret Nowak: New Year's Eve.

Stanley Nowak: New Year's Eve party. That's right. As the people went into the halls to celebrate their New Year's eve, they would raid them and stay there, and arrest everyone who came into the hall, and take them to the police headquarters. And then from there, for a time, for weeks, the families could not locate their sons or their husbands, at what station they were kept, because even the police department didn't know. They were not prepared for these kind of raids. There was something like ten thousand people—so-called Reds and radicals—arrested throughout the country. How many of them were in Chicago, I don't know. But that was my introduction to it. And later on—

Margaret Nowak: What made it more impressive for him, he told me—as we tried to write his book, he had to dig into his memory—is that many of these people who were arrested were people who had come from his village, his community. He knew them. And to a boy who had been educated in American schools about our great traditions and so on, and he saw these things happening to these people who had never done anything to anybody and it disturbed him.

■ HORACE SHEFFIELD

How did you feel when they enacted the Taft-Hartley Act in 1947?

I felt as the trade unions did all over the country. In the kind of climate, and the people who sponsored it, it was an antiunion act. . . . That was universal.

What about that act's non-Communist affidavit?

I had worried then, as I would have now, when you begin to single out one political group. I saw it as regressive.

■ JOHN SAARI

During the Taft-Hartley drive we lost a few; and, in fact, . . . one of them was a very prominent individual and a very good fighter, Joe Couser. He was an officer of Local 600, and he just simply refused to sign that [Taft-Hartley affidavit]. But others, well, I don't know what they done, but some of them signed, and they capitulated. . . . A lot of people quit [rather than sign].

When they couldn't beat us in Local 600, they called in the un-American Activities Committee. Paul [Boatin] was taken off. Let's see, five building chairmen were just arbitrarily taken off. I was a district committeeman. I was taken off. Several other committeemen were taken off. In other words, they got to our core—the core forces we had. . . . I went back on the job. Some didn't. Some that were accused, they flocked over. . . . They were out to get us; and they were using the arm of the government to get us.

"They" meaning Reuther? The right wing? Ford? They were all out to get you guys?

Oh, definitely, definitely. It's as plain as . . . can be. . . . We knew what we were doing, but our forces were limited. . . . A lot of people don't know what we're up against [during the Red Scare]. You got TV, you got radio, you got, at that time, you had three Detroit newspapers. You had every community newspaper. Gee whiz, that's a tremendous thing to face. Those are big odds. They threw the book at us. They hurt us, oh they hurt us, but they didn't drown us. We're not drowned by any means. We got hurt real bad, and a lot of them, it split their families, wives got divorced. It was a terrible blow. McCarthyism especially.

Workers were influenced by red-baiting sometimes?

Oh, yeah, yeah. They were. What happened is, a silence fell upon them.

■ KENNETH ROCHE

I was never in the leadership of the local, except for being a district committeeman. I never made any decisions or anything. Actually, the first political job I had was under one Paul Boatin, as committeeman in the old aircraft building (it's now the Dearborn engine plant), where they make Pratt-Whitney motors. I worked there. That's where I was removed by [Walter] Reuther. . . . Whitey Saari, myself, and Mike

Casper were committeemen in that unit, in the aircraft building. And
Nelson Samp came into the labor relations office with a letter; and he
told the labor relations man that he wanted to see all three of us in
the office. So, in we go, and he read the letter, from Reuther, demand-
ing—telling us—that we were removed from our [union] jobs for the
[UAW's] good.

■ HORACE SHEFFIELD

*How important do you think the 1952 House un-American Activi-
ties Committee's investigations were, when they came to Detroit?*
   In what respect?
In terms of the political struggles inside the local itself.
   Well, I don't think they had much impact. . . . The people that were
leading [it] were so unprincipled, Martin Dies and that ilk. It was a
witch hunt. . . . That was a very low point in our history.
*Do you think that was the general attitude of the right wing to-
ward the HUAC hearings—that the right-wingers disapproved?*
   Well, you had within the right-wing movement now, you had ideo-
logues just as passionately as you did now in the left wing. And, of
course, some of them took glee in it. I didn't, I didn't. But I think
most—a significant number—of the people in the right wing saw it
for what it was, really. "It's there now, and if we don't oppose this
thing, one day it will be the Methodists or the Baptists." And so they
took a rational attitude towards it. . . . Clearly there were those within the right-wing movement who took glee in it [the HUAC investiga-
tions] because they so passionately opposed the left wing, in the same
way that some of the Commies would have taken the same attitude if
it had been the reverse.
How about Reuther himself?
   Well, Reuther had a very principled position on it, the same as
[mine]. I mean, he opposed it on principled grounds.

■ VICTOR REUTHER

*In 1952 the House un-American Activities Committee came to De-
troit, and it focused its investigation on Local 600. Do you recall that?*
   Not the details of it. But I know that throughout the history of the
UAW, and certainly throughout Walter's activities that I know, we never welcomed the House un-American Activities Committee sticking
their nose into any internal matters of the labor movement. We always
looked upon them as the reactionary force they were. They were more

interested in grabbing headlines and smearing people than they were in being helpful in getting out the facts. So we are not one to encourage the House un-American Activities Committee.

In the Wayne State Archives is a letter, dated March 8, 1952, which was the second half of the correspondence between your brother and Chairman John S. Wood of the committee. It was Wood's reply, saying that your brother had written him to ask to appear before the committee, and that Wood couldn't fit him in the schedule during the Detroit hearings. But he could schedule him in Washington. Do you know if he ever testified?

I don't know whether he did or not. But I know that when the McClellan Committee had its hearings underway, Walter had to fight to get a hearing before them.[71] They were constantly smearing the UAW by various references to the Kohler strike, and so on, and Walter had to really raise hell and insist on a hearing. I don't think the House un-American Activities Committee was ever anxious to have Walter Reuther be a witness, because he would have been too effective in exposing them and what their antilabor smear actions always led to.

So that's the kind of thing that he wanted to bring up if he'd testified?

Oh, I'm sure he would have been a hostile witness. He would have said, "The record of our union on dealing with the Communist issue doesn't need any assistance from the House un-American Activities Committee. We are quite capable of dealing with that ourselves, and don't welcome your sticking your nose into it." I think that would have been the general tenor of what he would have said had he been privileged to testify.

■ JOHN ORR

There were a lot of Socialists. Hell, Walter Reuther was a Socialist once. So was Victor, [and his other] brother [Roy]. Most of the original UAW leaders were. A Socialist in the union at that time under Walter Reuther [was] not of the left wing; he was clean. [Reuther] was after the Communists. And as far as I'm concerned, that was just a whipping boy. . . .

How did the House un-American Activities Committee's hearings in Detroit affect the goings-on in the local?

Well . . . I never wanted to know who was a Communist and who wasn't. When a guy was charged he had a right to defense. . . . Quite a number of tool-and-die men were issued subpoenas to appear before that committee. Not all of them got to testify, but they were called down there. They lost work and everything else. And I put on a drive to pay their defense bills. . . . I raised $1,200. I never had a harder time in my life raising $1,200.

How did you go about doing it?

Took my best committeemen, and went man to man on their constituents. Not based on whether the guy was a Communist or whether he wasn't: "Was he a good committeeman, and whatnot? He's in trouble now." . . . We went man for man for $1. I remember one guy I went to, [to raise money for] Tom Jelley, [who] was a committeeman, and [this guy] said, "The best committeeman ever was in this plant."[72] He was crying. He handed over the $1, and he said, "If I thought for one minute that guy was a Communist, I would spit in his face. I wouldn't hand you a dime." He was the best committeeman he ever saw, but he was just so anti-Communist. I never saw emotions like they did then.

So, you had 1,200 contributors then, to that fund?

Well, maybe some people—I didn't raise it all personally. . . .

So, do you think that the HUAC hearings had an effect on the influence of the left in the local?

Oh, sure it did, it was intended to. Some still say that Reuther and the international union invited them to do a job that they couldn't do politically within the plant to them. Get their names before the general public.

So what happened?

Nothing. There was never anybody convicted or anything as a result of those hearings. And most of the guys just went down and used the Fifth Amendment.

So, how was it effective in reducing the force of the left in the local?

That was during the McCarthy days. . . . My God that McCarthy really raised hell in this country. Everybody was afraid to say anything. When he could indict guys like George Marshall—the secretary of state—as being an agent of the Communist Party, holy mackerel! He always used to go around waving a big sheet of paper. "Here, I have a list of twelve thousand dues-paying members of the Communist Party, and engaged in the State Department and other higher jobs." He never let that list go down so you could look at it. He just waved it. He started naming the names and, my God, some of the ones he named.

So, do you think the Ford workers were intimidated?

Yes, they were, sure they were.

■ WALTER DOROSH

Well, I did every kind of job [in the union] you could think of. I was department committeeman, district committeeman, [on the] bargaining committee. I was recording secretary of the tool-and-die unit, vice president of the tool-and-die unit, president of the tool-and-die unit, General Council delegate, convention delegate almost every convention, and president of Ford Local 600, [and] administrative assistant for Leonard Woodcock.[73]

Which years were you president?

1965–75, ten years.

That's a long time. During the early 1950s, you were on Carl Stellato's staff?

Oh yeah. Well, I was in charge of publications in 1950, until about 1952, when the un-American Activities Committee came to Detroit; and then I resigned and went back to work. Then I got elected again, committeeman.

■ SHELTON TAPPES

I was subpoenaed [by HUAC in mid-1951]. . . . "Contempt of Congress" is easy for those people; it's easy. They had a stack of steno notebooks; and each one had a year on it, had my name on it, and had a year on it. They didn't ask me questions; they told me. This was the preliminary hearing. The public hearing is just show. The hearing is held in privacy, in a room with one congressman and a battery of people from the Attorney General's Office [and] FBI. And you are there. Talk about Star Chamber, you are there sweating; and they just keep giving you coffee.

What are the steno notebooks about?

They got this record of you, reports they got from people, and all that, over the years. They had down there 1938, 1939, 1940, 1941. He had a stack of them. They'd ask questions; and I would answer. "Wait a minute," he'd say. You would get halfway through your answer, and he'd say, "Wait a minute." Then he would take his book, and he would go and find it, and then, "What did you say? It wasn't just quite that way, Mr. Tappes."

I was involved in a divorce too. I was divorcing my first wife; and there was a big question of custody of the children. And I wanted custody of the children. I was really—I was really frightened on that.

They'd say, "Mr. Tappes, on October 23, 1939, there was a meeting at St. — Do you deny that the meeting was [held]?" "No, I don't deny it. It probably was held." "Then if you feel that it probably was held, then do you remember that so-and-so said such-and-such and such-and-such?" "I don't know. I don't know. So and so and so and so? It's possible." All that kind of stuff, and it just goes on and on. They drone and drone and drone. This went on for about six hours, I guess, with a break for coffee, that's all, or [to] relieve yourself, and come right on back.

■   ART MCPHAUL

Shelton Tappes, I think, was one of the best, one of the most basic, trade unionists from the inception of the union at Ford's. He got off on a tangent during the un-American Activities Committee and testified against some of us, including me. This was a sort of self-serving thing for him. Well, I can understand why he did it. I didn't agree with why he did it, but I understand clearly why he did it. He felt that he had been let down by the left, that he stuck with the left when the left was in trouble; and then there was a certain incident that happened that hurt him and he figured the left was responsible for it—which they were.

Are you referring to the meeting with William Allan?

Well, I don't know if I'm talking about the same meeting. I don't know what happened with the meeting.

He talked about it in his testimony.

Say what?

He talked about it in his testimony at the House un-American Activities Committee.

What did he say generally?

Well, he said that he was called in to a Communist meeting where he thought he was going to speak; and actually they asked him why he didn't join, and—

Oh, no, no, that isn't the one I'm talking about. I don't know anything about that.

See, he was the first black—well, he was the first recording secretary of Local 600; and, of course, he was considered left, while never a member of the Communist Party. He was considered left, and supported the policies of left and even, in many instances, the policies of the party. But he never joined the Communist Party. Finally, there was another person that joined the Communist Party for opportunistic reasons, because the party had a lot of power there, and could get people elected.

Billy Allan was one of the guys that insisted that, "Why not elect Bill

Johnson?" I was opposed to it, I was opposed to electing Bill Johnson, because I knew he was an opportunist of the first magnitude. I knew that even though Shelton Tappes was not a Communist, he was a good solid trade unionist, and fought for those things that were in the best interests of the workers. There was no question in my mind about that. But he was defeated because the caucus endorsed—the Progressive Caucus, the left caucus—endorsed Bill Johnson. So, he defeated Shelton, and Shelton never quite got over that. So, that's why I say I could understand why he did—I didn't agree with him—but I can understand why he did [testify against some of us].

■   WALTER DOROSH

We were named. . . . They named about three hundred guys that were Communists. Shelton Tappes and Lee Romano, both worked for Reuther, named us. . . . Nothing happened out of it. They just sold everybody's names. The committee, they just asked us if we were Communists. Of course, we couldn't answer, because if you answer, you have to be a stool pigeon. And so, on advice of lawyer, you say that you stand on grounds of, I don't want to be intimidated. . . .

In the 1953 election, I was elected again to recording secretary to the bargaining committee in the tool-and-die building; and it was a very hot, heated election. They used the un-American Activities Committee material and everything, and that I was a "big Red." Workers said, "I don't care what he is. All I know is he's on the job. He does the job." They said, "I don't care." It didn't bother them.

■   DELORIS AND KENNETH ROCHE

How did the workers in Local 600 respond to the HUAC hearings?
    Kenneth Roche: As a whole they accepted the red-baiting. They were passive. They never would come out in the defense. Only as individuals, they would say, "Well, we don't agree with what is being done, but they're doing it anyway, it doesn't make no difference."
    Is that because of intimidation?
    Maybe intimidation, maybe self-preservation. Nobody wants to stick their neck out. A lot of people know what's right. You just can't get them to do it. They know it—you know it as well as I do—people aren't stupid. I don't care if they're workers or anything else. They actually do know what's going on. But because of fraternal organizations, religious organizations, churches that they go to, they cannot move. They're in a straitjacket, because [if they] open their mouth and say,

"Hey, I don't agree with you on this," they [will be] isolated. Nobody
wants to be isolated. I've been isolated in this town for a long time.
This is Dearborn, a sea of reaction, home of Mayor Hubbard, biggest
racist there is. I survived here but, so did she [my wife]. I was born
here, born and raised here. They say, "What do you live in Dearborn
for?" Hell, I was born here, right next door, sixty-two years ago in April.
That's the way it is. Background was there, Roman Catholic background, "Labor union radical, . . . you're red, you're this, you're that,
you're the other."

Deloris Roche: Would you believe that it even affected the kids in
school?

Kenneth Roche: Oh, yeah. The kids—

Deloris Roche: Fortunately, they absorbed what was said at home,
and (they) were able to hold their own, or fight back. Or he'd say, "You
have trouble with your teachers, and you can't straighten them out,
I'll come do it."

■ SAUL WELLMAN

I was arrested on September 17, 1952, for violating the Smith Act. I
was taken to the court of Judge Thornton at one o'clock in the afternoon, and the United States District Attorney for the Southern District
of Detroit read off the indictment against me. I didn't get up to respond
to it. So, he [an FBI agent] came over and said, "You're supposed to
get up, Saul." I said out loud—it was a big courtroom, and packed with
reporters and the curious, "They've got the wrong 'Saul Wellman.' That
doesn't apply to me. I never advocated 'the violent overthrow of the
United States government.'" . . .

One of the problems that Communist activists have— . . . it's in the
nature of things—is you're like a fire horse; you go from one activity
to another activity.

I came home from [fighting in] Spain on the 20th of December,
1938. I took two weeks to get reacquainted with my wife; and on the
6th of January, 1939, I was already in a new assignment—no time to
reflect on that enormous event that was to be the most important
experience in my life.

The Smith Act trial was a similar thing. It was a very profound event.
This time I determined that I was going to take time out to look at it.
So, that's where the jail thing came in. It turned out to be extremely
useful and helpful. . . . The trial had raised many questions that we
were unable to deal with. Every time we ran across a disturbing question we put it aside and said we'll deal with it at a future time. There

were very sharp differences between the defendants and the attorneys as to trial strategy and so on.[74] And then there were human differences between us. It's like a marriage, except instead of two people being married it was six people being married. . . . We managed to curtail all these tensions while the trial was going on. We put them on the side. At trial's end, we decided to really go into them. It was an ideal situation because, in a sense, we were in an encapsulated environment. We were separated from all the problems of the world. . . . In a sense, if I try to mark where, at what point, I began to move in the direction of leaving the party (I left the party in 1958), it may have begun in 1954. I had no ideas of leaving in 1954 or anything like it. But these questions confounded me, and I was beginning to confront them. . . .

There's nothing nice about prison life, it's terrible, it's demeaning; you're ordered around by people you don't respect but who carry guns. Someone else is running your life, and so on. Yet how do you create the illusion that you haven't lost control of yourself? This is what we did. I was a Communist all my life. I had been a Communist for maybe twenty years, up until 1954, but I read *Capital,* the first volume of *Capital,* for the first time in my life, [in prison]. I found a copy of the first volume of *Capital* in the prison library! One of our guys (Nat Ganley, the guy who was in the UAW) was an extremely able, self-taught Marxist economist, so we even had direction; it wasn't the blind leading the blind. . . . We really studied Marxian economics. I studied American literature. Some guys studied Spanish, and some guys studied economics. It was really a very rich period. So, when the bail was raised to get us out (because that's what we were waiting for) the last day, I was the last one out, of the five men. I was in no hurry to leave because I was in the midst of two books I had to finish that belonged to the prison library. . . . In 1958, the court overturned my conviction.

■ MARGARET AND STANLEY NOWAK

Margaret Nowak: [Stanley] was indicted in 1952, and came to trial in 1954, and then that went all the way through the Michigan Supreme Court, and then through the Federal Appeals Court in Cincinnati, and then it went before the Supreme Court of the United States. It was a landmark case, which [they] threw out of court. It was a long, hard period for us. Very difficult. But we didn't regret it after it was all over, as hard as it was, because we had worked in so many areas during all those years of our life that we were able to rally a great deal of support behind ourselves. We raised money to pay for the case; naturally we didn't have the money to pay for it out of our pocket.

Many of the people who were being threatened with deportation did
not have resources like that, that they could fight with. And a lot of
people kept saying, "Well, why don't you just give up and go to Poland?
You could probably have a very good position in Poland," and so on. . . .
He said, . . . this is his country. He's been here since the age of ten. He
was an American, not a Pole. . . . So, we decided to fight it out to the
last ditch. And it is good that we did, because his case, when it went
into decision, threw out hundreds of cases that were in the lower courts.
. . . His case was a reference in throwing out those cases.

Stanley Nowak: [I'd] only add to it this. The attorney general . . . at that
time (I don't recall his name now) made a statement that ten thousand—

Margaret Nowak: [Herbert] Brownell.

Stanley Nowak: Brownell is right. That's right. That ten thousand
naturalized citizens would lose their citizenship and thirteen thousand
aliens, or noncitizens, will be deported. And he made that speech at a
banquet—

Margaret Nowak: The Sons of St. Patrick.

Stanley Nowak: Yes, that's right. Well, what they did, they started
and they had two or three cases before me and each one they won.
The people lost them. Then my case came up, and no doubt that there
was a number of things. First of all, the whole period of McCarthyism
was coming to a climax. There was a point where there had to be some
change. That was one factor. The second factor, how do you denatu-
ralize a person who served ten years in the Michigan senate? . . .

Margaret Nowak: I think that's what intrigued them into reviewing
it because they had refused to review other cases.

Stanley Nowak: They reviewed this case. They made this two-point
decision. First, that the government failed to prove their case . . . that
I advocated violence. . . . Of course, they had a difficult time to get any
kind of evidence. They never did have it and the court recognized that
I had never—

Margaret Nowak: They even took notice in their decision . . . of how
the prosecutor prodded the people who were testifying to try to dig
statements out of them that they wanted. And even their statements
were not the kind that were really—

Who defended you?

Stanley Nowak: Ernie Goodman and George Crockett.

Margaret Nowak: George Crockett wrote the briefs, and Ernie Goodman did the arguments before the Supreme Court. . . . And I worked
for them for fourteen years in the office later.

Stanley Nowak: So, that was the first point. . . . Second, that *advo-
cacy* of violence is permissible by the Constitution, under the tradi-

tion of freedom of speech. But *practice* of violence is prohibited. They separated the two things.

Margaret Nowak: And in no case did they prove that he had—

Stanley Nowak: They never tried to.

Margaret Nowak: They didn't even prove that he had advocated violence. . . .

Stanley Nowak: That's probably as far as the Supreme Court has ever gone on that question, to the best of my knowledge. And my two attorneys were completely surprised by it.

Margaret Nowak: Well, they didn't expect that they were going to win the case.

Stanley Nowak: Not by that kind of a decision, and it was six to three. [John Marshall Harlan II] the [associate] justice . . . who wrote the decision [was] a very conservative person.[75] And that was the contribution—that's why all the programs Brownell had was knocked off completely by that decision. He couldn't go any more, and they dropped the whole case. So, that's the contribution we made.

Purge

■ HENRY MCCUSKER

There is no doubt about it that the people that were in the left wing contributed much to the organization in the plant. But after that it become a question of "rule or ruin." They weren't satisfied to be organized; they wanted to rule, and if they couldn't rule, they wanted to ruin. You see, big changes took place in this international union of ours, starting in 1946. In 1946, Walter Reuther was elected president of this international union but the executive board was still under the control of R. J. Thomas and the other people. . . . Although none of those people were Communists or real left-wingers, the left-wingers had a lot of influence on those people at that time. Then in 1947 that was changed. Reuther . . . had a majority [on] the executive board of the international union; . . . [and] they cleaned practically all of these people out, so far as regional directorships was concerned in the UAW.

■ DAVE MOORE

Local 600 was carrying the torch—"black and white, unite." And we got to a point where if you wanted to say anything about integrating the UAW executive board with a black, you were called a Communist. . . . They would just have the majority, and we could never beat them. . . . Beginning in 1947—1946 and 1947—you will find that the issue of Communism was the main wedge and the main hammer they had to use against those who were advocating the black people on the UAW executive board. As a result of that, we were branded. Some guys got defeated in their local union by others who claimed to be "red, white, and blue Americans." . . . This is what the UAW record shows. And if you care to look at the proceedings of the convention, you will find out. Starting in 1947, you will find out that that lasted all the way up through the McCarthy era.

I had been one of the guys [saying it's time for a black to be on the executive board], and I'm proud of it. And if I had to do it again, I would do it with more determination. And I would do it with more force. And I would do it with more knowledge than I had at that time. And I would never retreat on it.

You're talking about a "democratic union." . . . But dammit to hell demonstrate it to me in action. . . . Beginning in the late 1940s, Communism become a big issue, not only in the labor movement but throughout the country. . . . If [you] knew Dave Moore, . . . the FBI, the Red Squad in that city, would come to your . . . house. "I know that Dave Moore was over visiting you. How long have you been knowing him? What's his activities? Has he ever asked you come to a social affair? He's black and you are white. Why would you go?" And if you were to tell them, "Well, he's my friend. I don't give a damn what his political affiliation is. I don't know his political affiliation. . . . I never have asked him." . . . "Well, we want you to keep inviting him over. But we want you to make a report to us every time he comes over. What he says to you blah, blah, blah." And you say, "Well, I'm not going to be a damn stool pigeon." Then they brand you. Then you lose your job. The word passes on wherever you go.

But anyway, back to the UAW again. Beginning in 1946 and '47 the change began in the UAW; and that change, in my opinion, was not for the better, but for the worse. That's when the McCarthy era began to come in. And sometimes you sit back and you wonder: people who you have been so close to, and people who have sat at your table and ate with you, people you have fraternized with, people you'd loan money to when they needed money, people that your wife or your kids went over and helped when they were sick, or they needed assistance, whatever, . . . and they turned on you. They will see you coming and they wouldn't speak to you. You know, they would tell their kids, "Don't play with them. Don't you go over there anymore." Even in the church, they wouldn't sit beside you in the church. This happened to my father, not because my father was involved or anything, but because of me.

■ ART MCPHAUL

After the [1950] election, [Carl] Stellato began to red-bait and bring people up on charges and this sort of thing. And Reuther, of course, began to weed out "Communists," so to speak, and made a big Red issue and took over, put an administrator over, the local.[76] It was a political thing of the first magnitude, really that's what it was. There was no reason why they should have an administrator put over that local. There was no reason for it.

What were the ramifications of it? What happened as a result?

I think that it resulted in the severe weakening of the left wing, because the left wing was never able to really control the local there any more as it had in the past. As a matter of fact, it was part of that thing of my being discharged. It was [at] the same time that Stellato got in that I got discharged. . . . They got rid of most of the militant people. They either got rid of them or they prevented them from holding office for a number of years; and, of course, if you can't hold office you soon, lose your [support]. And that's what happened. . . . They discharged three or four of my supporters, my committeemen . . . not "my committeemen," but committeemen that was in the caucus that I headed. Let me put it that way. Just in my building. . . . Now what happened in other buildings, I really don't know too much because I was no longer in the plant after that. . . . I was discharged in 1950, [before] . . . the administrator was put over the local.

See, this was a part of this ongoing thing. . . . In 1952, the un-American Activities Committee came here. . . . But it was all part and parcel of this whole thing. But most of the people that was called before the un-American Activities Committee were the people that—and then they had what they call a loyalty oath; and, of course, certain people wouldn't sign the loyalty oath. And then some did sign it, and they claimed that they were lying, that they were Communists, that sort of thing. So, all of this was part and parcel of the destruction, shall I say, or demise rather, maybe is a better word, of the left wing at Ford's.

■ JOHN SAARI

If a guy was a right-winger, and he runs for office and wins, and he does his job, well, it makes no difference whether he's a right-winger or a left-winger. If he's doing his job. But that wasn't the case here. So, when the red-baiting and everything started, there was a lot of worms crawled out of the woodwork. And a lot of good people got hurt, a lot of good people got hurt, yeah.

I remember when they came in and told me that a guy by the name of Nelson Samp (he was on the international staff, and he came in to the labor relations office), and they called me in, and Nelson Samp says [it's the] official policy of the UAW that [they] don't recognize me as representative anymore. And Nelson Samp gives me a letter, . . . and they charge me—guess what they charge me with? "Malfeasance." I said, "Nelson, take this letter back, will you? I would rather you, they, charge me with Communism or whatever you have, than with malfeasance." I had no trial, no nothing. Although the five building chairmen, they had a trial, but it was all cut and dry; it was all cut and dry. "Take them out." One guy got fired, a fellow by the name of Art McPhaul. He got fired. A few others got fired. And, so, then the right wing took over solid. Then you went downhill.

■ KENNETH ROCHE

So, in 1952, when the UAW executive board put Local 600 under an administratorship, you were just banned from being in office at that time?

That's all, removed from office.

After the administratorship was taken away, and the elections came up, were you allowed to run again?

I was allowed to run again. It was only five of them that was out for five years. That was [Johnny] Gallo, Dave Moore, Nelson Davis, Ed Lock, and Paul Boatin. Incidentally, my father-in-law was the defense lawyer at the trial for them at the local. Percy Llewellyn, he defended the five at the local. Ellsworth Hanlon was the prosecutor.

■ WILLIAM JOHNSON

In 1952, when Reuther put the administratorship over the local, what was the reaction in the plant?

Well, it was bitter. [The plant] almost became an armed camp because the membership felt it was done for political purposes. There was no other justification for it. I think by and large they felt that Reuther was trying to consolidate his hold on the UAW and the biggest local, being that Local 600 consistently opposed Reuther and Reuther's policies. . . . But Reuther was always one who didn't take too well to criticism. We wouldn't hesitate to criticize Reuther if we thought he was wrong. In fact, we kept a running gunfire of a barrage of criticism against Walter Reuther. . . . As a result of that we got Reuther to change a lot of his policies. . . . We had an obligation to criticize him and keep him on his toes, and it got hot and heavy and in 1952—or was it 1951? Reuther put [an] administratorship over the local twice. He did it in 1947 because he wanted to get—we had a big argument over the Taft-Hartley, over compliance with the Taft-Hartley Act and signing non-Communist affidavits. A lot of the people felt that, "Why the hell should union people have to sign the affidavits when management people were not required to sign?" They felt it was an undue imposition on union leaders, in presumption that they were all Communists. Therefore, they have to sign these affidavits saying they weren't. So, we had a big fight with Reuther over that issue. Reuther was in favor of it.

In 1947 they put a limited administratorship over the local, supervising elections. . . . Someone had been tampering with the ballots. I was a local officer myself. I really never knew what the hell went on, but they claim[ed] one or two members on the election committee had ballots in their pockets or had stuffed ballots. . . . I never knew whether it was true or not, but, based on those allegations, they [the UAW executive board] put in a supervisor . . . to control the election, brought their own people in. And to a large extent they were successful in that election. We thought they actually just stole the election, because the results would never have gone that way ordinarily. Some of Reuther's people, well some of our people who felt they had to go along were elected. . . . We never could prove it.

And then in 1952. . . . they put the local under the administration, under what they call a board of administration, and they actually ran the local for about a year I guess it was. . . . They set all the local officers aside, and brought in one regional director and several people from the international staff. Jack Conway, who was Reuther's chief administrative assistant at the time, came, along with one or two guys from [Emil] Mazey's office, who were mostly in the auditing setup. The regional director, who was Joe McCusker, was part of that team; and they actually ran the local until they thought they had it ready for a take-over.

So, when they held the election, we defeated everyone of them. The membership returned all the guys to office. . . . We had a certified public accountant who supervised the election, and we swept the election and defeated all of the Reuther team. So, after that time we sat down, and we felt, "Well, maybe the fight has gone on long enough. Maybe, we ought to seek an accommodation on each side"—and that's what happened.

When did that happen?

In 1952–53, and from then on, there was very little infighting between the local and the international union.

Was that a policy of Carl Stellato?

It was a policy that we all more or less agreed to. I myself felt that it was becoming destructive, and it was not really doing the local union, or the international union, for that matter, any good. So, we just felt, "Well, we'll just extend the olive branch if they will, and we'll sit down and quit fighting each other and start working together." That was basically what we did.

Red-baiting had taken place during the House un-American Activi-

ties Committee [hearings]. The House committee came in 1951, I
guess.

*How did that go over in the plant? Were the workers frightened
by it, do you think?*

The only ones that were really frightened were foreign-born. . . . The
McCarran Act, of course, was involved at the time.[77] The FBI was involved, and they scared the hell out of a lot of foreign-born people,
because they felt they would be deported. . . . It didn't really affect any
one who was born [here]. The threat of deportation was the biggest
fear that a lot of the foreign-born had. . . . But I don't think anyone else
was bothered by it too much.

*Do you think that the removal of the five progressive candidates
from their positions in office—*

[Nelson] Davis, [Paul] Boatin, [Dave] Moore, [Johnny] Gallo, and—
I can't think of his name; he had been president of the plastics
plant . . .—Lock, Ed Lock, yeah.

You think that was very important?

No. It was important to them, because they were rendered ineligi-
ble to hold office. And a lot of the membership resented the hell out
of it, because these guys basically had been very active in organizing
the union, and had been very active in the early days of the
union. . . . Lock had been a chairman of one of the units. Boatin had
been chairman of a unit. Dave Moore had never been a chairman because he was in a unit where there was just a handful of blacks, but
he had always been very active in the unit. Nelson Davis, of course,
had come out of my unit, and he, as much as any single individual,
probably did more to organize the union in the foundry than possibly
anyone else. (In fact, he had run-ins with the Ford goons that tried to
run him out of the plant, because of union organizing, and that was
one of the work stoppages we had. Everybody left the job and chased
the Ford so-called plant protection men, and hired goons, at Ford Motor
Company, chased them out of the plant, and ran them a substantial
distance down Miller Road. They felt that much about Davis.)

None of them were engaged in any activities that you could even
remotely ascribe to being Communist. We didn't know what their
political inclination was, but we knew what they did in the union; and
they were basically solid-rock unionists. But it was a politically con-
trived thing, and for some reason they [the international] felt that they
wanted to make examples out of these guys. Of course, in the trials
in the local, they were exonerated. But as a result of the administratorship put over the local, they were expelled.

■ WALTER DOROSH

Right after [the HUAC hearing], Reuther put an administrator over
Local 600—this was 1952 I believe—and . . . took everybody out of
office, took all the staff, and put his guys on. I went to work in a plant.
Everybody went back to work in the plants. . . . I went to work building dies, I was a tool-and-die maker. . . . Walter wouldn't allow us to
schedule new elections at 600 until he thought we were ready for an
election. . . . Six months went by, and we started raising hell, and we
took about a thousand guys, I guess, out to Solidarity House. I guess
that scared him. We had a big riot out in front of the building
there. . . . His administrators [were] coming down to the buildings, and
we told [them], "The next one comes into this building, we are going
to throw his ass out." We told them, "If you won't let us come in and
see Reuther, don't you send your administrators out to our buildings.
We'll throw them right through the door without opening the doors."

*Reuther's administrators were acting as the committeemen and
chairmen?*

Well, they were in charge. The regular committeemen functioned,
but they were the overseers. . . . They were over the chairman and
everybody. . . . They went through all the buildings. Walter made an
announcement shortly after that [rally] that elections would be scheduled; and so we ran an election. Walter ran the international reps; Gene
Prato ran for president (he was Ken Bannon's administrative assistant);
Jack Peligreno ran for vice president (he was administrative assistant
to the regional director). I think there was about fifty thousand votes
cast. I think [Carl] Stellato got about thirty-five thousand, and, I think
the rest got about six thousand. Reuther took such a beating there
that—in them years we used to have elections every year—the next
election, Reuther wouldn't support nobody in the race. No place.
Everybody [on our slate] went uncontested, the left wing, all the left-
wing elements. And then after that Reuther started making overtures
towards the local. Stellato was bitter about it. And he wouldn't trust
Walter, because he'd run [in 1950] with Walter, as the candidate for
the international union against Tommy Thompson. Thompson was a
left-wing candidate; and that was a bitter campaign. Stellato ran in 1950
as a right-winger. (John Fitzpatrick, who was chairman of his campaign
committee, was chairman of the ACTU at the plant.) After he got elected [in 1950], within three months, he broke with Reuther, because
right after that it was when the five-year contract deal came up. And
that's where the fight started.

*What about Stellato's trial of the five left-wingers right after he
got elected?*

This is still during the Reuther period. [Reuther said,] "If you want to stay there, and since you didn't run on the left-wing ticket, you got to smash all these left-wing leaders." It's a grandiose scheme. I talked to him [Stellato] about it a number of times. He said, "I was young. I [was] just sold a bill of goods. Reuther said, 'You are very successful; and if you don't, the left wing is going to defeat you in the next election.'" (We used to have elections every year. Before the ballots would, the ink would be dry, they would start another campaign.)

[Stellato] . . . pressed charges against [the] five, [but] the council [of Local 600] voted it down. The trial was thrown out. . . . I think that the guys seen in that, that it was just a divide-a-union technique; you called this guy a Catholic, or called this guy a Communist, or called this guy a Socialist, or Trotskyite, or whatever. . . . The council at that time was still made up of the guys who helped build this union. . . . It was almost unanimously voted out, even . . . some of the right-wingers, that were identified with the right wing, couldn't conceive of it [the trial], except again the strong ACTU. I think John Fitzpatrick said that he was strongly behind it [the trial]. . . . When the hearings were held, and [the] trials, hundreds of people used to come there; and they intimidated the trial judge and the committees. The committee was made up of five ACTU guys, as a matter of fact.

Oh, really?

I think so, yeah, if I remember their names. We [Stellato and I] talked about it many a time. I said to him, "How can you be so stupid? You know, I have never known you to be a guy that believed in these techniques." "Young and stupid," he says. But he stayed fifteen years as [Local 600] president; and I succeeded him.

■ JOHN ORR

I was certainly opposed to it [Reuther's administratorship of Local 600]. I was chairman of the tool-and-die unit at that time, president or whatever you call it; and it isn't only those five they took out, they started taking individual committeemen, job stewards out, too, who they suspected of being Communists or fellow travelers.

Well, how many in all do you think?

I don't know, really, maybe fifty in the whole plant. In my unit, they took out two. They took out Mack Cinzori . . . and Tom Jelley.

What happened to those guys?

They all came back stronger than ever. It's another story. When the international union took over the local they, well anyway you call it, they were a dictatorship. They put an administrator in there. Jack Conway, who was approved as administrative assistant, took over the office of the presidency. An auditor from the international union took over the financial secretary's office. [The] recording secretary [was black], so a black guy took over the recording secretary's office. . . . They put a guy in the vice president's office too. . . . They had control of our local dues. They were running the local out of our dues money. The dues collection still went up. It was during that time, I wrote, in 1952, the latter part of '52, I wrote a leaflet that got wide circulation in the plant and in other plants too. The title [was,] "I Disagree." Because they were running our local newspaper *Ford Facts;* and one of the headlines they had in there was "Democracy Prevails in Local 600. Workers Still Have a Right to Disagree." I decided, "Well, I will avail myself to that right to disagree." I wrote a four-page tabloid and I headed it, "I Disagree"—told them I was taking this opportunity they said was provided for all the Ford workers to disagree.

Did you notice the level of democracy change during that administratorship?

Oh, did they [cut down]. . . . No local, no unit officer, could call a meeting without the presence of an international rep. They assigned an international rep to every unit, and only he could call meetings. Our elected chairman called a meeting, and he'd [the rep] be there, and I let the guy chair; and then he would tell them what subject matters could be brought on the floor and what party could vote, and whatnot. But I challenged them to have an election. They did; and, I tell you, that was the sorriest thing Walter Reuther did. If he ever took a licking, boy, it was in that one. We elected the local officers by two-thirds. I won by two-thirds in my unit, whereas I've been in close elections before. But these five they removed never got back in for about five years. [The] international held to that one.

What about the other fifty? Were they out that long?

Soon [as the] administratorship was lifted, they were put back in office. In the case of my two, they didn't want to go back in with that stigma over their heads. They were going to be accepted by the membership or not. They demanded elections, and I gave it to them; and they both overwhelmed.

Why did the international allow those people to come back?

They only charged five people with adherence to the Communist Party programs. The others were all taken out as "sympathizers" or [other legalisms].

So, how did the five that were ousted get back in five years?

They appealed to the international union. The way to get back was to appeal to the international convention; and after that time, finally somebody decided in the higher-up—Reuther was president—five years was enough. Don't ask me how he established the time.

Did that mean they were out of the plant altogether, or just inac-
tive leadership?

No, no, no, under the UAW a guy could [be] removed from office,
[but] the Ford Motor Company or any other company could not kick
them out of the plant. . . . They were allowed to stay in the job.

They pretty much remained active, except that they didn't have
official leadership?

Some did and some didn't. Some were so disgusted, they just
dropped out. Paul Boatin come back and became president. He defeated Carl Stellato's brother for president in the engine plant. John Gallo
came back and was elected president of the engine plant. Ed Lock, to
my knowledge, never ran for election again. A colored by the name of
[Nelson] Davis was reelected to the bargaining committee in the foundry; and Dave Moore, another colored guy, was elected vice president
in the axle building; that's where he was before. And eventually, [he]
became an international representative.

■   HORACE SHEFFIELD

I had no problems with it [Reuther's administratorship of Local 600],
because I had come out of the local, and I know some of the things
that happened in the local. . . . He had constitutional grounds to do [it,]
or he couldn't have done it. And, really, the first interest had to be
protecting your union. You know, the good name of the union. And
so that, yeah, I supported it. . . .

What was the reaction in the plant, when it was maintained that
long?

There was no general uproar. I mean, in other words, there was no
meaningful uproar. Clearly, the left wing agitated against it. But in terms
of any huge groundswell, there was none, because by and large, after
all, the local union took care of the workers' business just as usual; and
the grounds for their taking it over were well established. People understood it out there. . . . The UAW has never had the reputation for
being a dictatorial union or one that abused workers' rights and some
of the bad things, the dishonesty and other things that prevailed in
some of the other unions.

So, the right wing in Local 600 was pretty solid behind the ad-
ministratorship effort?

Oh, sure. There's no question about that. . . .

Did you think that was an important step in preventing the Com-
munist influence from being so big?

I don't think it is that significant a step, because really, I got elected out there [with] almost seventeen thousand votes [for me]. So, look,

I think their influence had begun to wane. . . . It may have had some minimal impact, but I really don't think that was any crucial watershed or anything like that. Yeah, [it] started to wane, . . . [because of] effective leadership [by] . . . people who really weren't Commies, and who were . . . articulate and addressing the workers' needs. A whole range of reasons why the [left's] hold on the local unions began to wane.

■ HENRY MCCUSKER

Do you think that the UAW administratorship over Local 600 succeeded?

Yes, it did. This has become a quieted down local union, and a well-behaved local union, and made a big contribution so far as the international union is concerned, and still does, still does.

■ PAUL BOATIN

I say that up to 1950, with the Korean War and all the red-baiting and patriotic jingoism that occurred, every worker and every leader in the Ford Rouge plant was a militant, aggressive, forward-looking liberal or progressive. And the dead weight of red-baiting created such a division and such suspicion, and it played into the hands of the company so successfully, that from that day on, things were beginning to go to hell in a basket. 1950 was a decisive year, and . . . the labor movement became so weak at the plant level that the company was able to decentralize, to move the Rouge plant down to the point where, as I've said, it went from eighty thousand to near fifteen thousand now [1983]. And it's better not to blame it all on the bad economy. It was this internal division and weakening of the union that made it possible for the company to do whatever they wanted. A Communist leader was sent to jail; union leaders remained silent for fear of suffering a similar fate; and the rest of the union went to sleep, and it is sleeping today.

The workers learned that the period of red-baiting and internal division [had] permitted the Ford Motor Company to decentralize the Ford Rouge plant—taught everybody a bitter lesson. Everybody looks back upon those days as days that were tragic for the worker, and therefore that mistake should not be repeated again. And Local 600, in its present form [or] some other form, and the workers in it will rise to fight militantly again.

The un-American Activities Committee came here for the first time in 1952. They had been investigating every one of my neighbors. I lived here since 1953, but prior to that I lived not far from here. My neighbors there and my neighbors here, and all were questioned by Army G2, by the FBI, by the Red Squad. And you can get discouraged because no matter how hard they [the FBI censors] try to cover up or blot out the names of the informants, [in the FBI file I got through the Freedom of Information Act,] once in a while a name sneaks through. They use one guy against another, you see? And it comes through. You have to. The un-American Activities Committee was brought here at the instigation of the ACTU, the Association of Catholic Trade Unionists, and the Reuther administration. It was to be a thing operated in sequence. You get your picture in the paper, you're called a bunch of names, and . . . they usually get the photos when you've got your mouth open, and you look like an arrogant son of a bitch. And then the union comes in and says, "We don't care about your politics; we're not concerned about that, but [for] the good name of the union and the rights of those workers. They voted for you, it is true, but they didn't realize what they realize now—that all this negative publicity is hurting the union. We have to go [to] contract negotiation. We have a strike to settle, we have this or that."

They [the UAW executive board] appointed an administrator, and it's an arbitrary decision. You're not asked anything. In fact, the un-American Activities Committee at least put you on the stand and gave you a right to talk, [not] the international executive board of the UAW. . . .

I don't want you ever to think that I'm castigating the principle of unionism at all, or that I'm really bitter against these guys. . . .

And the General Council only meets once a month. So, as time passes, because the workers resented—a lot of workers went down to the local. People wrote letters which were never published. But the leadership felt that the membership resented the autocratic method in which this had been done. So, they then decided to prefer charges, and that called for setting up a trial committee: "You'll have your opportunity. You'll have your day in court." They were backtracking at that point, because they had you out, and they had themselves in. In order to conserve finances, so that there would be no lost time paid, the trial committee met at night. And there you are, eleven or twelve o'clock at night. . . . You have defendants, you have a trial committee, and you have a defense committee, you have lawyers, [and] the damn thing never starts on time. So, it goes on week, after week, after week, after week. At the beginning, workers would come down there, but workers have got to go to work the next morning. Or some of them work afternoons or work at midnight. Attendance fell off, and they felt that, we got it. They may have had support in the plant originally, but you could see that that support is disappearing.

So, at a given point, they brought in high-powered CIO representatives. The director of the United Steel Workers from Chicago, Germano, came. And . . . he took up an entire evening. "Because of the exceptional circumstances that existed in Chicago and in the Steel Workers, President Philip Murray found it necessary to do this. . . . Now, the union is able to go ahead and negotiate," and so forth and so on. And without attacking us directly, he was trying to show that the type of rejuvenated climate that had been created in Chicago could be recreated here; and the workers and everybody would benefit from it. So, under that type of thing who is going to argue with a representative of Philip Murray?

"The Communist danger has been squashed." . . . It's like putting up a sign: "New management has taken over here." . . . The Local [600] had a General Council. The General Council is going to take the matter up. And the [UAW] administrator, Jack Conway, confessed to being a Socialist, a Catholic capitalist-Socialist. . . . He is carrying out the decision of the international executive board. It's just like [Klaus] Barbie saying, "I only took orders." What he was really saying is, "You can't talk. There's nothing you and I can talk about. The [UAW] international executive board decided, on the basis of certain facts that they had." And the red-baiting nationally continued.

The trial committee at a given point said, "There is too much time wasted," and they set a time limit, and they had the accusing parties that made all of the goddamned speeches. But when it came [to] the defense . . . [it's] last, right? So, we had, I don't know, a couple of evenings, and workers were angry, and they would holler, those who were there. The trial committee found us guilty. The trial committee had been created by the [local's] General Council, hence it had to report to the following meeting of the General Council; and the General Council turned down the verdict of the trial committee. Okay? But the ball game had been played out. Four, five, six months had passed. Their boys were in office. We were removed. And the fact that the General Council, which is the highest body in the local, had turned down the verdict of the trial committee, didn't do anything for democracy, because we weren't reinstated. . . . It took five years to get me reinstated.

In the meantime, of course, the Senate Internal Security Committee was brought into the picture and we heard rumors around. So in 1957, two days before an election for top offices being held at the local, the press corps of the whole United States, I'm telling you, were there. People got lost because there were so many goddamned newspaper people and cameras, and so forth, [to cover] the election campaigns: a full slate of candidates in the local, and [in] every one of the units, and people running for various committee positions, and so forth. There were a hell of a lot of people out there campaigning.

So, it had been arranged that I would be served (incidentally, I was the only one served) a subpoena right there, outside, in front, on the local steps . . . with all of the papers and the cameras churning, and so forth. That made the papers on the final day of the election; it got into the evening paper; it was on the radio, and so forth. It was part of the game to defeat left-wingers.

■ DAVE MOORE

I was put on trial in my local union. Five of us. They called us "the Ford five." . . . No charges were leveled against us. . . . I found out in the paper. I was on my way to work. . . . I was vice president of the bargaining committee at the gear-and-axle plant at that time. And on my way to work one day, I picked up a paper [saying] the administrator had been put over the local, and, "Five UAW officials removed from jobs." Nobody ever said anything to me about me. Lo and behold, I got [to] the plant, and [they] said, "You are to go back on your regular job classification." I had been elected, democratically elected. "I'll be damned if I'm going back on the job. I was elected, if the people want to send me back on the job, it's the people who voted for me, then they vote me out of office." Well, the hierarchy of the UAW sent a communication to the Ford Motor Company and said, "These people are no longer holding union positions here." Well, we raised hell about it. So, finally they put us on trial. The trial lasted almost two-and-a-half years.

All this time you were off?

Yeah, the only thing that saved me completely, out at the plant, was the Taft-Hartley Act itself, as much as I fought against the Taft-Hartley Act. But the Taft-Hartley Act had in it a clause, "No union official can ever be denied his right to work. He will be denied his right to hold elected or appointed office, but he cannot be denied his right to work for the plant." With my record with the Ford Motor Company at that time, when I had to go back on the job, they were glad to see me come back. They were glad to see me come back because they were going to give me one hell of a time; and they did. The job that I had before I got elected to the union position was as an inspector. . . .

We went through one hell of a deal . . . trials and the like, and we won. Accusations without any witnesses. No dealing of particulars. . . . "Hey you, we don't want you, either a member of or subservient to the Communist Party." Well, the administrators over at Local 600 took out all the elected officers, the president on down. That lasted for some time. Then [workers] were raising so much hell, that they lifted the administratorship, put some of the officers back and others they kept out, including me. I appealed, went all through the appeal stages, and the UAW executive board, UAW convention. . . . I was found innocent by the General Council, the highest legislative body of the Local 600, I was found innocent by the membership of Local 600. Despite all of that, the international union said, "The hell with what the membership, what the board, says, what the General Council says. We say he's guilty." Without any trial. Finally, came up at the convention, and . . . after four years, they decided to [give] us a trial. We threatened to go to court. And the trial committee—you can understand who held the trial—the trial committee was composed of all the present UAW officers at that time. Naturally, they found us guilty.

And we raised hell the next eight to nine years. In 1963, we got a lawyer and threatened to go to court. The lawyer called Walter Reuther one morning and said, "I got five guys from Local 600 sitting in my office. You can put them back on their elected jobs and give them full status in the union and the UAW, or we'll go to court." And all of a sudden they wanted to meet with us. We decided to go down for a meeting; and then they wanted us to sign a paper, and I wouldn't sign a goddamn thing. "This is the same thing you offered me about twelve years ago. That I'm not a member of the Communist Party. I'm not subservient to the Communist Party. I don't know anybody who is a member of the Communist Party, and all that junk." But [with the] threat of going to court, they . . . put us back.

I guess they played their politics wrong. Three months later, after they put us back with full citizenship and full status, they had an election in the Local 600. All five of us ran for election and got elected. After all those years. We beat guys who had been entrenched, who was unbeatable. All five of us got elected with overwhelming votes. Overwhelming votes, we got elected. And we stayed elected. Ed Lock, Johnny Gallo, Paul Boatin, Dave Moore, Nelson Davis. And, as I said, we held our positions. At the time they took us out, they couldn't defeat us. They had been trying to defeat us all the time, with candidates running against us. I know, I don't *think*, I *know*, what kept us in office. Despite the pressure, despite the awesome power of the UAW and all of its officers, and despite the FBI, and despite the Red Squad in the city of Detroit, and despite all of the federal and local and county agents who at that time was just looking for every Red under a bed, we stayed in office. We got elected, . . . based on what . . . we have stood for in organizing the UAW in the first place.

This understanding of solidarity, we had with the rank-and-file people. They trusted us with any kind of problem they had. They knew that if they had a gripe with the supervisor or foreman, that we wasn't going to sell them out, that we were going to go all the way with their case, which we did. "We are going to make a fight of it. I don't know whether we are going to win, but we are going to push them to the wall. We are not going to give an inch." People really appreciated it.

■ SAUL WELLMAN

The impact of the cold war is so overwhelming and powerful, and that's the thing that really changed. It influences everything. If the cold war had not unfolded as it did, with [such] intensity and power, then even Walter Reuther would not have played the role that he did. . . . I mean the cheap shots he took at the Communists. . . . He took more than "cheap shots," he destroyed the Communists and the left and militant influence within the UAW, within the working class. But if the cold war was not coming on . . . then the character of the struggle within the CIO would have been different, the character of the struggle within the left-led unions would have been different, the character of the struggle within the country would have been different—and that cannot be underestimated. It's like an avalanche or a fire or a hurricane that's hitting you, and it shapes everything that you do, and you really have no control over that hurricane. I would argue that the cold war was not something we could have stopped. The cold war was not the result of wrong policies. The cold war was the result of a fundamental change which the ruling class had decided to make over which there were no counterforces strong enough to resist or to reject or to hold back a defeat. The results are there. The fact is that there was resistance to the cold war. There was resistance to everything that was happening, but it didn't work out.

Maybe these are the expressions of a tired old man. I'm not really tired, but I'm an old man. I'm looking back at it and saying, "Well, hey, there's certain things we could do, and there's certain things we could not do, and I'm not going to be held responsible for the success of the cold war. I tried my damnedest. I went to jail and I did everything. So, I couldn't do anything more than what I did, and it couldn't have been done by any other way."

Biographical Appendix

Table 1. Rouge Workers and Local 600 Officers Interviewed

Name and Date of Interview	Birthplace[a]	Nationality or Race	First Hired at Ford	Union Positions at Ford[b]
Archie Acciacca (8/84)	Detroit, Mich. (1913)	Italian	1935	Committeeman, 1941; Bargaining Committee, 1942–43; v. pres., 1944–45; president, 1948–52 (Press Steel); staff member, National Ford Department
Ken Bannon (9/86)	Scranton, Pa. (1914)	White	1936	Committeeman, Unit Bargaining Committee, Rouge; chairman, Bargaining Committee; president, UAW Local 400; dir., National Ford Department, 1947; member, UAW International Exec. Bd. 1962; v. pres., UAW 1970
Paul Boatin (9/83 & 8/84)	Italy (1909)	Italian	1925	Rec. sec., 1943; president, 1950–52 (Motor); president, 1957–59 (Engine)

Table 1, continued

Name and Date of Interview	Birthplace[a]	Nationality or Race	First Hired at Ford	Union Positions at Ford
Walter Dorosh (1/84)	Ansonia, Conn. (1919)	Slavic (?)	1934 (HFTS)	Department committeeman; dist. committeeman; Bargaining Committee; v. pres. 1945; rec. sec. 1955–56; president (Tool & Die); president, UAW Local 600, 1965–75; admin. asst., UAW President Leonard Woodcock
William Johnson (8/84)	Detroit, Mich. (late 1920s)	Black	1936	Committeeman, president, 1948–50, 52 (Production Foundry); rec. sec., UAW Local 600, 1946–47, 1953–57
Henry McCusker (9/83)	Tannochside, Scotland (1900)	Scottish	1925 (HP) 1927 (Rouge)	Committeeman, fin. sec., 1943; president, 1945 (Aircraft); staff member, National Ford Department
Art McPhaul (9/83)	Oklahoma (1909)	Black	1928	Committeeman, dist. committeeman, Bargaining Committee; elected v. press (Press Steel); fired, never served

Name	Birthplace	Ethnicity	Joined	Positions
John Mando (8/84)	Pennsylvania (1921)	White	1940	Dist. committeeman, 1950–51; president, 1952–62 (Rolling Mill); UAW International staff
Dave Moore (1/84)	South Carolina (1912)	Black	1935	V. pres, 1949–51; fin. sec., 1947; Bargaining Committee (Gear & Axle); UAW International rep.
John Orr (9/83)	Canada (1915)	White (Scottish)	1929 (HFTS) 1933	V. pres., 1947–48; president, 1950–51 (Tool & Die); v. pres, UAW Local 600, 1953–63
Kenneth Roche (1/84)	Dearborn, Mich. (1922)	Polish	1940	Committeeman (Aircraft); committeeman, district committeeman (Tool & Die)
John Saari (8/84)	Central Heights, Mich. (1915)	Finnish	1936	Committeeman (Aircraft); district committeeman, 3-yr. trustee (Motor); district committeeman (Engine)
Horace Sheffield (1953)	Vienna, Ga. (1914)	Black	1933	UAW International staff, 1941–44; president, 1946 (Production Foundry); UAW International staff
Shelton Tappes (9/83)	Omaha, Nebr. (1911)	Black	1937	Rec. sec., UAW Local 600, 1942–44; president, 1947 (Production Foundry); UAW International staff

Table 1, continued

Name and Date of Interview	Birthplace[a]	Nationality or Race	First Hired at Ford	Union Positions at Ford
Thomas Yeager (1/84)	(1906?)	White (father Yugoslavia)	1928	Committeeman, district committee-man; Bargaining Committee, presi-dent, 1944, 1946–48 (Miscellaneous)
Mike Zarro (8/84)	Detroit (?), Mich.	Italian	1929 (HFTS) 1931	Chief steward, 1940; Bargaining Committee, president, 1944–45 (Glass)

Key: HFTS = Henry Ford Trade School; HP = Highland Park Plant

a. Includes birthdate, when known.
b. Information in tables 1–3 is derived primarily from House un-American Activities Committee hearings, FBI files released under the Freedom of Information Act, and *Ford Facts*, as well as from Fink, ed. (1974)

Table 2. Others Interviewed

Name	Birthplace[a]	Nationality or Race	Union (and Other) Positions
Stanley Nowak	Poland (1903)	Polish	Steward, Amalgamated Clothing Workers (ACW), 1922; UAW organizer, Michigan state senator, 1938–48
Victor Reuther	Wheeling, W.Va (1912)	White	UAW organizer, Detroit; UAW director of organization, Indiana, 1937; UAW International representative; head, CIO European Office, 1951; admin. asst., CIO president, 1953; admin. asst., UAW president, 1955–71; asst., UAW president, retired
Saul Wellman	New York (1912?)	Jewish	President, Teamster Local 806; president, New York Printer's Local; staff member, Young Communist League; staff member, Communist Party of America (National Staff in New York, coordinator of U.S. Autoworkers); acting chairman, Communist party of Michigan; left Communist party in 1958

a. Includes birthdate, when known.

Table 3. Local 600 Officers Not Interviewed[a]

Name	Birthplace[b]	Nationality or Race	First Hired at Ford	Union Positions at Ford
Robert "Buddy" Battle III	Detroit (1917)	Black	—	President, 1952–59 (Specialty Foundry); second v. pres., UAW Local 600, 1967–74; first v. pres., UAW Local 600, 1975; UAW Region 1A dir., 1976–83
Mack Cinzori	Coalbluff, Pa. (1909)	White	—	Committeeman (Tool & Die)
Nelson Davis	Ripley, Tenn. (1896)	Black	1922	V. pres., 1943, 1950–51 (Production Foundry)
John Gallo	Holden, W.Va. (1913)	Italian	1935	UAW Local 600 guide, 1942–47, 1961–65; rec. sec., 1950–51 (Motor)
Wilfred G. "Bill" Grant	Smethwick, England	Anglo-Gaelic	1922	Fin. sec., UAW Local 600, 1942–44; president, 1944; UAW Intl. rep., 1945–46; Bargaining Committee (Tool & Die), 1948; fin. sec., UAW Local 600, 1950–61; political action dir., 1961
Joe Hogan	—	—	—	V. pres., 1946; president, 1947–50 (Axle); challenged Stellato for presidency of Local 600 in 1951 and received 16,682 votes to Stellato's 17,111

Name	Birthplace (year)	Ethnicity	Year	Notes
Tom Jelley	Dayton, Ohio (1907)	White	1925	Sergeant-at-arms, 1945; v. pres., 1959 (Tool & Die)
Robert Lieberman	—	Jewish	—	Editor, *Ford Facts*; Wayne County CIO Council
Percey Llewellyn	Fayette City, Pa. (1905)	White	1937	Appointed UAW Local 600 president, 1939–41; elected president, UAW Local 600, 1943; UAW International Exec. Bd., director, UAW Region 1A; president, Dearborn Labor Council
Ed Lock	Michigan (1912)	White (father English)	1931 (HFTS)	President, 1947–51 (Plastic)
Joseph McCusker	Tannochside, Scotland (1904)	Scottish	1927	Rec. sec., 1941–44 (Tool & Die); pres., Local 600, 1945; UAW International Exec. Bd.
Bill McKie	Carlisle, England (1876)	White (Scottish)	1927 (HFTS)	Propaganda sec., Social Democratic Fed., Edinburgh; chairman, Socialist party, Scotland, 1914; president, AFL Federal Labor Union, Ford Motor Company; UAW Local 600 3-yr. trustee; ed. dir., State Committee Communist Party of Michigan
George Pluhar, Sr.	Hulch, Russia (1909)	White	—	V. pres., 1951; president, 1952–55 (Plastic)

Table 3, continued

Name	Birthplace[b]	Nationality or Race	First Hired at Ford	Union Positions at Ford
Lee Romano	Udine, Italy (1912)	Italian	1937	President, 1946–47 (Press Steel); UAW International staff
Carl Stellato	—	White	—	President, Local 600, 1950–55
Paul Ste. Marie	—	White	—	President, Local 600, 1942
Tommy Thompson	England	White	—	President (Aircraft); v. pres., UAW Local 600, 1944–45; president, UAW Local 600, 1946–49
Bagrad Vartanian	Turkey (1893)	Armenian	1925	Committeeman (Spring & Upset)
James "Jimmy" Watts	Georgia (1920)	Black	—	V. pres., 1952 (Production Foundry)

a. Includes only names prominently mentioned in the text.
b. Includes birthdate, when known.

Table 4. UAW Officials[a]

Name	Birthplace[b]	Nationality or Race	Union Positions[c]
George Addes	La Crosse, Wisc. (1910)	White	Sec. treas., UAW, 1936–47; CIO Executive Board
Jack Conway	Detroit, Mich. (1917)	White	Chairman, UAW Local 6, 1942–45; assistant, UAW president, 1946–61; exec. director, Industrial Union Dept., AFL-CIO, 1963–68; exec. director, American Federation of State, County, & Municipal Employees, 1975
Richard Frankensteen	Detroit, Mich. (1907)	White	President (company union, reorganized into Automotive Industrial Workers Association, later merged with UAW); v. pres., UAW, 1937; asst. gen. manager and labor relations consultant, Allen Industries, Inc., Detroit, 1950
Douglas Fraser	Glasgow, Scotland (1916)	White	President, UAW Local 227; UAW International representative, 1947–51; admin. asst., UAW president, 1951–59; co-director, UAW Region 1A, 1959–62; UAW International Exec. Bd., 1962–70; v. pres., UAW; president, UAW
Richard Leonard	New Straitsville, Ohio (1902)	White	President, UAW Local 227; UAW Exec. Bd., 1939–43; director, UAW Ford Dept., 1941–47; v. pres., UAW, 1946; president, UAW Local 227; CIO staff, 1948; asst., Philip Murray, 1950; asst., Walter Reuther, 1951–55

Name	Birthplace (date)	Race	Biographical information
Warren Homer Martin	Marion, Ill. (1902)	White	Baptist pastor, Leeds., Mo., 1931; president, UAW federal local, GM Chevrolet plant; v. pres., UAW-AFL, 1935; president, UAW-AFL, 1936; led the UAW into the CIO, 1936; led a small group of UAW locals back into the AFL, 1939
Emil Mazey	Regina, Sask. (1913)	White	Organizer, Detroit Unemployed Citizens League; UAW International representative; president, UAW Local 212, 1937–41; UAW International Exec. Bd., 1946; co-director, UAW Region 1
Dave Miller	Dundee, Scotland (1881)	White	V. pres.,AFL Federal Labor Union, Ford Motor Co.; first president, UAW Local 22
Walter P. Reuther	Wheeling, W.Va. (1907)	White	UAW organizer, Detroit; president, UAW Local 174, 1935; UAW International Exec. Bd., 1936; director, UAW General Motors Department, 1939; v. pres., UAW, 1942; president, UAW, 1946–70; v. pres., CIO, 1946; president, CIO, 1952–55; v. pres.,AFL-CIO, 1955; led UAW out of the AFL-CIO, 1968
R. J. Thomas	East Palestine, Ohio (1900)	White	President, UAW Local 7, 1936; v. pres., UAW, 1937; president, UAW, 1939–45; v. pres., CIO; v. pres., UAW, 1946; asst. director of organization, CIO, 1947; asst., CIO president, 1955
Leonard Woodcock	Providence, R.I. (1911)	White	UAW staff rep., 1940–44; admin. asst., UAW president, 1946; director, UAW Region 1D, 1947; v. pres., UAW, 1955; president, UAW, 1970

a. Includes only names prominently mentioned in the text.
b. Includes birthdate, when known.
c. Information provided in this table is derived mainly from Fink, ed. (1974).

Table 5. Other Labor Leaders[a]

Name	Birthplace[b]	Nationality or Race	Union Positions[c]
John L. Lewis	Lucas, Iowa (1880)	White	President, local of United Mine Workers, Panama, Ill.; AFL field rep., 1910–16; v. pres., UMW, 1917; acting president, UMW, 1917; president, UMW, 1920–60; president, CIO, 1938–40
James Matles	Rumania (1909)	Rumanian	Recording secretary, local of Metal Workers Industrial Union (MWIU), 1930–31; district secretary, MWIU, 1932–33; national secretary, MWIU, 1933–34; secretary, Federation of Metal and Allied Union, 1934–35; Grand Lodge representative, International Association of Machinists, 1936–37; director of organization, United Electrical, Radio & Machine Workers (UE), 1937–62; general secretary-treasurer, UE
Michael Widman	Westville, Ill. (1900)	Italian/Austrian	Representative, United Mine Workers, District 12, 1929–36; UMW International representative, 1936–48; asst. director of organization, CIO, 1939–41; director, UAW-CIO Ford Organizing Drive, 1941

a. Includes only names prominently mentioned in the text.
b. Includes birthdate, when known.
c. Information provided in this table is derived mainly from Fink, ed. (1974).

Methods Appendix

Oral history, unlike history that is glimpsed and reconstituted by historians on the basis of written documents, reproduces events and sentiments through the participants' eyes as they retell them in their own voices, as they remember living and making them. Hence, it provides insights into what the participants thought they were doing and how those perceptions oriented their actions. Oral history, then, transforms objects of study into subjects and thereby makes history and social analyses richer, more vivid, and truer.

This book is constructed so that a number of leading participants in the same historical processes all talk about them and their various aspects at once. The chapters often immediately juxtapose the words of several individuals on different sides in the local's politics, talking about the same events (or persons), so that their memories, interpretations, and assessments can be considered in tandem. In this way (and knowing who the speakers are) we can obtain a better, more nuanced, understanding of "what really happened in history." Excerpts are juxtaposed, for example, on Bill McKie as a political leader and as a union organizer. Although it is clear that not all respondents shared McKie's radical political perspective, they all agreed on his stellar personal qualities and the fact that he was crucial in the local's organizing efforts. Similarly, respondents' descriptions converged on other Communist Party members as pioneers and builders in the early period of auto unionism, on the orientation of southerners to unionism at the Rouge, and on the role black workers played in the early union years (compared with the later ones).

At the time they were interviewed, all of the respondents were retired from their union and production work. On the one hand, this serves to remove them from the self-interest and advantages to be gained in giving particular (institutional) accounts of an event, and as a result enhances the likelihood that the accounts are authentic. On the other hand, aging respondents and long time lapses between the events and the recall pose possible problems of faulty memory and memory loss. We were, after all, asking respondents to recall events that had occurred some thirty to fifty years earlier. To what extent could we rely on their long-term memories?

The literature in the social psychology of memory suggests that such problems are not serious. Memories are almost photographic in the few minutes after an event is experienced. Immediately after that, people discard certain parts of the event and select others to organize in their memories. The process of discarding continues over time, yet it is the initial discarding, which affects even contemporary witnesses, that is most drastic. The loss of memory during the first nine months is as great as during the next thirty-four years. Equally important, when individuals consider the objects of their memories to be significant, they are more likely to remember them. Little decline occurs in the accuracy of recall of friends' names and faces, even over fifty years.[1]

What about the aging process? How does it affect memory? Memory loss with increasing age is gradual. Recent memory rather than distant memory is the first to be affected. Older people tend to be more willing to remember, and they don't care as much about fitting the story to the social norms of the audience. "Interviewing the old, in short, raises no fundamental methodological issues which do not also apply to interviewing in general."[2]

Our aging respondents typically recalled events and persons in extraordinary detail and described contexts vividly. They often reported the exact dates, along with the precise contexts, on which they started a new job or were first elected to a union office.

Still, like all other forms of historical evidence, memories of events must be evaluated carefully. When memories are set into a context of time and place, especially when they contain comparisons drawn from that date, we can assess the degree to which the respondent has accurate recall of aspects beyond direct personal experience. When respondents are successful at placing their memories in specific contexts, this is a pragmatic ground for accepting what they remember as reliable historical evidence.[3] The credibility of these accounts is enhanced by comparison with other oral testimony (in juxtaposed accounts) and documentary evidence (in "Highlights").

■ THE SAMPLE

Rouge workers' collective experiences and struggles against rival workers' political groupings, within Local 600 and in the UAW, and against their main antagonist, Henry Ford and his company, are recalled here by some of the organizers, leaders, and activists who built the local from the ground up. Only two top UAW officials (Victor Reuther and Ken Bannon) and only workers who had been active unionists were interviewed. Our final "sample" of seventeen former Rouge workers is composed of everyone active in the union during the 1930s and 1940s whom we were able to contact and persuade to be interviewed.

Stepan-Norris, as part of the work on her Ph.D. dissertation (1988), reviewed the local's newspaper, *Ford Facts,* for information on the local's organizing battles during the 1930s and 1940s and on its internal political struggles through the 1950s. From this research, she put together a list of more than a hundred names of people who participated conspicuously in these historical events.

These names were checked against current telephone books for the greater Detroit area, and those listed were sent a letter describing our research and requesting an interview. Some who responded said that they were not the person being sought, still others declined to be interviewed. A few who initially agreed to be interviewed refused at the last minute when the interviewer was at their door.

This book contains excerpts from the interviews of sixteen former Rouge workers and Local 600 activists (and the wives of two of them) and four other men (and the wife of one of them).[4] Each of the twenty-three respondents gave us permission to use materials from the interview in our research and writing and to publish excerpts from it in this volume. Of the four men who were not Rouge workers, two (Victor Reuther and Stanley Nowak) were involved in Local 600's organizing but were never among its officers; one (Saul Wellman) was involved from the outside (as an official of the Communist Party) in the postwar period; and the father of one (George Pluhar, Jr.) worked at Rouge and served as a Local 600 unit officer.

Nowak was an "outside" UAW organizer at Rouge in 1936, but he suddenly found himself out of a job as an organizer two years later when—as an innovative organizing tactic—he ran for a seat in the state senate. He and his fellow organizers used the campaign in the Democratic primary to reach otherwise nearly unreachable Ford workers who were afraid to attend a union rally but would come to a campaign stop to hear a bona fide candidate for state office. Running against the incumbent (who had suddenly changed his name to Roosevelt), Nowak, to everyone's surprise, won the election and went on to serve in the state senate for a decade.

Reuther and Wellman, who never worked at Rouge, both played important roles on opposite sides in the political struggles in the UAW and Local 600. Reuther, along with his elder brothers Walter and Roy, was an outstanding participant in the organization of the UAW and later in the leadership of its anti-Communist forces. Wellman was the secretary of the Communist Party's National Auto Commission after the war. He came to Detroit, as he says, to coordinate and "maximize the response of . . . Communist auto workers" to the "devastating event" of Walter Reuther's reelection in 1947 as UAW president and his slate's sweeping victory over the left's other executive board candidates (including long-time secretary-treasurer George Addes).

Bannon, one of the sixteen Rouge activists, was an "in shop" organizer and then committeeman at Rouge for several years before going on to become president of Ford Highland Park Local 400. After Reuther was reelected as UAW president in 1947, Bannon became the UAW's Ford director and, later, a UAW vice president. He was allied with the Reuther caucus in the political battles within the UAW.

■   THE INTERVIEWS

The oral history interviews that make up this volume were conducted in and around Detroit, Michigan, between 1983 and 1986. We both conducted the first interview, with Shelton Tappes, in 1983, and Stepan-Norris then did the rest of the interviews herself, in person, usually at the respondent's home.

Interviews with Kenneth Bannon, Victor Reuther, and Horace Sheffield, however, were conducted on the telephone. Rick Norris operated the tape recorder during most interviews, leaving his wife better able to focus on asking the
questions and listening to the answers. The length of the interviews varied
from six hours (Walter Dorosh) to thirty minutes (Henry McCusker).[5]

Each interview began with a loose protocol of questions. Respondents were
asked to talk about their personal backgrounds, jobs at Rouge, positions in
the union, and roles in the political life of Local 600 and in its relations with
the International UAW. They were also encouraged to initiate new directions
and raise issues and topics. As the interviewing progressed, the list of questions changed somewhat. Some were dropped from subsequent interviews
because they elicited the same information repeatedly from different respondents. Other, new areas of inquiry that had been initiated by one or another
of the respondents were carried over into subsequent interviews (respondents
interviewed earlier were contacted again and asked about some of the new
topics). Some questions were tailored to an individual respondent's distinc-
tive role in the local, the international, or outside organizations in order to
elicit specific information.

The activists talked freely about their experiences, impressions, and views.
Most were pleased that we were trying to reconstruct the history of Local 600
and evidently enjoyed recounting their experiences. Yet full rapport was established only after the respondents' up-front questions had been answered.
Typically, they wanted to know about Stepan-Norris's background and how
she became interested in the Rouge; they also wanted to know about the
research's sponsorship and funding. Once they learned that Stepan-Norris's
father is a union carpenter, that the sponsor was not a corporation, and that
she and her professor wanted to reconstruct Local 600's unique historical
place in American labor, rapport was (usually) firmly established. Most also
tried to help by bringing out scrapbooks and copies of old newspapers and
flyers from the local's heyday. In many cases, the activists tried to identify other
potential respondents.

■   CREATING THIS BOOK

All of the interviews were recorded on tape. Transcription was a lengthy, te-
dious, and exacting process; many words and portions of each interview had
to be listened to over and over to get words and phrases exactly right. Stepan-
Norris proofread the transcriptions (which, finally, filled more than two thousand double-spaced typed pages) to ensure their accuracy. She coded the interviews using the Ethnograph computer program, which allowed them to be
sorted by topic. Then, both Stepan-Norris and Zeitlin searched through the
transcriptions of the interviews and selected portions to be included in this
book. From these, Zeitlin edited the excerpts as they are presented.

In an open-ended, free-flowing interview, particular incidents, issues, subjects, and persons can be touched upon at many different points. On inspection, however, they may constitute integral parts of a single narrative or

thought. Some passages (and often different sentences in the same passage) can touch on quite different issues, events, or persons. In editing these excerpts, Zeitlin tried to preserve the extracted passage's original integrity as an analytical, descriptive, or esthetic unit. He eliminated some redundant phrases ("oh yeah, oh, yeah," "no, no, no, no") or needless repetitions used repeatedly as verbal punctuation marks ("well," "you see," "you know," and "and" when it was used as a running conjunction between otherwise independent sentences). He also occasionally deleted a false start (the italicized words were deleted in the following phrase, for example: *"I had a—* well, I don't think the hall was much bigger than this"). In rare instances Zeitlin also transposed a passage within the excerpt so as to enhance its overall clarity or coherence. Otherwise, except for the insertion of appropriate punctuation marks, the excerpts appear as they were spoken, recorded, and then transcribed. Occasionally, grouped excerpts from different portions of the same person's interview are presented out of the order in which they were spoken; these are separated by an extra space rather than by ellipsis.[6]

Notes

■ PREFACE

1. Marx ([1852] 1963, 15).
2. See Lynd and Lynd (1973), in which we hear the voices of other rank-and-file unionists; also see Terkel (1972).
3. Bernstein (1970, 217).
4. Piven and Cloward (1977, 173).
5. This work of oral history is the most recent product of a research program focusing on the role of the left, right, and center in American labor from the 1930s through the 1950s. The issue of the history-making role of activists, organizers, and leaders—of "militant minorities" (Montgomery 1987, 2; also see Foster 1952, 117)—and so of the theoretical problem of the "relative autonomy of politics" is addressed in Stepan-Norris and Zeitlin 1989, 1991 and Zeitlin and Stepan-Norris 1992. Other studies produced in this research program are: Bartle 1983; Campbell 1990; Jepson 1988; Kimeldorf 1983, 1985, 1988; Regensburger 1983, 1987; Shiffman 1983; Stepan-Norris 1983, 1988; Stevens 1994; Weyher 1994; Wilson 1993; Zeitlin and Kimeldorf 1984; and Zeitlin 1983, 1987. For a study of the independent effects of political struggles in the shaping and transformation of basic social relations, in another time and in another place, see Zeitlin 1984.

■ INTRODUCTION

1. Missing here, alas, is Carl Stellato, who served as Local 600 president from 1950 through 1965, when he retired. Despite repeated requests, he refused to be interviewed. Of the twenty men interviewed, sixteen were Rouge workers and Local 600 officers, three others were involved in Local 600's organizing, and one (George Pluhar, Jr.) is the son of a deceased Local 600 unit officer. Brief notes on these men are given in the tables in the Biographical Appendix (except on Pluhar, whose father's note appears). Ken Bannon, Stanley Nowak, and Victor Reuther, although active in organizing Local 600, were not Local 600 officers. Saul Wellman was head of the Communist Party's National Auto Commission. The three women interviewed are Ann Boatin (wife of Paul Boatin), Margaret Nowak (wife of Stanley Nowak), and Deloris Roche (wife of Kenneth Roche). Ann Boatin worked as a secretary in the office of Local 600 for many years.

2. *Detroit Times,* April 2, 1941, 1; *Local Union No. 600 v. Ford Motor Co.* (1953, 837).

3. No other plant anywhere has employed as many workers. Ford had eighty-seven thousand hourly-rated production workers on its Rouge payrolls in 1941 (Wayne State University Archives [hereafter WSUA]: Leonard to Roosevelt 1941), when Local 600 won its first contract and far more during World War II. According to the company, it had some seventy thousand a decade later after Ford started to "decentralize" (Allan 1951b, 8). During the second half of the 1950s, and even after the acceleration of Operation Runaway, as the local called Ford's decentralization, fifty thousand production workers were still employed at Rouge.

4. When it was born on the eve of World War II, the local had more members than all but six of the CIO's thirty-eight international unions; at the end of the war, it still had more members than twenty-six of these internationals.

5. The quoted phrase is from "Ballad for Americans," music by Earl Robinson, words by John Latouche (1939).

6. Father Charles Edward Coughlin was pastor of the Shrine of the Little Flower in Royal Oak, Michigan. During the 1930s he used his weekly radio pulpit to rail simultaneously against such enemies of the workers as Henry Ford, "international bankers," Communists, and Jews. He denounced FDR and the New Deal and preferred, he said, "the road of fascism." His organization, the National Union for Justice, founded in 1934, advocated a number of fascist measures, and its magazine *Social Justice* was filled with anti-Semitic and pro-Nazi propaganda. He and Ford patched up their differences in the summer of 1938 and formed an alliance to fight the UAW. When the United States entered the war, the government barred *Social Justice* from U.S. mails as enemy propaganda under the Espionage Act, and it ceased publication in 1942. Later, Father Coughlin was silenced by his church superiors, although he was allowed to continue his parish duties.

7. Seaton (1981, 24).

8. Conot (1974, 174-76).

9. In a sit-down strike, the workers effectively occupy the plant or other work place and prevent the employer's importation of strike-breakers and resumption of production.

10. The NLRB (National Labor Relations Board), established under the National Labor Relations (Wagner) Act in 1935, is responsible for administering the act. Among its major activities are the determination of appropriate bargaining units, the certification of union representation in these units, and the adjudication of disputes concerning unfair labor practices.

11. Conot (1978, 372).

12. The battle between Reuther and Local 600 was part of the internecine struggle in the CIO between the so-called right and left. In the postwar era, after a brief interlude of renewed militancy and continuing unity of the left, center, and right, the CIO soon began to split apart, both over domestic and foreign politics. They differed about the correct political strategy in the fight against resurgent reaction and antilabor legislation and, far more sharply, over

the formation of a third party as a vehicle to advance labor's interests and oppose the emerging cold war policy of Soviet "containment" embodied in the Truman Doctrine and Marshall Plan.

In January 1948 the CIO executive board, after having wavered in the preceding months on the issue of endorsing Truman or launching a third party, overwhelmingly voted to endorse him and oppose formation of a third party. The board also gave its support to the Marshall Plan. In subsequent months, in the CIO's local and regional PACs and industrial union councils throughout the country (uniting the locals of various CIO unions to consolidate their political and economic strength), the CIO executive board enforced loyalty to the Democratic Party and support of Truman's candidacy and purged anyone who refused to go along. Truman's reelection and "Henry Wallace's dismal showing [as the presidential candidate of the newly formed, Communist-supported, Progressive Party], . . . demonstrated that in national politics the Left was a paper tiger." The returns were hardly in when "CIO liberals turned [the November 1948 CIO national convention] into an anti-Communist spree," and Reuther warned the Communists and their allies to "repent before it is too late" (Levenstein 1981, 280, 282, 337).

A year later, at the CIO national convention, two of the major Communist-led unions, the United Electrical, Radio, and Machine Workers (UE) and Farm Equipment Workers, were expelled, and the CIO's now totally non-Communist executive board voted to hold trials on the expulsion of other unions charged with consistently following "the Communist line." The trials began in early January 1950, and by midyear another nine "miscreant unions . . . claiming to represent over one million members had been drummed out of the CIO" (Levenstein 1981, 306).

The CIO national office resorted to the trials and expulsions, as Oshinsky (1974, 125) observes, "because the anti-Communist factions within the various left-wing affiliates were unable to dislodge the Communists from power. In only three . . . of the pro-Communist unions were the right-wingers successful in gaining control—an indication, perhaps, that despite their pro-Soviet, anti-Truman position, the Communists were still respected for their ability to run effective trade unions." (Reuther was also unable to dislodge Local 600's indigenous, freely elected left leaders, so he resorted to putting the local under a trusteeship and then throwing out five of its top elected officers on charges of being Communists.)

After their expulsion from the CIO, the Communist-led unions were the target of continual raids by warring CIO unions and were subject to unrelenting attacks by an array of government institutions: The NLRB discriminated against them; the Justice Department scrutinized their officers' non-Communist affidavits; the attorney general prosecuted them; the IRS combed their tax returns; the FBI harassed, infiltrated, and sabotaged them; and the Immigration Department tried to deport the foreign-born among them.

A swarm of congressional committees, including the House un-American Activities Committee, the Senate Internal Security Committee, the McCarthy Committee, and Hubert Horatio Humphrey's Senate Labor and Public Welfare

Subcommittee, held hearings on "Communist infiltration" and "Communist domination" in city after city across the country in 1950, 1951, and 1952, concentrating on subpoenaing "unfriendly" witnesses from locals of the expelled unions. In 1954 the coup d'grace came in the form of the Communist Control Act, which authorized the Subversive Activities Control Board to declare the left unions "Communist-infiltrated" organizations and thereby deprive them of the protection of the NLRA (Caute 1978, chs. 18–21).

13. WSUA: Stellato (1950); *Detroit News*, December 17, 1950. A press release of July 10, 1950, quotes Stellato's "statement of policy," passed a day earlier by a vote of 75 to 63 of the local's General Council: "The American workers are caught between two fires—one [is] monopoly capitalism that the unions in America has [*sic*] fought for years—and the Communist Party that, like termites[,] are boring away within our union" (WSUA: Stellato 1950).

14. Interview, August 31, 1983. Tappes is referring to Leonard Woodcock and Douglas Fraser, both of whom were active in organizing the UAW and later (after Reuther's death) became presidents of the UAW. See Table 4 of the Appendix for biographical notes on them.

■   HIGHLIGHTS OF LOCAL 600'S HISTORY

1. Stolberg (1938, 115–16).
2. Cochran (1977, 63); also see Keeran (1980, 37); Saperstein (1977, 20).
3. Federal labor unions were newly organized locals given a temporary AFL charter to "store workers" until they could be parcelled out to AFL craft affiliates (Bernstein 1970, 355).
4. "The Grand Old Man of Ford Local 600," 3.
5. Rankin (1939, 131, 173).
6. Meyer (1980, 78).
7. The Workmen's Circle (Die Arbeiter Ring) was a fraternal benefit society organized in 1892 by Jewish socialists.
8. Keeran (1989, 385).
9. Bonosky (1953, 59).
10. Conot (1974, 284).
11. Sward (1948, 233).
12. Sugar (1980, 34).
13. Conot (1974, 285–86). Five marchers died of their gunshot wounds—four immediately, a fifth later. Bonosky (1953, 85–86) puts the number of funeral marchers at seventy thousand plus another thirty thousand spectators lining the route of the march. Sugar (1980, 69) puts the number of marchers between fifty and sixty thousand.
14. Howe and Widick (1949, 91).
15. Sward (1948, 389–93).
16. See Table 4 of the Appendix for a biographical note on Reuther.
17. Bonosky (1953, 156–58).
18. Sward (1948, 397).
19. Howe and Widick (1949, 97).
20. "CIO Backs Ford Drive," 3.

21. Ford's rehabilitation of Inkster, a mostly black village, was highly publicized, but not his regular deductions from the paychecks of black employees who lived there, in order to pay him back for the money he spent on it.

22. "40 Servicemen Attack UAW Members," 1.

23. Sward (1948, 379).

24. See Table 4 of the Appendix for a biographical note on Martin.

25. Keeran (1980, 86-87). *This* Progressive Caucus in the *international* union was on the political right and is not to be confused with the left-wing Progressive Caucus in Local 600.

26. Levinson (1956, 270); Spivak (1940, 11). In Ford's view, reiterated often in interviews and in his writings, "'radical unions' are organized by Jewish financiers, not labor. . . . A union is a neat thing for a Jew to have on hand when he comes around to get his clutches on an industry." Ford had published *The International Jew* in 1920, in which he claimed that Jewish bankers financed Communism. Hitler borrowed many of his ideas from Ford's diatribe and incorporated them into *Mein Kampf:* "Not only did Hitler specifically praise Henry Ford in *Mein Kampf,* but . . . there is a great similarity between *The International Jew* and Hitler's *Mein Kampf,* and some passages are so identical that it has been said that Hitler copied directly from Ford's publication . . . . There can be no doubt as to the influence of Henry Ford's ideas on Hitler" (Pool and Pool 1978, 100, 91).

Ford also brought the notorious anti-Semitic preacher Gerald L. K. Smith to Detroit and subsidized his activities. Smith, a radio evangelist, tried to reach Protestants (especially newly arrived southerners) as Coughlin was reaching Catholics, with diatribes against Communists, Jews, the UAW, and the CIO. Ford, who would be awarded the second highest Nazi decoration in a public ceremony in Dearborn on July 30, 1938, also encouraged organizing at Rouge by the "Nazi-fronting National Workers League, fulminating against Jews and Negroes" (Conot 1974, 367-69).

27. Although Frankensteen had agreed with Martin in late 1937 to try to arrange a meeting with Ford personally, their alliance split apart, and Martin fired him as director of the Ford organizing drive in April 1938.

28. Sward (1948, 380-83).

29. Sward (1948, 383).

30. Conot (1974, 369).

31. Stolberg (1938, 170); "Text of Ford and Other Resolutions," 6.

32. WSUA: Tappes (n.d. 16-18) and ACTU 1939.

33. See Tables 3 and 4 of the Appendix for biographical notes on Llewellyn and Leonard.

34. A year earlier, in August 1938, Martin had provisionally chartered Ford Local 600 (WSUA: ACTU 1939, 2).

35. WSUA:ACTU (1939, 4). In 1942 Local 600 would elect Ste. Marie (who until then had been the local's secretary) as president. The next year, they would reelect Llewellyn president, an electoral see-saw indicating the roughly even political balance between the left and right in Local 600 during these years. See Table 3 of the Appendix for a biographical note on Ste. Marie.

36. WSUA: Tappes (n.d., 25).

37. See Table 4 of the Appendix for a biographical note on Thomas.

38. See Table 5 of the Appendix for a biographical note on Widman.

39. "$100,000 Appropriated," 1.

40. "UAW-CIO Locals Back Ford Drive," 1.

41. Cochran (1977, 151).

42. Bonosky (1953, 160).

43. Widman hired McKie despite the fact that UAW president R. J. Thomas had refused to hire him in the past unless he signed a non-Communist loyalty oath. McKie would not do so, and simply went on organizing on his own while supporting himself by selling pamphlets and union buttons.

44. Bonosky (1953, 160, 165–66).

45. "UAW-CIO Locals Back Ford Drive," 1.

46. Nowak (1989, 165).

47. WSUA: Tappes (n.d., 24).

48. Galenson (1960, 181).

49. Sward (1948, 404).

50. WSUA: "History of the Production Foundry Unit Local 600 UAW" (n.d., 6–7). See Table 3 of the Appendix for a biographical note on Davis.

51. Sward (1948, 402–7).

52. Sward (1948, 402–12); Conot (1974, 370–71). Some ten thousand blacks were employed in all Ford Motor Company plants during the late 1930s (Conot 1974, 370), apparently, nearly all of them at the Rouge plant—which, as of 1937, employed 9,825 blacks among its 84,000 or so production workers. The number of blacks employed at the Rouge rose substantially during World War II.

53. Howe and Widick (1949, 104).

54. Conot (1974, 372).

55. According to Galenson (1960, 183), the tally was 51,866 votes for the UAW-CIO, 20,364 for the UAW-AFL, and 1,958 for neither out of a total of 74,188 votes cast—which is some 9,300 votes less than the total of 83,500 votes cast, reported in Conot (1974, 372). But the percentage distributions for both sets of figures are virtually identical.

56. Sward (1948, 419–21); Conot (1974, 372).

57. The leaders of the center-left coalition were Addes, UAW secretary-treasurer from 1939 through 1947; Richard Leonard, member of the UAW's executive board from 1939 through 1943 and director of the UAW's Ford Department from 1941 through 1947; and R. J. Thomas, UAW president from 1939 through 1945 and vice president in 1946 (after his defeat for the presidency by Reuther). The coalition was supported by Communists and allied radicals until its defeat by the Reuther faction in 1947. See Table 4 in the Appendix for a biographical note on Addes.

58. Five candidates split 37,194 votes cast on the first ballot: 12,516 went to incumbent Tommy Thompson and 11,883 to Stellato. In the run-off election, Stellato won with 15,317 votes to Thompson's 14,758. Thompson also had attacked the Communists in his campaign, and months earlier, in Novem-

ber 1949 at the CIO convention, he had presented a resolution urging CIO officials to formulate procedures to purge "Communists and Communist sympathizers" from the leadership of its international unions (WSUA:Thompson 1949). See Table 3 of the Appendix for a biographical note on Thompson.

59. WSUA: Stellato (1950).

60. See Tables 1 and 3 in the Appendix for biographical notes on these men.

61. *UAW* (1947, 22). The clause had been passed at the 1941 UAW convention, without opposition from its Communist members. They went along with it (obediently if uneasily), in accordance with the party's Popular Front strategy (Keeran 1980, 11, 24).

62. WSUA: Zwerdling (1950).

63. Allan (1951a, 5). The trial committee chair later charged that Stellato had made a deal with the left wing that effectively prevented a majority vote of guilty. He also charged that Stellato stopped the printing of the trial committee's transcript in the local's paper in order to prevent full disclosure of "the facts" (WSUA: Savage n.d.).

64. See Table 1 of the Appendix for a biographical note on Bannon.

65. In June 1953, now running officially as the left-center candidate of the Unity Coalition (which allied his Unity Caucus and the Progressive Caucus), Stellato overwhelmingly defeated the candidate of the (self-named) Right-Wing Caucus. In the run-off election pitting Stellato against Reuther's candidate Gene Prato, chair of the UAW Ford Conference (and a signatory of the September 4, 1950, five-year contract), Stellato got 20,139 votes to Prato's 8,400 (Morris 1953, 4; "Stellato Re-elected"; "Carl Stellato Re-elected"). Stellato went on to serve as Local 600's president until his retirement from office in 1965. His papers have not been deposited in the Wayne State University Archives.

66. Reuther wrote to the committee to request an opportunity to testify, but the committee's "tight schedule" precluded his testimony (WSUA: John S. Wood to Walter Reuther, March 11, 1952).

67. WSUA: Stellato et al. (1952).

68. "Stellato Re-elected," 3.

69. "Carl Stellato Re-elected," 3.

70. Lichtenstein (1986, 27).

71. As early as 1946, when the company was considering the relocation of its motor assembly operations, an internal memorandum noted: "The concentration of Ford Motor Company facilities in the Detroit area may be the best arrangement, but it is possible, even probable, that the concentration is so great as to amplify, unnecessarily, the labor and management problems" (Ford Industrial Archives: Analysis of Motor Assembly Move, 1946).

72. Ford Industrial Archives: Executive Communication (1949).

73. Ford Industrial Archives: Bethlehem Steel Company (1949, 2–3).

74. WSUA: Averill (1950, 1–2).

75. Bugas also sent the local a letter on June 8, repeating the company's claim that it could not give the local specific answers to its questions because its "plans for the future will be determined first of all by the over-all economic situation which in turn will determine the demand for car and truck pro-

duction" and "by [its] ability... to remain competitive in a highly competitive industry" (WSUA: Averill 1950, 5-7). Carl Stellato's subsequent letter of
June 15 to company president Henry Ford II, reiterating the local's questions
and requesting that Ford meet with him and other Local 600 officers, apparently did not receive "the courtesy of a reply." Ibid., 7.

76. WSUA: Stellato to Reuther (1951).

77. Cranefield (1951) reviewed a draft of the proposed suit. A copy is in
the Wayne State University Archives (WSUA, [no author given], Civil action
1951).

78. WSUA: Cranefield (1951).

79. We have not found any document with Reuther's (or the UAW executive board's) specific reply either to Cranefield or to Local 600.

80. Two months later, Stellato reported to the local's membership: "The
company's attorney argued, time and time again, that since the international
union and not the local was on the contract, the case could not be continued without the international. We pointed out in reply that the local and its
members were the only workers affected. While we believe that we are correct on this argument, the case would be strengthened if the international
union joined in. I again urge the international to come into the case . . . because the issue involved is one which affects every member of the UAW-CIO,
as well as every union member in the country" (*Ford Facts,* January 19, 1952,
1-4).

81. Not only were the assurances false, but the company's representatives
"well knew at the time that they were false. [They constituted] a fraud upon
the [union], in that at no time prior to, or during the negotiations which led
up to and culminated in the current agreement, was there any communication or intimation . . . that the defendant was planning, or had planned or
intended any substantial transfer or contracting out of the usual and custom-
ary production operations, maintenance and construction activities and
facilities . . . then being carried on at the Rouge plant . . . but, on the contrary,
were denied by the defendant" (*Local Union No. 600 v. Ford Motor Co.* [1953,
839]).

82. Ibid., 844. Goodman (of the firm of Goodman, Crockett, Eden and
Robb) drew up the suit and also represented the local before the court.

83. Ibid., 843-44.

84. Paul Boatin told us that the left leaders in Local 600 opposed UAW's
ceding the so-called managerial prerogative to Ford. "They [the internation-
al] consciously recommended to the workers that the company shall retain
the sole right about the location and the kind of things the plants do. . . .
[They] allowed a trade-off—'We'll give you three percent annual wage increases but [we keep] the prerogatives, the rights of management.'. . . This is carried to the ridiculous extreme where even the pension money of the workers is managed by the company."

Throughout the CIO era, the contracts won by the locals of Communist-
led unions were far less likely to cede the managerial prerogative than the
contracts won by their rivals in other political camps. Their contracts were

also less likely to bar strikes during the term of the contract or require a cumbersome, time-consuming, bureaucratic grievance procedure that removed the resolution of workers' grievances from the factory floor. The pattern was the same from 1938 through 1950 in the national contracts that the CIO's "Big 3" made with the major employer in their industry. All of UAW's contracts with GM and all of USWA's with U.S. Steel, but *none* of the contracts of the red-led UE with GE, ceded management rights (Stepan-Norris and Zeitlin 1991).

85. WSUA: Averill (1950, 8).

■ TALKING UNION

1. The company fired the trouble-makers, that is, union men, and kept a list of them.

2. Marshall, himself black, supervised the hiring of blacks at Rouge.

3. See "Highlights" for a discussion of the Ford Service Department.

4. On this complex question, see Milkman (1987).

5. See "Highlights" for a discussion of the Unemployed Council.

6. The Civilian Conservation Corps was created by Congress in 1933 to provide young unemployed men with employment on public conservation and community beautification projects. The Public Works Administration was created under the National Industrial Recovery Act to provide employment on public works for those in need but not on relief rolls. The Works Progress Administration was created under the Emergency Relief Act of 1935 to provide employment to those on relief or in need of assistance.

7. The so-called Bonus Marchers consisted of more than twenty thousand veterans (calling themselves the Bonus Expeditionary Force), who were mostly unemployed and in desperate financial straits. They spontaneously converged on Washington, D.C., in the spring of 1932 to demand passage of Congressman Wright Patman's bill authorizing immediate payment of the World War I bonus promised them. They assembled peaceably and camped (with police permission) in parks and government buildings. But when the Senate defeated the bill on June 19, they refused to go home. Herbert Hoover ordered the army to evict them. Gen. Douglas MacArthur ordered their camps burned, and the army drove them out of the capital by force, resulting in many casualties among the veterans.

8. The Stout cargo airplane (designed by the engineer William B. Stout) flew faster and had more carrying load than previous cargo planes. Henry Ford bought Stout's company and brought the Stout's production to the Rouge plant.

9. The Battle of the Running Bulls was a confrontation between police and strikers during the major sit-down strike at the General Motors plant in Flint, Michigan.

10. See Table 4 of the Appendix for a biographical note on Frankensteen.

11. See "Highlights" for a discussion of Homer Martin's role in the UAW organizing drive. Also see Table 4 of the Appendix.

12. For a discussion of the Auto Workers Union (AWU), see "Highlights."

13. The so-called Taft-Hartley (Labor-Management Relations) Act of 1947

abolished many of the gains organized labor made under the Wagner (National Labor Relations) Act of 1935 and nullified parts of the Norris-LaGuardia (Federal Anti-Injunction) Act of 1932. The Taft-Hartley Act empowers the government to get an eighty-day injunction against any strike that it deems a peril to national health and safety and allows companies to sue unions for breach of contract. It outlaws the closed shop and permits the union shop only on a majority vote of employees. It prohibits secondary boycotts (a boycott of an already unionized company doing business with another company that a union is trying to organize); forbids unions from contributing to political campaigns; and outlaws strikes by government workers. It also requires union leaders to swear and sign a non-Communist affidavit to confirm that they are neither members nor sympathizers of the Communist Party. Without such affidavits by union officers, the union cannot be certified to use the facilities of the National Labor Relations Board.

14. See Table 3 of the Appendix for biographical notes on W. G. Grant and Cinzori.

15. In 1933, when Reuther was fired from his job at the Ford plant, he and his brother Victor went on a "hand-to-mouth world tour." This included a visit to the Soviet Union, where they worked in an auto plant near Gorki for sixteen months. At that time, they wrote a letter home praising the Soviet regime. Victor has insisted that parts of the letter were forged (Howe and Widick 1949; Reuther 1976).

16. See Table 4 of the Appendix for a biographical note on Mazey.

17. The so-called no-strike pledge was taken by top AFL and CIO leaders at the initiation of American's involvement in World War II. The labor leaders agreed to forestall all strike activity for the duration of the war.

18. Grievances are formal complaints by union members concerning the employment relationship. The first step of a grievance usually involves the aggrieved worker, the committeeman (or steward), and the foreman. Additional steps of the grievance procedure are handled by higher-level officers of the company and union.

19. The Ford National Negotiating Committee is responsible for negotiating the Ford collective bargaining agreements.

20. The UAW Resolutions Committee is appointed by the UAW executive board for the purpose of proposing resolutions to UAW conventions.

21. See "Highlights" for a discussion of the Ford Hunger March.

22. See "Highlights" for a discussion of the Dearborn leafleting ordinance.

23. See "Highlights" for a discussion of this NLRB case.

24. Deloris Roche is the daughter of Percy Llewellyn, the progressive president of Local 600, 1939–41, 1943.

25. Widman arrived in Detroit in 1940.

26. Smith's first name was Norman.

27. See "Highlights" and Table 3 of the Appendix for a biographical note on McKie.

28. The International Workers Order (IWO) was a fraternal benefit society formed in 1930 and led by Communists (see "Highlights").

29. Paul Robeson, son of a runaway slave, was a four-letter man at Rutgers University, a distinguished actor (*The Emperor Jones, Othello*) and a bass singer (he appeared in the original *Show Boat* and was noted for his rendition of spirituals). He was also an outspoken man of the left and a Communist ally. He was awarded the Stalin International Peace Prize in 1952.

30. On the UAW Unity Caucus, see "Highlights."

31. The *Dearborn Independent* was published from 1919 to 1927. *The Ford News* was published through 1942. Because Nowak is speaking about 1938, she must mean *The Ford News*.

32. The Black Legion was a right-wing, anti-immigrant (i.e., anti-foreign-born), anti-Jewish, and antiblack vigilante secret society active in the Detroit area and in some other cities in the immediate prewar years. In 1935 an estimated one hundred of the seven hundred delegates to the convention of the Wayne County Republican Party (Detroit is in Wayne County) were legion members. They made deep inroads into police departments in the Detroit area and in some other cities.

33. Labor's Nonpartisan League was established on August 10, 1936, to act as organized labor's united political arm. It aided in the reelection of Franklin D. Roosevelt in 1936.

34. The United Electrical, Radio and Machine Workers Union (UE) was the CIO's third-largest union. In 1944 it had a half-million members, compared with a million in the UAW and eight hundred thousand in the USWA; together, at that time, the Big 3 constituted 46 percent of the CIO's thirty-eight affiliated international unions. UE was known as the "red fortress" in the CIO, and its leadership was supported by a broad base of Communists and other radicals spread throughout its independent locals.

In 1949 the CIO officialdom expelled UE as a Communist-controlled union. UE's local and international collective bargaining agreements were by far the most consistently prolabor of the Big 3 on a set of crucial provisions involving management prerogative, strike prohibition, contract duration, and grievance procedure (Stepan-Norris and Zeitlin 1991). Although UE is not what it once was, either politically or in size and significance, it has had a far higher rate of success in organizing new members (and winning NLRB elections) in recent years than the CIO's International United Electrical Workers (IUE). When UE and IUE have competed head-on for the workers' allegiance, that is, in jurisdictions in which they both already had sizable bases, the UE has won 97 percent of the elections (Goldfield 1987, 298).

35. Matles was one of the top three officers of the UE. See Table 5 of the Appendix for a biographical note on Matles.

36. See Table 3 of the Appendix for a biographical note on Lieberman.

37. Ford had "recruited perhaps as many as two thousand unemployed Negroes, including some boxers and street-fighters, for use as strikebreakers" (Meier and Rudwick 1979, 84).

38. The union set up a relief system to assure that the strike and shut down of production did not damage plant and equipment, so they kept such things

as the furnaces and electric turbines running during the strike (Meier and Rudwick 1979).

39. Grand Circus Park was a regular meeting place during the 1920s and 1930s for ethnic, labor, and left-wing organizations.

40. The Young Communist League (YCL) was the youth organization of the Communist Party. Its name was later changed to the Labor Youth League (LYL).

41. Flying squads were mobile union trouble-shooting units and often came to the defense of unionists confronted by company security forces.

42. A wildcat strike is a work stoppage (usually spontaneous) by a group of union members that is not authorized by the union local or international leadership.

43. Incentive pay is a system of wage payment that provides incentives for increased production. During World War II, a wage freeze was in effect, and so one of the few routes to increased pay was the adoption of an incentive wage plan. Unions have historically opposed incentive plans because management has used them to speed production or raise production norms.

44. See "Highlights" for a discussion of Ford's decentralization.

45. A straw boss is a work-group leader who does the same work as other workers but also has some supervisory responsibility.

46. Trumbo, who died in 1976, was a three-time Academy Award-winning screenwriter. In 1947 he became one of the "Hollywood Ten"; he was jailed for ten months because of his refusal to cooperate with HUAC and subsequently blacklisted. Still, he turned out a substantial number of screenplays under pseudonyms, notably *The Brave One* (1956) as Robert Rich, which won an Oscar for best writing. In 1960, with the support of Kirk Douglas (whose hit film *Spartacus* was based on the novel by Howard Fast, another blacklisted writer) and the producer Otto Preminger (*Exodus*), Trumbo's name again began appearing in film credits.

47. Sometimes seniority applies only within individual departments. Interchangeable seniority means that the seniority a worker earns in one section of the plant can be applied in another section.

48. The *Daily Worker* was the official paper of the U.S. Communist Party.

49. "Thirty-four Americans died and more than one thousand others were wounded in the streets of Detroit—in the heart of the 'Arsenal of Democracy'—during Negro-white clashes the week of June 20, 1943." Indiscriminate attacks—shootings, beatings, property destruction, car burning, and the wounding, maiming and killing of men, women, and children—were carried out by both whites against blacks and blacks against whites. So, what Attorney General Francis Biddle wrote in a letter to President Roosevelt on July 15 after an extensive investigation is all the more significant. Despite the ferocity and massive scale of the violence in the streets, "There was no disorder *within plants,* where colored and white men worked side by side, on account of efficient union discipline" (emphasis in the original). The letter was printed in full in the *American Labor News,* August 10, 1943, a shop paper supplement published by the UAW (Lee and Humphrey 1943, 2, 61).

50. See Table 3 of the Appendix for a biographical note on Watts.

51. See Table 4 of the Appendix for a biographical note on Conway.

52. George Crockett founded and directed the UAW's Fair Practices Committee from 1944 to 1946. Fired by Walter Reuther in 1947, he became a partner in the law firm of Goodman, Crockett, Eden and Robb, which in 1951 brought Local 600's suit against the Ford Motor Company to try to halt its decentralization of production. He was elected to the Recorder's Court in Detroit in 1966 and served as a judge until 1980, when he reached the age of mandatory retirement (seventy). He then ran for Congress from Michigan's Thirteenth Congressional District and has been reelected regularly since. In 1990 he was reelected with more than 88 percent of the vote.

53. Again, Attorney General Francis Biddle reported privately to FDR that "there was no disorder *within plants,* where colored and white men worked side by side, on account of efficient union discipline."

54. The IWW, whose members also bore the nickname "Wobblies," was a revolutionary, syndicalist, industrial union organized in 1905 by forty-three labor organizations and led by such men as Eugene V. Debs, "Big Bill" Haywood, and Daniel DeLeon. The Wobblies advocated direct action and opposed collective bargaining. In opposition to the AFL, they stood for solidarity between black and white and native and foreign-born workers in waging the class struggle for socialism. At its peak on the eve of World War I, the IWW had as many as one hundred thousand members, most of whom were unskilled workers. The federal government suppressed the IWW during the war. Its entire leadership was arrested for fomenting strikes, and it declined in the aftermath.

55. Italian anarchists weren't the only leftists lauding Ford's policies in the early 1920s. In response to Ford's chartering a "peace ship" to cross the Atlantic in an antiwar gesture and his 1914 labor reforms that instituted the eight-hour day and the $5 day, John Reed, William Z. Foster, the Michigan Socialist Party, and others joined in the praises. It was not until 1929 that left critiques of Ford proliferated (Roediger 1988).

56. In a discussion of the U.S. government's "hunt for subversives," in particular, its persecution of the men who had fought as volunteers in the Spanish civil war in defense of the Republic against Franco's fascist troops, Bernard Knox writes: "The authorities descended to measures that can only be described as despicable. [Saul] Wellman, for example, who had served as commissar with the Mackenzie-Papaneau Battalion was, it is true, a high Communist official and had been convicted under the Smith Act, but there is no possible justification for the action of the Veterans Administration which cancelled the disability pension he received for serious wounds suffered as an infantryman in the Battle of the Bulge in 1944 and sent him a bill for $9,000 for back payments [for his medical care]" (1994, 38).

57. The Proletarian Party, based primarily in Michigan and with its headquarters in Detroit, came out of the split in the Socialist Party in 1919. Aiming at a "majoritarian revolution," its main focus in practice was on mass education (Nowak 1989). The main Trotskyist organization during this period was the Socialist Workers Party, formed in 1938.

58. The Abe Lincoln Club and the Foster Section were local clubs of the Detroit Communist Party.

59. The USSR bore the brunt of the early fighting in Europe against Nazi expansion. This was the main front of the war. The Soviet government called on the Allies to launch a second front in the West to relieve the pressure of the Nazi advance in the East.

60. Excerpted from WSUA: "Boatin Statement" (1957). After a decade as a member of the Communist Party, Boatin was expelled in 1949.

61. See Table 3 in the Appendix for a biographical note on Miller.

62. The Knights of Columbus is a fraternal organization of Roman Catholic men.

63. *The Wage Earner* was the official newspaper of the Association of Catholic Trade Unionists (ACTU).

64. In a check-off system, the employer collects union dues and assessments for the union by deducting them from the workers' paychecks and turning them over to the union.

65. Art McPhaul was called before HUAC in 1952. He refused to "name names" (HUAC's standard demand of a hostile witness was to provide the names of their political associates) or turn over to the committee the records of the Civil Rights Congress in Detroit, of which he was an officer. "I wonder," he told the committee, "if the Kluxers of Georgia have ever been asked to produce their records." The committee brought a contempt citation against him, and Congress approved it unanimously. He was sentenced to nine months and a fine of $500. On appeal, McPhaul's conviction was upheld in 1960 by the Supreme Court on a 5 to 4 vote, justices Black, Brennan, Douglas, and Warren dissenting. The majority ruled that the Fifth Amendment did not protect a witness from the requirement that he submit records kept in a representative capacity, even if submitting them might tend to incriminate him.

66. Joe Hogan, the Progressive Caucus candidate, ran against incumbent Local 600 president Carl Stellato in 1951. He ran on a program that opposed five-year contracts, no-strike pledges, and discrimination against blacks in hiring and upgrading and received 16,682 votes to Stellato's 17,111 (Lock 1951). Stellato was first elected president in 1950, when he defeated incumbent president Tommy Thompson, who had been aligned with the Progressive Caucus.

67. See "Highlights" for a discussion of the HUAC hearings in Detroit.

68. See "Highlights" for a description of the trial of the five at UAW Local 600.

69. See Table 3 of the Appendix for a biographical note on Romano.

70. The Palmer Raids, aimed at ridding America of the "revolutionary threat," were initiated by Woodrow Wilson's attorney general, A. Mitchell Palmer, in 1920. As a result of the raids, four thousand suspected radicals were arrested; and one thousand of those arrested were ordered deported.

71. The McClellan Committee (also called the Select Committee on Improper Activities in the Labor Management Field) hearings led to the passage in 1959 of the Landrum-Griffin Act—which, while it established formal pro-

visions protecting union democracy, also strengthened the antilabor provisions of the Taft-Hartley Act.

72. See Table 3 of the Appendix for a biographical note on Jelly.

73. See "Highlights" for a description of the General Council of UAW Local 600.

74. The other five that were convicted with Wellman were: Thomas D. Dennis, Jr., Nat Ganley, William Allen, Philip Schatz, and Helen Allison Winter.

75. Justice Harlan wrote the decision on May 26, 1958, in *Stanley Nowak v. the United States, Chief Justice Earl Warren presiding:* 356 U.S. 660.

76. See "Highlights" for a discussion of the UAW administratorship over Local 600.

77. The McCarran Act (also known as the Internal Security Act) outlawed "conspiracy" to establish a totalitarian dictatorship in the United States, required the registration of "Communist front organizations," and created the Subversive Activities Control Board.

■ METHODS APPENDIX

1. Bahrick, Bahrick, and Wittlinger 1975.

2. Thompson (1988, 117).

3. Lummis (1987, 130).

4. The interview with one of the seventeen respondents was brief and uninformative, so no excerpts from it are included here.

5. The interview with Saul Wellman was somewhat different: the first one was over the telephone, then subsequent interviews with him occurred in person over several days at Stepan-Norris's home.

6. The tapes of the interviews, the original unedited transcripts, and the edited transcripts (that is, the originals showing the editing) are available for use by other scholars.

Works Cited

"AFL Leaders Help Ford in Union-Busting Campaign." 1941. *The Militant* (April 26).

Allan, William. 1951a. "Ask Reuther Back 30-hr Week Demand." *The Daily Worker* (November 20).

———. 1951b. "Ford Local Throws Out Witch Hunt." *The Daily Worker* (June 12).

Bahrick, H. P., P. O. Bahrick, and R. P. Wittlinger. 1975. "Fifty Years of Memory for Names and Faces." *Journal of Experimental Psychology* (104:1).

Bartle, Kathleen. 1983. "Short-Term Employment: Women and Unions in World War II." Pages 128–97 in *How Mighty a Force? Studies of Workers' Consciousness and Organization in the United States.* Edited by Maurice Zeitlin. Los Angeles: Institute of Industrial Relations, University of California.

Bernstein, Irving. 1970. *Turbulent Years: A History of the American Worker.* Boston: Houghton Mifflin.

Bonosky, Philip. 1953. *Brother Bill McKie: Building the Union at Ford's.* New York: International Publishers.

Campbell, Alec. 1990. "Political Generations in Ford Local 600, UAW-CIO." M.A. paper. Department of Sociology, University of California, Los Angeles.

"Carl Stellato Re-elected over Gene Prato." 1953. *The Wage Earner* (June).

Caute, David. 1978. *The Great Fear: The Anti-Communist Purge under Truman and Eisenhower.* New York: Simon and Schuster.

"CIO Backs Ford Drive, Says Lewis." 1937. *The United Automobile Worker* (November 20).

Cochran, Bert. 1977. *Labor and Communism.* Princeton: Princeton University Press.

Conot, Robert. 1974. *American Odyssey.* New York: William Morrow.

Fink. Gary M., ed. 1974. *Biographical Dictionary of Labor Leaders.* Westport: Greenwood Press.

Ford Industrial Archives. 1946. Analysis of Motor Assembly Move. AR 65-71, box 38.

———. 1949. Bethlehem Steel Location Company: A Study Relating to the Best Location for the Proposed New Body Stamping Plant of the Ford Motor Company. AR 65-71, box 41.

———. 1949. Executive Communication. April 25, 1949. To Henry Ford II, E.

R. Breech, J. S. Bugas, L. D. Crusoe, and D. S. Harder on location of a new pressed steel plant. AR 65-71, box 41.

"40 Servicemen Attack UAW Members." 1937. *The United Automobile Worker* (November 6).

Foster, William Z. 1952. *History of the Communist Party of the United States*. New York: International.

Galenson, Walter. 1960. *The CIO Challenge to the AFL*. Cambridge: Harvard University Press.

Goldfield, Michael. 1987. *The Decline of Organized Labor in the United States*. Chicago: University of Chicago Press.

"The Grand Old Man of Ford Local 600." 1946. *The Daily Worker* (November 17).

Howe, Irving, and B. J. Widick. 1949. *The UAW and Walter Reuther.* New York: Random House.

"Inside the Ford Campaign." 1937. *The United Automobile Worker* (August 21).

Jepson, Mark C. 1988. "The Making of the Western Working Class: The Sources of Western Working Class Formation in the Nonferrous Industry, 1848-1893." M.A. paper. Department of Sociology, University of California, Los Angeles.

Keeran, Roger. 1980. *The Communist Party and the Auto Workers Union*. Bloomington: Indiana University Press.

———. 1989. "The International Workers Order and the Origins of the CIO." *Labor History* (30:385-408).

Kimeldorf, Howard Alex. 1983. "The Social Origins of Radical and Conservative Union Leadership." Pages 307-69 in *How Mighty a Force? Studies of Workers' Consciousness and Organization in the United States*. Edited by Maurice Zeitlin. Los Angeles: Institute of Industrial Relations, University of California.

———. 1985. "Reds or Rackets? Sources of Radical and Conservative Union Leadership on the Waterfront." Ph.D. dissertation. University of California, Los Angeles.

———. 1988. *Reds or Rackets? The Making of Radical and Conservative Unions on the Waterfront*. Berkeley: University of California Press.

Knox, Bernard. 1994. "In Another Country." *New York Review of Books* (December 1): 32-38.

Lee, Alfred McClung, and Norman D. Humphrey. 1943. *Race Riot*. New York: Dryden.

Levenstein, Harvey A. 1981. *Communism, Anticommunism, and the CIO*. Westport: Greenwood Press.

Levinson, Edward. 1956. *Labor on the March*. New York: University Books.

Lichtenstein, Nelson. 1986. "Life at the Rouge: A Cycle of Workers' Control." Pages 237-59 in *Life and Labor: Dimensions of American Working-Class History*. Edited by Charles Stephenson and Robert Asher. Albany: SUNY Press.

"Local Union No. 600, United Automobile, Aircraft & Agricultural Implement

Workers of America, UAW-CIO et al. v. Ford Motor Co." 1953 (June 5). Pages 834-45 in *Federal Supplement* [113 F. Supp. 834]. Minneapolis: West Publishing.

Lock, Ed. 1951. "Ford Vote Rocks Reuther." *March of Labor* (April).

Lummis, Trevor. 1987. *Listening to History: The Authenticity of Oral Evidence.* London: Hutchinson.

Lynd, Staughton, and Alice Lynd. 1973. *Rank and File: Personal Histories by Working-Class Organizers.* Boston: Beacon Press.

Marx, Karl. [1852] 1963. *The Eighteenth Brumaire of Louis Bonaparte.* New York: International.

Meier, August, and Elliot Rudwick. 1979. *Black Detroit and the Rise of the UAW.* Oxford: Oxford University Press.

Meyer, Stephen. 1980. "Adapting the Immigrant to the Line." *Journal of Social History* (14:67-82).

Milkman, Ruth. 1987. *Gender at Work: The Dynamics of Job Segregation by Sex during World War II.* Urbana: University of Illinois Press.

Montgomery, David. 1987. *The Fall of the House of Labor: The Workplace, the State, and Labor Activism, 1865-1925.* New York: Cambridge University Press.

Morris, George. 1953. "The World of Labor." *The Daily Worker* (June 4).

Nowak, Margaret. 1989. *Two Who Were There: A Biography of Stanley Nowak.* Detroit: Wayne State University Press.

"$100,000 Appropriated by CIO and UAW-CIO to Further Big Drive." 1940. *The United Automobile Worker* (October 1).

Oshinsky, David. 1974. "Labor's Cold War: The CIO and the Communists." Pages 117-51, 310-15 in *The Specter: Original Essays on the Cold War and the Origins of McCarthyism.* Edited by Robert Griffith and A. Theoharis. New York: Franklin Watts.

Piven, Frances Fox, and Richard A. Cloward. 1979. *Poor People's Movements.* New York: Vintage.

Pool, James, and Suzanne Pool. 1978. *Who Financed Hitler? The Secret Funding of Hitler's Rise to Power.* London: MacDonald and Jane's.

Rankin, Lois. 1939. "Detroit Nationality Groups." *Michigan History* (23:29-211).

Regensburger, William. 1983. "The Emergence of Industrial Unionism in the South, 1930-1945: The Case of the Coal and Metal Miners." Pages 65-127 in *How Mighty a Force? Studies of Workers' Consciousness and Organization in the United States.* Edited by Maurice Zeitlin. Los Angeles: Institute of Industrial Relations, University of California.

———. 1987. "Ground into Our Blood: The Origins of Working Class Consciousness and Organization in Durably Unionized Southern Industries, 1930-1946." Ph.D. dissertation. University of California, Los Angeles.

Reuther, Victor. 1976. *The Brothers Reuther and the Story of the UAW.* Boston: Houghton Mifflin.

Roediger, David. 1988. "Americanism and Fordism—American Style: Kate Richards O'Hare's 'Has Henry Ford Made Good?'" *Labor History* (29): 291-352.

Saperstein, Lou. 1977. "Ford Is Organized." *Political Affairs* (56:19-25).

Seaton, Douglas P. 1981. *Catholics and Radicals: The Association of Catholic Trade Unionists and the American Labor Movement, from Depression to Cold War.* Lewisburg: Bucknell University Press.

Shiffman, Michael. 1983. "The Rise and Decline of Communist Leadership in the Transport Workers Union (CIO), 1933-1949." Pages 128-97 in *How Mighty a Force? Studies of Workers' Consciousness and Organization in the United States.* Edited by Maurice Zeitlin. Los Angeles: Institute of Industrial Relations, University of California.

Spivak, John. 1940. *Shrine of the Silver Dollar.* New York: Modern Age Books.

"Stellato Re-elected." 1952. *The Wage Earner* (October).

Stepan-Norris, Judith. 1983. "The War Labor Board: The Political Conformity and Bureaucratization of Organized Labor." Pages 198-230 in *How Mighty a Force? Studies of Workers' Consciousness and Organization in the United States.* Edited by Maurice Zeitlin. Los Angeles: Institute of Industrial Relations, University of California.

———. 1988. "Left Out: The Consequences of the Rise and Fall of Communist Union Leaders in the CIO." Ph.D. dissertation. University of California, Los Angeles.

Stepan-Norris, Judith, and Maurice Zeitlin. 1989. "'Who Gets the Bird?' or, How the Communists Won Power and Trust in America's Unions: The Relative Autonomy of Intraclass Political Struggles." *American Sociological Review* (54:503-23).

———. 1991. "'Red' Unions and 'Bourgeois' Contracts?" *American Journal of Sociology* (96:1151-200).

Stevens, Max. 1994. "Employer Resistance and Radical Union Leadership in the CIO." M.A. paper. Department of Sociology, University of California, Los Angeles.

Stolberg, Benjamin. 1938. *The Story of the CIO.* New York: Viking Press.

Sugar, Maurice. 1980. *The Ford Hunger March.* Berkeley: Meiklejohn Civil Liberties Institute.

Sward, Keith. 1948. *The Legend of Henry Ford.* New York: Rinehart.

Terkel, Studs. 1972. *Working.* New York: Random House.

"Text of Ford and Other Resolutions." 1939. *The United Automobile Worker* (April 8).

Thompson, Paul. 1988. *The Voice of the Past: Oral History.* 2d edition. New York: Oxford University Press.

"UAW-CIO Locals Back Ford Drive." 1940. *The United Automobile Worker* (November 1).

United Automobile, Aircraft and Agricultural Implement Workers of America. 1947. *Constitution of the International Union [,] United Automobile, Aircraft and Agricultural Implement Workers of America* (UAW-CIO). Atlantic City: UAW.

Wayne State University. Archives of Labor History and Urban Affairs [WSUA]:

———. Association of Catholic Trade Unionists. 1939. "Memorandum re situation in Ford Local 600 UAW-CIO." ACTU Collection, box 24, folder Local 600, 1939-45.

———. Averill, David. 1950. "Decentralization of the Ford Motor Company and the Union's Position in Relation to It."

———. Boatin, Paul. 1957. "Boatin Statement" and "Investigation of Irregularities." Walter P. Reuther Collection, box 250, folder 250-17 (April–September).

———. Civil action to enjoin Ford from violating contract of September 14, 1950, draft copy (October 31). 1951. Walter P. Reuther Collection, box 249, folder 249-23.

———. Cranefield, Harold A. 1951. "Inter-Office Communication [to Walter P. Reuther]." November 8. Walter P. Reuther Collection, box 249, folder 249-23.

———. Ford Local 600 By-Laws Committee. N.d. "Proposed By-Laws of Ford Local #600." ACTU box 24, folder Local 600—General.

———. "History of the Production Foundry Unit Local 600 UAW." Shelton Tappes Collection, folder 220.

———. Leonard, Richard T. 1941. Letter to Pres. Franklin Delano Roosevelt from R. T. Leonard, director, UAW-CIO Ford Division (December 8). Local 600 Collection, access no. 176, box 1, folder 1-3.

———. Savage, Frank. N.d. Untitled statement. Walter P. Reuther Collection, box 249, folder 249-24.

———. Stellato, Carl. 1950. "Statement of Policy" (press release Ford Local 600 UAW-CIO, July 10). Walter P. Reuther Collection, box 249, folder 249-19.

———. Stellato, Carl. 1951. Letters to Walter P. Reuther (October 30, November 12). Walter P. Reuther Collection, box 249, folder 249-23.

———. Stellato, Carl, and other officers. 1952. "Answer of Local 600, UAW-CIO Showing Cause Why an Administrator Should Not Be Placed over Local 600, UAW-CIO" (March 13). Walter P. Reuther Collection, box 249, folder 249-24.

———. Tappes, Shelton. N.d. Interview. Maurice Sugar Collection, box 54, folder 7.

———. Thompson, Tommy. 1949. Executive Board Minutes, Resolution of Local 600 Executive Board (November 1). Local 600 Collection, access no. 176, box 2, folder 2-12.

———. Wood, John S. 1952. Letter to Walter P. Reuther (March 11). Walter P. Reuther Collection, box 249, folder 249-24.

———. Zwerdling, A. L. 1950. "Statement of A. L. Zwerdling, attorney for Carl Stellato, President of UAW-CIO Local 600, Concerning the Trial of Five Local Officers" (carbon copy, October 12). Walter P. Reuther Collection, box 249, folder 249-19.

Weyher, L. Frank. 1994. "The Relative Effects of the Congress of Industrial Organizations (CIO) vs. the American Federation of Labor (AFL) in Reducing Racial Inequality." M.A. paper. Department of Sociology, University of California, Los Angeles.

Wilson, Valerie. 1993. "C.I.O. Unions and Gender, 1944–1946: Did Politics Matter?" M.A. paper. Department of Sociology, University of California, Los Angeles.

Zeitlin, Maurice, ed. 1983. *How Mighty a Force? Studies of Workers' Con-*

sciousness and Organization in the United States. Los Angeles: Institute of Industrial Relations, University of California.

———. 1984. *The Civil Wars in Chile (or the bourgeois revolutions that never were).* Princeton: Princeton University Press.

———, ed. 1987. *Insurgent Workers: Studies of the Origins of Industrial Unionism on the East and West Coast Docks and in the South during the 1930s.* Los Angeles: Institute of Industrial Relations, University of California.

Zeitlin, Maurice, and Howard Kimeldorf, eds. 1984. *Political Power and Social Theory: A Research Annual.* Greenwich: JAI Press [devoted to studies of the left in American labor, from the 1930s through 1950s].

Zeitlin, Maurice, and Judith Stepan-Norris. 1992. "The Insurgent Origins of Union Democracy." Pages 250–73 in *Reexamining Democracy: Essays in Honor of Seymour Martin Lipset.* Edited by Garry Marks and Larry Diamond. Newbury Park: Sage.

Index

Chicago, 21, 43, 175, 200, 224; packing-house strike, 130; and Palmer raids, 200

Chrysler Corporation, 5, 52, 56–57, 58, 62, 65, 66, 92, 93, 102, 144

Churches: Catholic, 53, 98; black, 58, 102; ministers, 5, 17, 102

Cinzori, Mack, 50, 72, 111, 159, 219; biography, 234

Civil rights, 139, 145, 195

Civilian Conservation Corps (CCC), 43, 255n6

Class struggle, 75, 123, 150

Coal miners, 47, 48–51, 112; black-lists, migration to Detroit, 50; and company store, 81; sense of solidarity, 51. *See also* United Mine Workers

Cold war, 227

Collective bargaining. *See* Ford Motor Company-UAW collective bargaining, and individual unions

Communism, 6, 73, 144, 217; Communists, 1, 2, 78, 87, 108, 139, 150–67, 212, 213, 214, 215, 219, 227; in unions, 9–11

—Communist Party, 20, 63, 81, 88, 178, 204, 224, 225, 226, 241, 243; Abe Lincoln Club, 260n58; affect on UAW Locals, 7, 51, 155, 157, 174, 190, 205, 208, 212, and 735, 156; affect on workers politics, 180; and black liberation, 153; clubs, 157; concentration policy, 70, 109; decline of influence on Rouge, 221–22; educational activities, 157, 160; fellow travelers, 1, 104, 145, 154, 158, 206; Foster Section, 260n58; influences among immigrant nationalities, 10; lines of, 157, 158, 161; members of, at Rouge, 139–40, 145–46, 148–49, 153–66, 212–27; National Auto Commission, 156; policies, 145, 147, 161, 162, 253n61; and Local 600 Progressive Caucus, 179, 206; role in Ford Hunger March, 11; role in Rouge organizing, 3, 9, 85–86, 108; role in Unemployed Councils, 104; reasons workers join, 152; sectarianism, 163; social activities, 155; strategy of black and white unity, 145, 147, 148. *See also* Young Communist League

Congress of Industrial Organizations (CIO), 1, 9, 14, 15, 16, 57–58, 68, 69, 73, 83, 85, 86, 90, 110, 114, 177, 180, 183, 191, 224, 227; Battle of the Running Bulls, 50; black white unity, 106; constitution, 105; expulsion of Communist-led unions, 248n12; Wayne County Council, 7

Conway, Jack, 147, 216, 219, 224; biography, 237

Conyers, John, Sr., 102

Cooper, William, 72, 142

Coughlin, Father Charles, 2, 13, 14, 17, 90, 168, 248n6, 251n26

Couser, Joe, 201

Cranefield, Harold, 23, 254n75

Crockett, George, 147, 210, 259n52

The Daily Worker (Communist Party newspaper), 19, 143, 157, 162, 163, 258n48

Dancy, John, 17

Darrow, Clarence, 99

Davidow [?], 142–43

Davis, Nelson, 16, 19, 103, 154, 157, 221; biography, 234; Nelson Davis forum, 157; reelected, 226; removed from office, 215, 217; support from foundry workers, 217

Davis, Roy, 150

Dearborn Independent, 257n31

Dearborn, Michigan, "Ford City," 1, 42, 61, 65, 82, 95, 110, 197, 208; anti-handbill ordinance, 66; city ordinances, 4, 12, 53; Jim Crow in, 148–49; police, 11, 17, 53

Debs, Eugene, 99

Democracy, 101, 144, 175–94, 220, 224, 225; union, 1, 7–8, 18, 213

Democratic Party, 94–95, 195–96, 248n12

Depression. *See* The Great Depression

Detroit, 11, 87, 95, 99, 104, 109, 110, 112, 131, 136, 138, 151, 152; 1943 race riot, 146, 148; and Abolitionist Underground railroad, 147; Belle Isle, 138; black community, 147–48; Cadillac Square, 138; Grand Circus Park, 108, 258n39; foreign-born workers, 87; Labor Day, 138; one-industry town, 109; Red Squad, 213,

JUDITH STEPAN-NORRIS is assistant professor of sociology at the University of California, Irvine. Her current research focuses both on the internal political life of UAW Local 600 and on the impact of the local's militancy and radicalism on the communities of the Detroit area.

MAURICE ZEITLIN is professor of sociology at the University of California, Los Angeles. He is the author of seven books, including *Revolutionary Politics and the Cuban Working Class; Landlords and Capitalists: The Dominant Class of Chile* (with Richard E. Ratcliff) and *The Large Corporation and Contemporary Classes*.